THE LIFE
AND DEATH
OF IMAGES

THE LIFE AND DEATH OF IMAGES

Ethics and Aesthetics

Edited by Diarmuid Costello and Dominic Willsdon

Tate Publishing

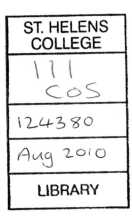
First published 2008 by order of the Tate Trustees
by Tate Publishing, a division of Tate Enterprises Ltd,
Millbank, London SW1P 4RG
www.tate.org.uk/publishing

A catalogue record for this book is available from the British Library

ISBN 978 1 85437 658 9

Designed by Turnbull Grey
Printed by Cambridge University Press

Front cover: Hans Haacke, *Stargazing* 2004 (detail of fig.12, p.205)

Measurements of artworks are given in centimetres,
height before width.

Contents

We need... to grasp both sides of the paradox of the image: that it is alive—but also dead; powerful—but also weak; meaningful—but also meaningless.

W J T Mitchell, *What do Pictures Want* [1]

INTRODUCTION
Diarmuid Costello and Dominic Willsdon

This is a book about ethics and aesthetics. More specifically, it is a book about the ethics *of* aesthetics. The recent revival of interest in aesthetic theory has made this topic central. As well as rethinking the range and nature of the aesthetic, contemporary aesthetic theory asks after the value of aesthetic value itself, often interpreting this value in quasi-ethical or political terms. Sometimes the questions concern art: What is art's capacity to embody human freedom? What is the function of art in the formation or negation of human ethos? Can art motivate us to ethical action? How can art contribute to social change? However, art is not the sole province of the aesthetic. There is an aesthetic dimension to our experiences of all images, and not only images, in the wider culture, and across cultures. It is this broader frame, which includes art as a specific component but is not exhausted by it, that this collection addresses.

This, then, is a book substantially, if sometimes indirectly, about artworks, but they are not its only focus. The scope is broader, partly because we believe that understanding the issues of ethics and aesthetics, even as these arise *within* art theory and practice, requires tracking them across the boundary, such as it may be, that separates art from non-art. Mainly, though, it is because we think that questions about the condition of art *matter* in as much as they are ways of asking questions about the condition of human being, as it unfolds in history. Thus, although this book deals with artworks and other forms of imagery, at a deeper level it concerns the value *of* aesthetic value, and the question of where, in art or elsewhere, such value is to be found. It offers an insight into the ways such questions have been approached across a range of disciplines in recent years, and seeks to advance these debates by bringing them into dialogue around artworks and other kinds of image. The book is a series of exchanges, conceived so as to test certain assumptions about the ethics of our encounters with visual imagery.

That said, in conceiving this project we began with art. Our starting point was a sense of how questions concerning the value of aesthetic value have played out in debates around modern and contemporary art over the last three or four decades. Art discourse has, since the crisis of modernism, been occupied with the relationship between ethics and aesthetics, whether or not it has been expressed in these terms. Often this has taken the form of *opposing* aesthetics to ethics, on the grounds that the aesthetic is a space apart from practical considerations, whether of an ethical or a political nature. This legacy can be traced back to Kant, and the separation of the value spheres, right through to Greenberg's definition of modernism as 'a kind of bias or tropism: towards aesthetic value, aesthetic value as such and as ultimate.'[2] Indeed, it is above all modernist theory's *claim* on the aesthetic, its co-option of the discourse of aesthetics to underwrite a particular kind of art and a particular kind of critical practice, that has dominated the fraught relation between art theory and the aesthetic since the 1960s. If it is possible to get beyond this tendency to identify aesthetics with modernism, then both might begin to be seen in a new light. In certain respects, then, this book is as much a reflection on late or post-modernism, and our current modernity, as it is a way of orienting ourselves towards questions concerning the ethics of artworks and images in general.[3]

Two phases in this recent history of art practice and discourse may be distinguished. The first is a working through of the apparent loss of ethical content once claimed for modernist art. It centred on the perception that modernism had become *merely* aesthetic, in the pejorative sense of the aesthetic as a function of good taste. This is the moment of the post-modern *anti*-aesthetic, manifest in art practice and theory, though arguably propelled more by the latter than the former. From the 1970s through to the early 1990s, prevailing tendencies in art theory rejected the discourse of aesthetics on the grounds that it was politically or ethically regressive. It was argued that claims for the aesthetic value of art were little more than covert ways of blocking the critical analysis of artworks, and sustaining cultural elitism, traditional authority, and the market. Recall Hal Foster, in his editor's preface to what became the seminal collection of this moment, *The Anti-Aesthetic: Essays on Post-Modern Culture*:

'Anti-aesthetic'… signals that the very notion of the aesthetic, its network of ideas, is in question here: the idea that aesthetic experience exists apart, without 'purpose', all but beyond history, or that art can now effect a world at once (inter)subjective, concrete and universal – a symbolic totality. Like 'postmodernism', then, 'anti-aesthetic' marks a cultural position on the present: are categories afforded by the aesthetic still valid? […]

The adventures of the aesthetic make up one of the great narratives of modernity: from the time of its autonomy through art-for-art's-sake to its status as a necessary negative category, a critique of the world as it is. It is this last moment (brilliantly figured in the writings of Theodor Adorno) that is hard to relinquish: the notion of the aesthetic as subversive, a critical interstice in an otherwise instrumental world. Now, however, we have to consider that this aesthetic space too is eclipsed – or rather, that its criticality is now largely illusory (and so instrumental).[4]

This critique of the aesthetic was not wholly new. It has been a strand in the history of modern art and culture that reaches back to the beginning of the twentieth century, to Dada for example, or even earlier. In part, the project of the anti-aesthetic entailed recovering and re-evaluating this history. In practice and theory, the anti-aesthetic developed into a program of opposition to the ways in which aesthetic modernism had established itself as the cultural manifestation of social and political power, and hence became a means of sustaining, in cultural and intellectual practice, progressive political and social agendas which had, in the 1970s and 1980s, by and large been defeated in the spheres of politics and society. While, for the most part, excluded from mainstream political, social, even cultural life – it was business as usual, in terms of the aesthetic evaluation of art by museums, dealers, collectors and the mainstream media – the post-modern anti-aesthetic, in its various incarnations, did gain substantial institutional power. It is important not to overestimate this power, however, which was confined to certain sectors of academia and specialised critical commentary. Nevertheless, within that sphere, it succeeded in establishing the idea that, in art, ethical value is *opposed* to aesthetic value and vice versa, thereby establishing itself as the principal mode of ethical and political rectitude in contemporary art discourse.

It no longer holds this position. Though inheritors of the anti-aesthetic still generate important critical analyses, not least of the increasing spectacularisation of art practice, they no longer determine the prevailing conception of what it means for art to carry ethical value. Its waning, if we can call it that, was accompanied, or even partially caused, by the increasing prominence of competing ways of thinking about the relationship between ethics and aesthetics: of the authors gathered here, Thierry de Duve's work contributed significantly to freeing aesthetics from its identification with late modernism and thus its status as the antithesis of ethical value from a post-modern viewpoint. Hence, the second phase in recent practice and theory may be seen as an attempt to rethink the relationship between ethics and aesthetics. It is less easily described, perhaps in part because we still inhabit it. But it may be provisionally characterised as an array of attempts to renegotiate or recover connections between aesthetics, on the one hand, and ethics and politics, on the other. Where for advocates of the post-modern anti-aesthetic it seemed clear that the privileging of sensuous affect in art was at odds with ethical criticality and political project, today a range of practices and theoretical positions are, in different, and often antagonistic ways, seeking to overcome this opposition. Let us outline three broad tendencies as a way of dividing the field (there are doubtless others): the return to beauty, participatory practice and engaged art.

The idea of a 'return to beauty' generated an extensive literature and exhibition history in the 1990s.[5] In part, the return to beauty was a protest against the apparent institutional power of post-modern anti-aestheticism. It was motivated by a feeling that, as Peter Schjeldahl wrote in 1996, 'Beauty [...] has been quarantined from educated talk'.[6] At least that was its specific, artworld manifestation. But it also often entailed an attempt to reinvigorate the ethical, or even political, claims of beauty itself, by tracing the conjunction of the beautiful, the good and the just back to ancient philosophy on the one hand, and pre-modern art on the other. Elaine Scarry, an influential exponent of this position, writes in *On Beauty and Being Just*, the starting point for Jay Bernstein's essay in this volume:

> The banishing of beauty from the humanities in the last two decades has been carried out by a set of political complaints against it ... Beauty is, at the very least, innocent of the charges against it, and it may even be the case that far from damaging our capacity to attend to problems of injustice, it instead intensifies the pressure we feel to repair existing injuries.[7]

To claims such as this, Gayatri Spivak's question 'Why Beauty Now?', the title of her keynote address to the 2005 'Re-turn of Beauty' conference at The House of World Cultures, Berlin, seems apposite. From the anti-aesthetic perspective, but not only from the anti-aesthetic perspective, the return to beauty has often come across as a reactionary grab for one of most contested and 'abused' – to adopt Arthur Danto's usage – terms in the critical vocabulary, so it is important to ask *why* beauty matters in art today.[8] Why, if beauty it must be, does beauty matter again or, if it has always mattered – perhaps as the 'promise of happiness,' or as a revivifying, enlivening force, or, as for Plato, the object of love that we seek to know better, as Alexander Nehamas, its most eloquent defender, has argued – does it matter more urgently *now*?[9] What is at stake politically, in such a return, if that is what it is? Is it more than a defensive formation against the explicit politicisation of culture, and if so how? Alternatively, if it need not be beauty, might art be seen to function in ways less traditionally construed and constrained, yet recognisably aesthetic nonetheless? In short: why should we accept beauty as *the* mark of aesthetic value in art today?

The second broad tendency is the re-emergence of art as social practice: the production of forms of participation in art contexts with a view to mobilising the potential of that sphere for transforming, or at least transcending, everyday social relations. There are as many divergent practices within this tendency as any other: from stagings in museums and galleries of interactions among a narrow artworld public, to strategies of art-activism, to the resurgence of community arts. To some degree, recent social practice draws on modes of exchange, interaction and community building developed online. In other respects, it recovers previously overlooked forms of collective and collaborative art practice dating back to the 1960s. From the late 1990s until recently, Nicolas Bourriaud's term 'relational aesthetics' was a loose and overpervasive designation for this tendency. For Bourriaud, relational art turns the space of art into a site that promotes a 'specific sociability', that is, a staging of social relations within a specific situation.[10] These situations, and participatory practices more generally, are said to rehumanise social relations, if only within that specific situation. Thus, a *social* dimension in contemporary art practice is credited with *ethical* significance. This tends to focus on an internal ethics of artistic production and participation, notably whether a given work promotes 'positive' or 'negative' relations between its participants.

That said, the content and social structure of participatory works can also refer to broader social and economic structures: one thinks of projects by Santiago Sierra, Harrell Fletcher and Jochen Gerz, among many others.[11] Forms of social practice that foreground this larger social frame often take themselves to be quite at odds with Bourriaud's thinking, and recently there has been something of a backlash against the latter's focus on the *form* of social relations, as opposed to their content or conditions. For some, there is a suggestion of political dilettantism about activities that foreground conviviality within an artworld context.[12] For others, whilst it may be clear what is *relational* (or social) about such practices, with their stress on open-ended interaction between the work's participants in specific social situations, it is less obvious what 'aesthetic' might mean in such contexts. To a significant degree, these concerns may be rooted in the fact that it is often unclear what these practices aim to achieve – is it, for example, real social change on whatever scale, or is it to develop awareness about how existing social systems and networks operate? For as long as this remains unclear, it will also remain difficult to assess how inhabiting art spaces and discourses matters to their achievement.

The third tendency might be described, doubtless too simply, as the return of the art of engagement. The globalisation of social, political and economic conflict post-Cold War, and the concurrent globalisation of art practice, exhibition and debate, has created a context in which artists seek to document, reflect, supplement or intervene in representations of those conflicts worldwide. These practices may be at odds with the art market and the conservative discourse of the aesthetic, quite as much as the anti-aesthetic, yet the aesthetic as such is no longer at issue. This is because *immanent* artworld politics – questions of aesthetics and anti-aesthetics, autonomy, authorship, commodification, the spectator, in fact much of the legacy of modernist discourse – are secondary. What is primary here is the possibility of representations and counter-representations of points of political fracture. Just as engaged art of the early- to mid-twentieth century lay outside modernist discourse, belonging mainly to a Realist tradition, so today it lies largely outside modernism's legacies. For instance, one of its most central genres, documentary, was deemed a minor art form for much of the modern period, and hence excluded from mainstream modernist aesthetics. What is significant for documentary is the political agency of artworks and images in a larger context of representation and reception: the context of print and broadcast media, mainstream filmic and photographic representations, the broader circulation of vernacular, digital imagery. Although these strands of practice and theory are committed to political agendas commensurable with those of the anti-aesthetic, the aesthetic itself is no longer considered at odds with their pursuit. Instead, a range of aesthetic strategies are mobilised in order to investigate how regimes of representation operate.

Consider the difference between the Documentas of 1997 and 2002 in this regard. Documenta X (the X functioning visually as a cross over the category of art or art exhibition) was widely seen as exemplary of the anti-aesthetic agenda: the transformation of art into a space of political representation to the exclusion of aesthetics. Its director, Catherine David, justified the omission of Felix Gonzales-Torres, an artist of subtle ethical and aesthetic sensibilities, on the grounds of her antipathy to the 'dramatic aestheticization of political debate in recent art'.[13] By contrast, Documenta 11, curated by Okwui Enwezor, articulated numerous functions for art and its aesthetic capacities in a global polity, notably its value for navigating contemporary political tensions worldwide.[14] The latter exhibition included artists guided by what might be called – adapting Jeff Wall's reference to the 'art concept of photo-journalism' – the 'art concept of the document' (such as Allan Sekula), alongside paintings of muted, though compelling, political force (by Luc Tuymans), together with artists comparable to Gonzales-Torres in their creation of icons of intimate ethical experience (such as Doris Salcedo and Mona Hatoum). In practices such as these, ethical and aesthetic moments become inseparable; what matters is how, through the deployment of which media and what iconographies, the work addresses matters of political or ethical concern. Aesthetics here is not primarily an issue of judgement or beauty, but a matter of rhetoric: a concern with *how* the mode or manner in which the work treats its content, and the point of view from which it is addressed, disposes its viewers to see the world. This is not to suggest the aesthetic dimension of such work is somehow inessential or epiphenomenal, as might be implied were one to call it *merely* rhetorical, but to understand art's aesthetic dimension as such as a matter of rhetoric, such that what is aesthetic about a work of art just *is* the way in which it presents what it presents.[15]

For sure, to describe three tendencies in this way is an abstraction from the field of contemporary art, in its unprecedented pluralism. Our reason for doing so here is simply to characterise some of the ways in which ethics and aesthetics are no longer set up as *antithetical*, and to suggest that what might most deeply, if only implicitly, be at stake in much contemporary art theory and practice is the various ways in which their relation might be recovered or reconceived in view of this fact. This state of affairs prompted a number of questions, or possible tasks, that served as our guide in developing this project – questions that circulate around the world of art, but are not only internal to it.

1. We wanted to ask again about the ethics of modernism. If the identification of modernist art with aesthetics no longer holds, what of the strands of modernist thinking that foregrounded its ethical value—such as the Frankfurt school? How do those claims hold up in the present context for thinkers who have worked through post-modernist theory or programmatically worked against it? Is it possible, given the situation we have been describing, to re-evaluate the ethical claims of modernism itself, those claims regarded as 'largely illusory', by Foster among others at the high point of post-modern anti-aestheticism?

2. Beyond the specific discourses of participation, dialogue and community that frame social art practice, and not only social art practice—discourses that remain within the modernist legacy – what constitutes the specific agency and capabilities of that community specific to art: the artworld? How are ethics and aesthetics intertwined in the structure of the artworld, understood not just as a sociological fact, but also as an object for the philosophy of art? In a broader sense, how should we understand the contested idea of community in relation to art?

3. Relatedly, how are interpersonal relations mediated or evoked by our encounter with artworks and other images? How are ethics and aesthetics intertwined

within such encounters, and what is the relationship between encounters with artworks or images and our encounters with one another? Do ethics and aesthetics exhibit structural parallels, ether at the level of their objects, or the structure of their respective judgements, or the forms of the encounters in which those judgements take place?

4. If artworks have the potential to operate as counter-representations, what are the ethical conditions for representation in the culture at large, the context in which they need to operate? How should we understand the ontology of images so as to grasp these aspects of the aesthetic: specifically, in what terms can we characterise an aesthetics of engagement? Under the current conditions of global culture, how can the aesthetic, in the context of art practice, be something other than fragile and ineffectual?

It seemed to us that addressing these questions and tasks required drawing on approaches that did not belong exclusively to the discourses of contemporary art. We wanted to contribute to these debates in art theory by bringing a range of theoretical perspectives to bear on a topic – ethics and aesthetics – that, while clearly central to art discourse, just as clearly goes beyond it. The project of this book therefore entailed staging a series of interdisciplinary encounters that brought ethics and aesthetics into dialogue across a range of humanities disciplines.

When we embarked on this project, which initially took the form of a series of four half-day, two-speaker events at Tate Modern, London, a number of books and conferences on the so-called 'return to aesthetics' had already been published or taken place.[16] But in one way or another, all of these seemed, at least to us, to limit the scope of potential debate. To varying degrees, each belonged *within* analytic *or* continental traditions in philosophy, to art history *or* visual studies, or other fields such as comparative literature or gender studies. By contrast, we wanted to set up a series of encounters that *crossed* these various fields, bringing what is particular to each to bear on related disciplines and traditions, so as to discover something about what might be at stake not just within, but also between and across, debates that were otherwise going on within discrete disciplinary or tradition-specific boundaries. Given this broader goal, we wanted to enable a real exchange to take place, rather than simply juxtapose contributors from different disciplines.

A principle of exchange was therefore built into the structure of the events themselves. Each took the form of a pre-circulated paper followed by a prepared response, a moderated discussion, a question and answer period, and then the same again, but in reverse speaker order: speaker 1 paper; speaker 2 response; discussion; speaker 2 paper; speaker 1 response; discussion. This structure generated a more substantial intellectual exchange than can typically be expected in a public forum. It also gave rise to unusually strong lines of argument between the paired contributors, as may be traced here in the way the themes of each contributor's paper tend to reappear as presuppositions or grounds for their response to their co-contributor in each of the four sections. This structure of paper response, paper response has therefore been retained in the revised versions of papers and responses published here.

Our goals for the project directed us not just in the choice of disciplines represented, but also in the choice of speakers to represent them, and even more critically, who would be paired with whom. The disciplines represented here include analytic and continental philosophy, art history, theory and practice, cultural history and visual culture, rhetoric and comparative literature. We arrived at specific pairings by looking for areas of potential dialogue and difference between the respective projects of exponents of these fields. The pairings were conceived so as to bring together thinkers from different disciplines and perspectives whose work nonetheless bears upon shared issues, and who could therefore respond to each other in valuable ways. Contributors needed to have enough common frame of reference to be able to understand the other's aims and sources, yet enough differences to ensure a critical interaction. Most importantly for our purposes, the work of each of these thinkers converges in fruitful ways in the region where ethics, aesthetics, and politics meet. Moreover, in several of the pairings (the exception being Thierry de Duve and Howard Caygill), the contributors were already fairly well known to one another, and to that extent the exchanges build upon existing, though largely unpublicised, intellectual relationships. Indeed, the structure of the original events encouraged a certain performance of these relationships as friendship and antagonism in the encounters themselves.

Thus Jay Bernstein, possibly the leading philosopher working in English who remains committed to sustaining and extending the legacy of Adornian Critical Theory, and by so doing, countering the supposed ethics of post-modern anti-aestheticism, meets Judith Butler, one of the most prominent figures in gender theory, whose work in recent years has increasingly focused on contemporary issues concerning ethics, State politics and the law.

Noël Carroll, both a respected film theorist and one of the most prominent analytic philosophers of art of his generation, with a special interest in the philosophy of the avant-garde, meets Adrian Piper, both a leading first-generation conceptual artist known for bringing political questions, notably questions of race, into the purview of conceptual art and, uniquely, also a professional philosopher who works on meta-ethics and conceptions of the self from a Kantian perspective.

Thierry de Duve, art historian, theorist, critic and curator, known for his work seeking to retrieve and reformulate Kantian aesthetics for art *after* beauty, meets Howard Caygill, continental philosopher and cultural historian, whose intellectual career began with a reconstruction of the *pre*-history of Kant's aesthetics, on the shared ground of the afterlife, if any, of Kantian approaches to aesthetics today.

Finally, Tom Mitchell, known for pioneering work on the relationship between language and images, which was to prove one of the central impetuses for the recent emergence of Visual Culture as a distinct discipline, meets art historian Griselda Pollock, a pioneer of feminist art history whose work now extends to the interface between ethics, aesthetics and politics, beyond academic art history.

In the process of developing the project, first the public programmes, then the book, in collaboration with the contributors, it became clear that lines of affinity and argument were being generated not only within the pairings, but across the series as a whole; we will try to make some of these explicit below. One theme in particular emerged: the question of how we might understand the image, often but not always the artwork, as a *form of life*, more specifically a form of damaged or endangered life – life threatened by death. This idea can be approached from either of two ends; from one perspective, ethical and political issues generate implications for aesthetics; from the other, issues in aesthetics generate ethical and political implications.

These exchanges took place during what might be called a 'war of images', one that continues as we write. This is the topic of Tom Mitchell's contribution. Like many critical intellectuals, several of the contributors to this volume – Caygill, Mitchell and Pollock stand out – chose to address questions concerning the aesthetics and ethics of the image in relation to contemporary political events. Others – such as Butler and Bernstein – though not directly focusing on those events, found themselves reflecting on fundamental questions concerning violence and the image, while themes such as the communities convened by, or for, works of art – addressed by de Duve, Carroll and Piper – take on new resonance when viewed in this light. This is not to say that any of these texts are merely 'occasional', nor that issues concerning the life and death of images are confined to present political conditions; rather, it is to say that the larger political context led to a foregrounding of questions concerning art and images as agents, even combatants, in a theatre of war. In different ways, through the book, this question of the *agency* of images feeds into reflections on the vitality, or even the virulence, of images and their various forms of political efficacy and ethical valence.

Looked at from the other end, however, matters concerning the ontology – perhaps even bio-ontology – of artworks are primary. Notably, they centre on the question of whether there are substantive analogies to be drawn between artworks and persons as both objects of experience and entities capable of making a particular kind of claim on our attention. A persistent theme concerns the implicit parallels between ethical and aesthetic judgements, and the way each mediates the other – questions such as how artworks and images mediate our claims on one another (de Duve), whether our care for art reflects our care for others (Caygill), and whether artworks and images function as a double for life (Bernstein, Butler, Mitchell). This theme is developed in relation to both art and non-art images. Bernstein and Butler suggest, in addition, that art is privileged over other forms of imagery, in virtue of its challenge to cognitive life. Their concern with art as a 'shock to thought' finds echoes, at one remove, in Mitchell and Pollock's interest in traumatic images, images that address us in ways we find hard to process cognitively. All the contributors to this volume are concerned, albeit in different ways, with the vitality of images or artworks, what it means to see images as forms of life, or with understanding human life through the life of images.

Butler's and, especially, Bernstein's essays consider the work of art as an analogue of human life, and as a substitute for the human body. Something like this thought returns in different ways in both Caygill's concern with the energetics of the artwork and what it means for it to be subject to care and destined to die and, again, in Pollock's analysis of the image, in its very materials, as a register of human death. In part, the debate between Carroll and Piper touches on the human lives convened by works of art, brought into ethical community, or neglected by them. Relatedly, de Duve's concern is ultimately with art as a vehicle through which we address one another in virtue of our common humanity. It is Mitchell, however, who takes the life of images as his central theme. His essay here is connected to his book *What do Images Want?* in which he makes a case for the analysis of image-life that sustains, despite their differences, all the contributions to this volume. In that book, Mitchell writes:

> Let me put my cards on the table at the outset. I believe that magical attitudes toward images are just as powerful in the modern world as they were in so-called ages of faith. [...] My argument is that the double consciousness about images is a deep and abiding feature of human responses to representation. It is not something we 'get over' when we grow up, become modern, or acquire critical consciousness [....] The specific expressions of this paradoxical double consciousness of images are amazingly various. [....] They include the ineluctable tendency of criticism itself to pose as an iconoclastic practice, a labour of demystification and pedagogical exposure of false images. Critique-as-iconoclasm is, in my view, just as much a symptom of the life of images as its obverse, the naïve faith in the inner life of works of art. [...]

We might even have to entertain what I would call a 'critical idolotry' or 'secular divination' as an antidote to that reflexive critical iconoclasm that governs intellectual discourse today. Critical idolotry involves an approach to images that does not dream of destroying them, and that recognizes every act of disfiguration or defacement as itself an act of creative destruction for which we must take responsibility.[17]

Mitchell is arguing that we cannot, and should not, deny the life of images; we might add that, given the increasing power of the icon in the culture at large, perhaps, more than ever, we cannot *afford* to do so. The life of the image has been given urgent global, political and cultural significance in the image wars that have irrupted since 9/11.[18] But this is also a response to the post-modern anti-aesthetic, named above in the phrase 'critique-as-iconoclasm'. For proponents of the anti-aesthetic, it was crucial, one might say, not only that images be dead, but that they be *shown* to be dead. Their assault on the aesthetic was or is to a large extent an assault on the claims of the image or artwork to an inner life. This thought dates back to a certain reception of Walter Benjamin within Anglophone art theory since the 1970s. For Benjamin, as is well known, art emerges from practices of ritual and cult, and the artwork in its enchanted form is a form of magic, credited with a semblance of life. On this account, the artwork is a residual vehicle or vestige of religious transcendence in an otherwise disenchanted world. Such animism, on this reading of Benjamin, is to be contested. It is above all this question of the transcendence or non-transcendence of artworks and images that our title refers to; as such it signals a quite different orientation to the question of ethics and aesthetics from that seen in preceding debates about beauty and the anti-aesthetic. In as much as this volume presents a set of resources for the reconsideration of the relations between ethics, aesthetics and politics – in the wake of modernism, and of post-modernism – it addresses issues fundamental to aesthetic theory in general. The perspectives collected here are diverse, but the questions they share may be framed in the terms outlined above. Mitchell offers one perspective among others, while also making most explicit the claim that connects, in different ways, all the essays in this volume – namely, that the issues raised by the vitality of images are unavoidable for contemporary interpretations of the relationship between ethics and aesthetics. The details of the lines of argumentation that connect these texts, within the pairings and across them, and the variations on the theme present here, will be apparent if we now consider the texts in some detail.

I

J M Bernstein and Judith Butler

Jay Bernstein's essay begins with a critique of Elaine Scarry's *On Beauty and Being Just*, cited above, which is one of the most impassioned defences of beauty, and its positive ethical value, to emerge from the return to beauty debate of the 1990s. Scarry argues that acknowledging beauty promotes a sense of justice among human beings as a function of its tendency to affirm a reciprocal 'aliveness' in people and things. She argues this explicitly in opposition to what she sees as beauty's banishment from the humanities by a set of 'political complaints', alluding to the discourse of the anti-aesthetic. It is a questionable thesis. Scarry caricatures the critical arguments against beauty, and relies herself on an objective idea of beauty as a property of things and people. Bernstein is not concerned with the merits and demerits of Scarry's argument as whole, but with the fact that she foregrounds a relationship between beauty and life. He limits himself to pointing out the idealism of Scarry's case for beauty. He notes how her account of beauty's extraordinary aliveness presumes a background of ordinary deadness. His essay can be read as an account of the dialectical relationship between these two moments, one which aims to understand how the experience of the aesthetic – which he sometimes continues to call 'beauty', and agrees is 'enlivening' – figures within what he sees as the pervasive deadening of experience characteristic of our historical era: modernity. Ultimately, his argument with a conception of experience, and hence of beauty, such as Scarry's is not only that it fails philosophically, but that it does not take account of the experiential failure of modern social life. Bernstein aims to explain how and why what remains of beauty – for him this is the 'violent', negative beauty of modernist art – has been motivated by the prevailing social conditions of modernity. In short, he would argue, the forces of modernity (technological reasoning and capitalism) transform experience into *mere* representation and the violence of modernist art is a violence against representation as such for the sake of experience.

   Bernstein's philosophy of aesthetic modernism is most comprehensively set out in his book *Against Voluptuous Bodies: Late Modernism and the Meaning of Painting*.[19] That book begins with a critique of Kant's conception of aesthetic experience and experience in general. Bernstein argues that although Kant posits that experience is a function of the reciprocity of sensory and cognitive awareness, effectively the former is subordinated to the latter. Sensory awareness is deemed inarticulate and meaningless until it is subsumed under concepts, and so does not count as awareness, on its own terms, at all. Bernstein argues that the possibility of experience in the fullest sense thus dissolves, and that this is a point at which philosophical and social modernity converge: 'In metaphorical terms, but terms that I argue are not merely metaphorical, Kantian conceptuality's increasing independence from its sensory bearer is enacted, cognitively, in the mathematical explanations of modern natural science, and practically in the rationalizations of the practices and institutions that legislate the shape and meaning of modern social life.'[20] Seen in this light, the ethics of modernist painting lies not in what it succeeds in doing but in the failure of ethical life to which its very existence testifies. This is because Bernstein's account of modernism centres on the idea that its autonomy from social and political practice is not modernism's achievement but a fate it has suffered. It is art expelled from everyday life under the conditions of modernity. Modernity is understood as a process of pervasive rationalisation incommensurable with full and free sensory experience. The idea of spontaneous mutual harmony between the faculties of understanding and imagination – underpinned by the idea of a universal ethical community – central to Kant's aesthetics of beauty, fails. Modernist aesthetics is the aesthetics of that failure. 'The task of the arts [which modernism takes up] is to rescue from cognitive and rational oblivion our embodied experience and the standing of unique, particular things as the proper objects of such experience, albeit only in the form of a reminder or a promise.'[21] Bernstein readily acknowledges that this line of argument is not fully his own but that of T W Adorno. In large part his philosophical project consists in sustaining and defending Adorno's thought, arguing for its ongoing necessity, and bringing it to bear on new topics. *Against Voluptuous Bodies* is an Adornian interpretation of a field of modernist practice that Adorno himself did not address: painting.

While Bernstein's allegiance is principally to Adorno, his critique of representation connects with another strand of continental aesthetics of the last forty years: the Nietzschean aesthetics articulated by, for example, Gilles Deleuze. In the present essay, his only sustained engagement with this strand of aesthetic theory, Bernstein agrees for the most part with Deleuze's account of artistic modernism, as it emerges in his book on Francis Bacon. For Deleuze, Bacon's paintings materialise a violence against representational or figurative painting, for the sake of sensation or experience. Bernstein questions, however, the choice of Bacon as an example. Bacon makes things both easier and more difficult for Deleuze. Easier in that Bacon's art advertises itself as an art of violence, so gives credence to Deleuze's claims. More difficult in that violence is depicted. If Bacon's paintings embody a violence *against* representation they are also undoubtedly representations *of* violence. Bernstein selects instead the example of Matisse in order to bring out the nature of modernism's *pure* violence, a violence immanent to painting and strictly against representation as such. Scarry's only extended reference to artistic modernism in *On Beauty and Being Just* is to Matisse. Scarry takes as given Matisse's conventional reputation as a painter of sensuous beauty, focuses on Matisse's least modernist and most representational period – the years in Nice following the First World War – and explicitly values these works for their representational power. Bernstein, selecting the most aggressively modernist – also and therefore for him the most 'beautiful' – of Matisse's paintings effectively switches the site of modernism's 'pure violence' against representation from one in which it can be confused with real violence, Bacon, to one in which it cannot, Matisse.

At the heart of Bernstein's essay is a characterisation of Matisse's modernist paintings as a certain kind of life form. His central claim is that the beauty of Matisse's paintings is a life-giving quality, as Scarry said, but one that *internalises* the deadened quality of ordinary experience in the world for which they are created. They exhibit a kind of less than fully human half-life, a shell-shocked consciousness, which Bernstein memorably describes as 'vegetable'. If a plant could breathe, he writes, it would look like a Matisse. His references to vegetable life are intended mainly to say something about Matisse's use of the arabesque; the arabesque – which Matisse learned from the Islamic cultures of North Africa – is a means to defeat representation for the sake of experience. But they also draw together a set of questions to do with the life of an artwork. What it is for an artwork to live? What are the relationships between the life of artworks and human life? What is it for an artwork to suffer and die? How would that relate to human suffering and death? Bernstein's essay centres on such questions, which recur in Caygill's notion of works of art as entities made to be destroyed. They also return in various ways in other contributions to this volume, not least in Judith Butler's.

Butler's essay pieces together remarks on aesthetics by Walter Benjamin dispersed through a number of posthumously published texts from 1917 to 1921, and then surfaces certain continuities with his reflections on ethics in writings of the same period, including his influential essay on law and justice, 'Critique of Violence' (1921). It is a close reading of Benjamin – a quite different Benjamin from that of the post-modern anti-aesthetic – that explicates his often elusive theological vocabulary, in order to connect a metaphysics of art to one of law. In so doing she presents an account of the 'critical violence' of modernist art, which is comparable to Bernstein's, and a reflection on ethics that supplements her recent writings on political power and State violence as well as those on ethics and theology.[22]

She begins with a distinction Benjamin makes between marks and signs in a short text from 1917. Signs are printed (from outside) on lifeless things, whereas marks are manifestations (from within) on living beings. In the case of the former he is thinking of writing or drawing (the graphic line), in the case of the latter he refers to how marks on living human bodies carry a moral meaning: in two vivid examples, blushing is a mark of guilt and stigmata are marks of innocence. Benjamin suggests, however, that painting is also a medium of marks. A painting differs from a drawing (and more obviously from a written text) in that it is not organised against a background. Its organisation is internal. On this basis he sees an analogy between paintings and living bodies that leads him to propose that we can understand something about moral being through understanding painting. This is what interests Butler. The mark is 'the juncture of aesthetics and morality', she writes. This juncture does not depend on just the examples of stigmata and blushing (which are, it is fair to say, too unusually loaded with ethical meaning). Benjamin's claim is rather that paintings are like living (human) bodies in that they are compositions of marks that appear to express an immaterial spirit that he calls 'the word'. This term can be misleading. 'The word' is not a linguistic entity (like the signs of writing or drawing), it is the metaphysical idea that informs painting: it is something like the principle of composition in painting. He argues that different kinds of painting are characterised by different relationships between word and mark. In classical painting, his example is Raphael, the word predominates over the marks, which is to say, the substance of the painting is subsumed under the idea it represents. In modernist painting, he is thinking of Kandinsky and Klee, the word 'enters' the mark – or, the idea is coextensive with the substance of the painting.

Butler elaborates on this fragment of a modernist theory by connecting it with Benjamin's no less fragmentary remarks on beauty. Beauty is the life of a work of art, and the life of a work of art is a *semblance* of human life. It is semblance because there is nothing behind it, it is like a mirage, and this is the source of its seductive power. But the ethical value of painting, as Butler finds it in Benjamin, its value as a kind of ethical exemplar, lies in the manner in which it acts against its own seductive power. 'If the ideal appears at all', Butler writes, 'it is always partial and fragmented, putting the work of art at risk, and even mandating its critical destruction.' The true task of the work of art (in modern times) is to destroy its own aspect of semblance, beauty and life. It is a matter of bringing to light that quality of the painting that acts against the seductiveness of beauty. Benjamin calls this quality 'the expressionless'.

Here it becomes clear how Butler's essay parallels Bernstein's. Both are contributions to an understanding of the ethical significance of the modernist aesthetic centred on modernist painting's action against painting itself as a semblance of life. There are similarities and differences between Butler's theory of modernism derived from early Benjamin and Bernstein's derived from Adorno. Both are theories of art's autonomy, which translates to an idea of anarchism ('order without law', as Bernstein writes) in art. Both are concerned with a recalcitrant quality in modernist painting. In both cases this quality is somehow inhuman. Bernstein writes of vegetable life. Butler writes of painting's mineral quality ('dead, petrified and without life'). The most important difference between them is that Butler argues for a metaphysical – Benjamin's word is 'divine' – dimension to the ethics of painting. There is something equivalent in Adorno to 'the expressionless', as Bernstein notes in his response to Butler, but whereas Benjamin interprets the inhuman quality of modernist painting as divine, Adorno sees it in purely materialist terms. Butler holds to Benjamin's theological frame of reference. Ultimately, she is interested in how painting can tell us something about the relationship between morality as a closed economy of crime and punishment – of retributive and restitutive justice – and what acts against it. Retribution, for her, belongs to an Old Testament and Judaic conception of law (law being instituted morality). 'The expressionless', as a divine force, is said to destroy the cycles of retribution in manner analogous to its destruction of the semblance of human life in painting. This is what is at stake for her in the juncture between aesthetics and ethics that she finds in Benjamin. It is also where the present essay connects, for example, with her arguments elsewhere against the revenge politics of the United States after 2001 with reference to new instances of administrative violence – specifically the practice of 'indefinite detention'.[23]

II   Noël Carroll and Adrian Piper

Noël Carroll argues, with echoes of Hegel, that until the modern period art functioned as a powerful vehicle for forming the self-understanding of a people or culture. Why, he asks, did this cease to be the case in the modern period? What developments in the artworld, on the one hand, and the philosophy of art on the other, were responsible for severing aesthetics from ethos?

With respect to the former question, Carroll attributes to the artworld a desire to constitute art as an independent and autonomous realm of value in an increasingly specialised world. But the resultant stress on art as something to be valued for its own sake has, he claims, unwittingly disabled art, by stripping it of its former substantive social functions; through the achievement of autonomy, art unwittingly made itself socially dispensable. Seen in this light, the autonomous artist's fiercely guarded distance from society, critical or otherwise, becomes little more than a mirror image of the indifference of society to autonomous art. For why, Carroll asks, should society care about what does not address its concerns, or if does address them, only ever does so as 'scold'? From this point of view, both anti-aesthetic post-modernists, who question artistic autonomy, and critical modernists who defend it, such as Bernstein, represent this negative tendency. But Carroll and Bernstein's positions are opposed in a deeper sense: in his account of art's increasing isolation from society, Carroll implies that the artworld has something approaching a collective agency, and through this agency inflected its marginalisation upon itself, albeit unwittingly. Autonomy is thereby figured as something akin to the attainment of an intentional goal, rather than a consequence of deeper social and historical processes, of which the artworld was as much an object as the subject. Bernstein's paper, by contrast, takes the latter way of thinking about artistic modernity as an expression of broader social forces for granted. In her reply to Carroll, Piper raises a related question about the apparent voluntarism in Carroll's historical account: the implication that if artists were free to choose self-expression, they must have been free to choose otherwise.

With respect to the latter of the two questions Carroll poses at the outset, he argues that the philosophy of art's attraction to the autonomy thesis is deeply rooted in the self-conception of analytic philosophy as a discipline, notably the way in which it aspires to define the essence of a given concept or practice in terms of necessary and sufficient conditions. The autonomy thesis appeals to philosophers schooled in this tradition, he argues, because it facilitates the essentialist project by providing, so it seems, a strong candidate for what everything that is art, and only everything that is art, is supposed to have in common; the standard interpretation of autonomy, in this context, being 'form valued for its own sake'. The problem with this conception of autonomy, for Carroll, is that it marginalises that in the service of which form functions, namely, meaning or extra-artistic purposes and commitments of one sort or another. Moreover, by ignoring the kind of work a given work is, this approach misperceives the nature of its object. In Carroll's example, this would include ignoring the way in which realist novels comment on particular social formations by focusing exclusively on the formal traits through which they do so. Given that in the realist novel form is in large part a *vehicle* for social and psychological commentary, appreciating their formal qualities in isolation from their rationale falsifies the art.

In all these claims, Carroll's paper reflects his broader philosophical project. It builds on earlier influential papers contesting aesthetics in general, and formalism in particular, in the philosophy of art. Like his work in film theory, it advocates what he has called 'piece meal' philosophising over grand theoretical abstractions about art as such or individual arts. His focus on the realist novel here (as opposed to, say, literature as such) is in line with his attention, in the philosophy of film, to various filmic devices rather than *the* medium of film as such. This reflects his antipathy for essentialism in philosophy more generally: not only does essentialism distort the data, in the case at hand it serves to isolate the philosophy of art. For on this conception only those already invested in art have any reason to concern themselves with it. In the light of this Carroll argues that both artists and philosophers should renounce the autonomy thesis: the latter to better understand the broader terrain of art's relation to ethics, politics and the like, the former to better engage the wider culture from something other than an adversarial perspective.

In her reply, Adrian Piper focuses on Carroll's recommendation that artists re-engage with the broader life-world by celebrating what is positive in their audience's ethos. On the one hand, Piper believes there is little to celebrate in an ethos in which all values, including that of 'free expression', are subjugated in advance to the profit motive. On the other, she believes that Carroll's proposed solution is distorted by a misperception: he is diagnosing a *conception* of art shared by 'Euroethnic' philosophers, critics and art institutions in the modern period, rather than by artists themselves. If that is right, Piper argues, Carroll's remedy will be misguided: for the problem lies not with how artworks function for their viewers, or with the attitudes or intentions of artists, but with how what they produce is *taken up* by the culture at large. One issue this raises is the extent to which artists share, or at least acquiesce to, the dominant conception of art within a given culture: if Euroethnic aestheticians, art critics and art institutions alike are internal to a particular conception of art, one might wonder how it is possible for artists to remain outside it. Be that as it may, from Piper's perspective, even were Carroll right in his diagnosis, his prognosis would be unworkable: in a free market if art does not sell it will not achieve the visibility required to achieve the positive effect Carroll advocates; but if it does sell, and thereby achieves such visibility, whatever positive ethos it might once have promoted will be subordinated in advance to the need to maximise profits. On this view, Piper argues, contra mainstream liberal free-market economics, that profits and social progress, on her understanding of the latter, are incompatible.

This view is at the heart of her own paper. Like Carroll, she takes issue with the dominant self-understanding of the contemporary artworld, albeit from a different perspective: she begins from a critique of the ideological uses to which the 'anti-originality' thesis central to much post-modern art and theory has been put. Piper sees this thesis as a strategic manoeuvre designed to legitimate pilfering from marginalised cultures that came to prominence in response to the increasing value attached to ideas of 'otherness' in the late 1980s. As she points out, the anti-originality thesis conflicts with a much deeper cultural investment in the rhetoric of innovation, and concomitant cycles of desire-satisfaction for the 'new and improved'. Piper coins the term 'advertainment' to characterise this anaesthetic combination of advertising and entertainment. For Piper, artworld investment in 'the new' reflects this wider phenomenon, and artists suffer to the extent that they do not play ball. Contrary to the view that free expression is compatible with an unrestrained free market, Piper argues, in a broadly Kantian vein, that such a conception of freedom – freedom to consume – amounts to enslavement to a cycle of manufactured desire and temporary satisfaction. Far from being compatible with such models, art that really does express a view at odds with manufactured desire is incompatible with the conflation of freedom and free market, which is why it suffers a marginalisation proportionate to the challenges it raises.

This is evidently one reason Piper maintains what she calls her 'day job' in philosophy. Since her own art practice falls within the category of *explicitly* political art, that is, art that is either ignored, or, if it cannot be ignored, attacked, it follows that Piper needs an alternative means to support herself. The belief that there is such a thing as *non*-political art is, for Piper, pure ideology: art that is not explicitly political is *implicitly* political. Implicitly political art, defined negatively, includes all works that do not fall within the former category. Piper's distinction between explicitly and implicitly political art might be read as descriptive rather than evaluative – were it not clear that Piper takes such work to function, wittingly or otherwise, as an endorsement of free market capitalism, to which she is evidently opposed. Thus, she argues, only *explicitly* political art's principled opposition to the market is compatible with the demands of free, non-instrumentalised, expression. Only this art, though it violates accepted norms for innovation within our society, nonetheless offers a glimpse of human freedom.

As with Carroll, Piper's essay reflects her broader project in various ways. As an artist, Piper's work has been persistently concerned with social antagonism towards marginalised identities, notably those structured around conceptions of race. But rather than deal with such issues abstractly or didactically, her practice has striven to make those who encounter it aware of their own tacit prejudices, through its direct address to its others in what Piper calls 'the indexical present' – the here and now of their encounter with the work. As a philosopher, Piper has contested dominant modern liberal conceptions of the self that combine an economic conception of rationality based on utility maximisation with a Humean theory of action as desire-based motivation. Against this, she argues for a Kantian conception of the self that takes its point of departure from the idea of a unified, rationally consistent experience of the world in the *Critique of Pure Reason*. Piper's contribution here draws out the implications of her larger project for ideas of originality and progress in art.

Carroll shares Piper's antipathy for capitalism, but he finds her division of art into the explicitly and the implicitly political too Manichean. He proposes adding a third category, the possibility of which Piper denies: that is, non-political art. Carroll's example is paying an artist to paint a portrait, outside any gallery nexus. He asks whether the fact that no overt criticism of the artworld or free market takes place in such a scenario may be equated with endorsement, arguing that to identify non-criticism with endorsement drains the latter concept of 'existential seriousness'. For Carroll, the exchange in question takes place, to all intents and purposes, outside the market and, to that extent, occurs off Piper's conceptual map. Carroll also takes issue with the apparent normativity of Piper's position that any art that *fails* to be explicitly political is implicitly political, where the latter is understood as a tacit endorsement of capitalism: why, Carroll asks, can't artists simply have 'other fish to fry?' From the perspective of his own paper, Piper's argument would be another example of art's self-marginalisation from positive social purpose. As a corrective, he suggests various possible roles within Piper's category of explicitly political art for art to be other than negative. Picking up the theme of his own paper, he suggests explicitly political art might instead celebrate what is positive in a given ethos or polis. For Carroll, the murals in Philadelphia's garment district suggest a whole range of possibilities for the promotion of a given ethos that are largely off the artworld's map: to think that art must *always* be adversarial to be explicitly political is to assume that there is nothing whatsoever to celebrate in a given ethos – and this implies a perfectionism bordering on the puritanical. On Carroll's account, resistance to the market is but one paradigm of free expression.

III   Thierry de Duve and Howard Caygill

Thierry de Duve's unique contribution to recent art theory is to have shown that Kant's aesthetics remains a productive resource for contemporary thought about art, particularly art after Duchamp. His paper here extends this program into new areas, and in doing so makes the ethical stakes of his aesthetics more explicit. It does this by addressing what de Duve calls the 'crisis of representativity' affecting artists with the advent of modernity. In the face of widespread scepticism, de Duve defends the idea that artists speak 'on behalf' of others. Indeed, for de Duve, the thought that artists speak on behalf not only of others, but of *all* others, is essential to the notion of art, however problematic it may seem. The question is what *legitimates* this assumption. De Duve proposes an alternative: either it is the artist's 'universal mandate' or it is the 'artwork's universal address', and his paper sets out to decide which.

De Duve begins by drawing attention to a key feature of Kant's account of aesthetic judgement: its normativity, the implicit claim that all others *ought* to agree with the judge. For de Duve this is crucial; it is the most important conjunction of ethics and aesthetics in Kant. The question is how judgements premised on subjective feeling could legitimately lay claim to the assent of all others. Kant's solution is to invoke a *sensus communis* – a community of shared feeling – grounded in a 'free play' of faculties that we are presumed to possess as human beings, in so far as they are required for cognition in general. What makes disputes about such judgements significant, on de Duve's account, is that refusing to endorse another's aesthetic judgement amounts to implicitly denying them their humanity – their participation in a community of sense. In Kant's day, *natural* beauty was the site where such 'hope in the ethical destiny of the human species was put to the test'; today, for de Duve, *art* has become this site. In making this case, de Duve focuses, in a way that has proved controversial for more orthodox Kantians, on Kant's theory of *pure* aesthetic judgement – that is, judgements concerning conceptually unconstrained, and hence predominantly natural beauty – rather than Kant's account of judgements of artistic beauty.[24] He does so because he holds that it is no longer our aesthetic judgements about nature, but about art, that testify that humanity *ought* to be living in harmony, in the face of pervasive demonstrations that it cannot. For de Duve, this is why the important parallel to draw is between the *significance* that the judgement 'this is beautiful' held for Kant, and the *significance* that the judgement 'this is art' holds today.

De Duve's reworking of Kant needs to be understood in the context of art after Duchamp. Duchamp's readymades – everyday objects presented as works of art for the aesthetic judgement of everyone and anybody – provided an enormous stimulus to theoretical reflection on art, one that de Duve's work has consistently sought to unpack. The readymades, and the art practices that have followed from them, institute a state of affairs in which art may be made from anything whatsoever, and presented for the judgement of anybody whomsoever. Everyone must judge for himself or herself, and in doing so they find themselves in the position of the artist. What judges are henceforth asked to do is to endorse the artist's judgement, addressed to all, that this is art, with their own. Hence the shift in the nature of aesthetic judgement, as de Duve sees it, from the Kantian 'this is beautiful' to the post-Duchampian 'this is art.'

Given this, the question becomes how to articulate the universality of aesthetic judgements after Duchamp. On de Duve's account, artists speak on behalf of others, not in virtue of some putatively universal mandate artists possess, but in virtue of their art being addressed to all others. To de Duve's mind, formalism and multiculturalism alike get this wrong: both claim mandate is the ground of address, rather than vice versa, the only difference being that the latter relativises the domain of such mandate to a specific group. For a way out of this impasse, de Duve invokes deictics: terms sometimes referred to as 'linguistic shifters' such as 'you', 'I' or 'we' that remain purely formal until they are fleshed out empirically in a particular linguistic situation. He demonstrates this by invoking in turn the audience and his co-contributor, Howard Caygill, with whom he was sharing a stage. The upshot, for de Duve, is to bring out the ethical implications of aesthetic judgement. Every aesthetic judgement contains a universal address which signals that the judge, in the position of the artist, claims to speak on behalf of all others, but only by virtue of addressing all others: in de Duve's terms 'you and me' legitimates 'all of us', and not vice versa. This universal address fulfils what de Duve calls the 'quasi-ethical' obligation to endow all others with the capacity to agree based on feeling alone. Works of art are the very embodiment of such an address.

In his reply, Caygill says that he shares both de Duve's premises and his conclusions, but not the arguments by which he gets from the former to the latter. He proposes rephrasing the question '*Do* artists speak on behalf of all of us?' as '*Must* artworks speak on behalf of all of us?' The move from de Duve's 'Do artists ... ?' to Caygill's 'Must artworks ... ?' realigns the question not only from artist to work, but from question of fact to question of obligation. Like Kant, de Duve privileges the moments of 'quantity' and 'modality' of judgements of taste. But, for Caygill, he overplays universality to the detriment of necessity. In Caygill's rephrasing, the question becomes: why *must* certain objects (works of art) provoke certain (putatively universal) responses? This question shifts the terrain of debate away from de Duve's emphasis on the subject towards the object, and with it to Kant's possible contribution to the ontology of art. Caygill's way of posing the question is designed to avoid an aesthetics of subjectivity. Caygill sees the problem such an aesthetic entails in the way de Duve's argument slides from claiming that *art* is the place where the ethical destiny of mankind, its capacity for living in peace, is put to the test, to using art as an occasion for *us* to test our claims to community vis-à-vis one another. Caygill's return to the challenge that works of art present, 'even to the point of their own destruction', flags the point at which his own concerns intersect with de Duve's, and demonstrate the consequences of his proposed reorientation in action.

His paper follows these through an analysis of works of art as entities 'made to be destroyed'. For Caygill this emerges from a consideration of the metaphysical categories of being, becoming and annihilation transposed into the aesthetic register of creation, conservation and destruction. The intuition that guides his paper is that the destruction of art is much closer to its creation than has generally been recognised by modern aesthetics, given its privileging of creation. Caygill proposes that works of art be understood as finite, pointing to the constant care required to prevent their passing out of existence. This leads to the question of what *right* artworks have to their continued existence. This question is foregrounded in cases of wilful destruction, which serve to throw the otherwise taken for granted care maintaining art in existence into relief. He argues that the standard terms in which such events are understood needs to be reoriented, since understanding destruction in general on the iconoclastic model leads to conceiving it as something that befalls the work from *without*, as opposed to something more like the *telos* of works of art in general.

Caygill thinks something of this logic can even be seen in cases of iconoclastic destruction. He cites the Bamiyan Buddhas destroyed by the Taliban in 2001, as an example of works whose destruction was inscribed from the outset, as the immanent possibility of a catastrophic 'future breakdown of care'. On this account 'the work of art is the possibility of its destruction', and iconoclasm is a particular, motivated, expression of a deeper ontological truth about works of art: namely, that they will go out of existence, if they are not destroyed first, for no reason at all. From this it is hardly surprising that, in response to the Kantian question, 'We have works of art: how are they possible?', Caygill proposes substituting the answer 'because they have been kept in existence' for the more Schillerian 'because they have been created'. On Caygill's view, the transcendental question about art is no longer 'we have works of art: how are they possible?' but, rather, 'works of art are made to be destroyed, why do some continue to exist?' On this account, a work is something that endures for a finite time between creation and destruction. To Caygill this suggests that the question of art should be oriented away from talk about objects to talk about events.

Caygill supports this argument by looking at a number of artworks, both historical and modern, that do not make sense on what he sees as the essentially Schillerian idea of art as creation, rather than as destruction temporarily forestalled. Caygill's key example is Picasso's *Construction with Guitar Player*, 1913, which, fittingly for his purposes, no longer exists, allegedly destroyed by Picasso himself. The evidence of the work's previous existence is a series of prints that may or may not be from a single negative. The prints themselves have been manipulated in various ways: they are cropped, on different sides and to different degrees; they are drawn on directly, obscuring the image; and various areas have been occluded during the exposure itself. All of this makes it difficult to determine precisely where the work should be located: is it the unfinished work depicted, but later destroyed, or the finished manipulated prints, or the whole ensemble taken together? The series is accompanied by a self-portrait of Picasso before the work, either before its creation, and hence depiction in the other photographs, or later, during or after the process of its destruction; it is impossible to say. Either way, destruction here becomes an animating moment *internal* to the creative process itself, not something external to it.

In his reply, de Duve teases out the implicit vitalist thread running through Caygill's paper. If works are finite, are they not like people in this regard? Depending on how strong Caygill wants to make his claim for the finitude of works of art, de

Duve seems to suggest, his argument might make more of the parallels between the ontology of artworks and the finitude of persons, and the respective roles of care in relation to each. This prompts de Duve to wonder whether it might not be so much the *destruction* of art as the *care* for art, and beyond that perhaps the care for others, that is Caygill's underlying theme. This is where the concerns of de Duve's paper intersect with Caygill's. The differences between them come out in de Duve's main criticism. He suggests that Caygill may be running destruction *in* art (Picasso, Rauschenberg) too close to destruction *of* art (the Taliban), and, against this, argues that we should respect a distinction between creating or destroying something *as* art (Picasso, Rauschenberg) and creating or destroying something in the *name of* art. Neither the creators, nor the destroyers, of the Bamiyan Buddhas, de Duve points out, took themselves to be acting in the name of art. The latter is a distinctly modern Western conception, predicated on art's institutional autonomy, which is obscured by talking about both in the same terms.

IV   W J T Mitchell and Griselda Pollock

Tom Mitchell and Griselda Pollock are concerned principally with images of human life threatened with death or being put to death. Their questions concern the ethical functioning of such images of trauma. The two essays deal, for the most part, with different historical and political contexts, but connect at points around images generated by the attacks on the United States of 11 September 2001. Pollock focuses on a single photograph of a summary execution carried out by a German soldier on the Eastern Front during the Second World War, but her analysis of that image leads into a discussion of painting, as well as of Richard Drew's photographs, ethically controversial at the time, of people who jumped to their deaths from the World Trade Centre on 9/11 rather than die inside. Mitchell's focus is on the period between 9/11 and the re-election to the US Presidency of George W Bush in November 2004, just a few weeks before he presented this paper in London. He seeks to understand the role of a certain breed of images in the new formations of power and ideology that took shape in those years. Mitchell and Pollock are writing about the ethics of pictures, and specifically about how and why certain pictures of human life on the threshold of death function in public consciousness the way they do. Both attend equally to images from across visual culture, including artworks, and they deal with them primarily as representations. In these respects, their perspectives diverge from those contributors who are concerned primarily with the value of art and for whom representation itself is the issue. So whereas Mitchell and Pollock are, in effect, asking after the ethics of pictures, Bernstein and

Butler, for example, are looking to articulate the ethical value of artworks that deny their condition as pictures. Although the pictures that have ethical value for both Mitchell and Pollock are ones made by artists, for neither is this a function of the ethical value of art as such. In each case it is a matter of specific artists making specific interventions into the image flows of a larger culture.

Mitchell's essay makes its argument to a significant degree through the juxta-position of images. He brings together, with images from news media and popular films, the photographs of the World Trade Center during the attacks, of the dental examination of the captured Saddam Hussain, and of the violent maltreatment of detainees in the Abu Ghraib prison near Baghdad. These last are his main concern. Mitchell explores the iconography that permeates these images as they circulate, are transformed and reproduced, at speed and with the reach made possible by digital technology. He is concerned with a period of very recent history, but it is still history in a significant sense. His subtitle, 'The War of Images 2001–4', implies that the war, or a distinct phase of the war, is over. For Mitchell, what ended with Bush's re-election was a widespread belief that these traumatic images – specifi-cally, those from Abu Ghraib, and those of the corpses of American hostages and civilians – would or could effect immediate political change, in the way, perhaps, that documentary images are said to have helped end the US war in Vietnam. He suggests that, because their political efficacy is no longer an issue, an analysis of an underlying syndrome in the social construction of visual culture becomes possible.

He calls this syndrome 'Clonophobia'. It is the fear of cloning, as the most vivid threat posed for many by biotechnology, but also the fear of terrorism, as the endless, viral reproducibility (cloning) of an indeterminate and almost invis-ible danger. His argument is that these fears are manifest in many ways, and attach themselves to many seemingly disparate images, but belong to the same underlying logic or syndrome. Clonophobia is described as a kind of image-medi-ated relationship to oneself, or to life itself, projected as a bad or evil other, or as the other of life (either artificial life or death), and then subjected to hate. In the passages from *What do Pictures Want?*, cited above, Mitchell argues that speak-ing about images as life forms may be a symptom of something incurable; the task is not to overcome these tendencies but to understand them through a kind of symptomology. Clonophobia is the particular pathology with which his paper is concerned, and Clonophobic images should be read as a special case of a general, even universal phenomenon. It is an especially vivid case in that it brings together anxieties around what constitutes life, the image of life, and the life of images. The fact and future possibilities of cloning unsettle our confidence in both the singular-ity and natural givenness of life, and in the reliability of images to picture life, or to distinguish between real and artificial life. At the same time, Clonophobia names, for Mitchell, a fear of the multiplication of fearful objects – in the context of the violence of the so-called 'War on Terror' – that is engendered by the multiplication of images of those objects, and which gives image life as much apparent reality as life itself.

Pollock is also centrally concerned with photographs of violence against human life. Her questions concern the ethics and aesthetics of our relationship, as viewers, to images from the Holocaust and historical images of deep trauma more generally. She begins by describing the ethical implications of a tension central to the very being of photography, that is, the tension between a photograph's indexical moment and its rhetorical moment – to focus on the index is to focus, like Mitchell, on the reality or artificiality of the image. Like Mitchell, she is concerned with the ethical implications of the image in its degree of reality. Her example is an often-reproduced photograph of the shooting of a woman and child by a German soldier during the Second World War, taken at the moment the shot is fired. As an index, the photograph functions as testimony. To attend to it at this level seems both ethically necessary, given the subject matter, and yet wrong, in that it activates a kind of complicity with the killing; in as much as the photographer was complicit so, by proxy, is the viewer. But if we suspend its indexical status, and regard the photograph as a cultural image from the historical archive, our ethical connection to the event is weakened. The image becomes meaningful – she notes how this particular image echoes (and is formatted to echo) the paintings of executions by Goya and Manet as well as how it draws on general and deep-seated representations of femininity – but that is at the expense of its being as traumatic fact. This latter is, for Pollock, the aestheticisation of the traumatic image. She tracks this issue through two other cases: Pieter Breughel's *Landscape with the Fall of Icarus* c.1558 and Drew's photographs from 9/11. She focuses on one image in particular, a single male figure framed against the stripes of the WTC printed only once in US newspapers, through self-censorship, after being criticised for its voyeurism. Her question concerns how images, specifically paintings, might operate between singular, ethical testimony and general, cultural-aesthetic meaning, and between present experience and historical memory. In a sense, it is the question of how, ethically, through images, we might inherit and live with trauma. Pollock describes how, for her, the art theory and practice of Bracha Ettinger offers an answer to this question. In Ettinger's painting, the key to this is a particular way of veiling and overworking the photographic image of trauma. In her theory, the key is a rethinking of the aesthetic, in psychoanalytic terms, as a vehicle of mourning.

Mitchell and Pollock's essays connect at several points: they deal with pictures of human beings poised, as Pollock puts it, between life and death, and the effects of the circulation of those pictures; they reveal the persistence in modern visual culture of the iconography of religious painting, and analyse its politics; and although they deal with image culture at large, they both conclude with examples of art. The differences between their examples reveal something of the differences between their theoretical positions. Mitchell concludes with examples of what could be called counter-icons, produced by artists: Sallah Edine Sallat's mural in Baghdad juxtaposing the image of the tortured 'Hooded Man' with a hooded Statue of Liberty; Guy Colwell's *The Abuse*; and Hans Haacke's *Stargazer*. These are works that seek to employ the same iconic power possessed by the Clonophobic images Mitchell has been analysing, but for the purpose of revealing the political logic behind them. Pollock concludes with Ettinger's paintings; by contrast, these aim, through formal devices, to mediate and lessen the iconic power of the image, as if it is the icon itself, and its digital reproducibility, that is the danger. The ethical stakes of this difference are played out in Pollock and Mitchell's responses to each other, which, next to the Carroll–Piper exchange, are the most conflictual pair of responses in the book. Mitchell suggests Ettinger's images aestheticise what they depict, and – for the needs of current politics – calls for a more direct form of address; Pollock charges Mitchell with eclipsing the real political substance of contemporary conflicts behind his discussion of the war of images. Their criticisms of each other are, on both sides, for the sake of political realism, but they disagree over how images can function in the service of politics.

The second point of disagreement between them concerns the digital. Pollock notes that the advent of digitisation finally breaks the indexical link between the photograph and reality, the link that underpins, for her, the ethical value of the photographic image as testimony – 'all reality is in potential virtualised'. In a sense, the achievement, as she sees it, of Ettinger's art is to reconcile the indexicality of photography with the material density of painting. It seems crucial to Pollock that images that are vehicles of mourning be painted. This is a consequence of painting's ability to embody the image, rendering it corporeal: Ettinger's paint is a 'membrane', she writes, of 'pulsing touches', and in this way a more tactile seeing is 'enfleshed'. It seems that for Pollock something of what she values in Breughel's *Fall of Icarus* returns in Ettinger's art: it is something realised specifically in painting – the fact that Ettinger is both a painter and a theorist is clearly important to Pollock, yet it is conceivable that her claims for painting might be extended to works by Gerhard Richter, such as *18 Oktober 1977*, or Luc Tuymans' works on National Socialism or Belgian colonialism. In Breughel, she writes, there is an aesthetic of painting that is 'at once an ethic – establishing the terms of relations to others that are the grounds of painting's production of its subjects, not as witnesses, documenters, but as visual thinkers'. For Pollock, Ettinger's practice reconciles this ethic of the aesthetic (of painting) with the ethics that attends the witnessing and documenting character of photography. Breughel's paintings are a vehicle of tragedy, Ettinger's of trauma. Mitchell's question is whether the aesthetic might not, to the contrary, detract from, or mute, the document of trauma. For her part, Pollock's political criticisms of Mitchell connect with her scepticism towards the digital as the virtualisation of reality. Her concern is that politically and ontologically, the field of imagery that fascinates Mitchell has lost connection with reality. Mitchell denies this, doubting whether there is any essential ontological difference between analogue and digital photography, the important quality of the digital being the potential speed of its dissemination, which has political but not ontological significance.

What the essays and responses collected here have in common, some more explicitly than others, is a concern with the life and death of images, their vitality, fragile or otherwise. When we initially solicited contributions for this volume, we asked our contributors to address the theme of ethics and aesthetics, broadly conceived: it is remarkable that a persistent concern with the vitality of images should have emerged from such a broad starting point. The result is a series of exchanges that in various, and often conflicting, ways prompt the conclusion that the idea of image-life remains crucial to contemporary discussions of ethics and aesthetics, across art and the wider visual culture. This is a thought that, in the context of recent debates about art and visual culture, would have seemed untenable until recently. Many will doubtless still want to question it. This is hardly surprising: the critical analysis of images – since the early twentieth century, but especially during the recent period of the post-modern anti-aesthetic – has been thoroughly, even constitutionally committed to the negation of any conception of image-life. The exchanges collected here question this assumption in one way or another; nonetheless, it should be clear that none of the authors gathered here wants *simply* to reverse that tendency; none argue for the animism of the image, nor for restoring an uncritical belief in the spiritual dimension of art. No one suggests the re-enchantment of art. Rather, the idea of the life and death of images is entertained in order to diagnose *how* images persist in existing for us, aesthetically, ethically and politically.

As such, the papers offer various diagnoses of the condition of images, the degree and manner of their aliveness, one might even say, their states of health.

These range from a dangerously virulent excess of life, through the half-life of vegetables and the inanimate condition of minerals and death, to entities created for the sake of their own destruction. These competing diagnoses of the health of images have, as their corollary, different perceptions of the agency or efficacy of images: their capability and susceptibility, their activity or passivity, the damage or violence they suffer, inflict or self-inflict. These include the efficacy of artworks and other images as convenors of community or political agents, their ethical significance as vehicles of mourning or the site of putatively universal form of address. Such reflections on the agency of artworks and images prompt, in turn, questions concerning the human life-worlds with which they interact, and the nature of that interaction. What is the role of images in moderating and generating subjectivity, inter-subjectivity and human ethos? In what ways does the health of images testify to health of our lifeworlds? Unsurprisingly, on several occasions these reflections on the life and death of images evoke, explicitly or implicitly, the figure of the icon or idol, understood as an image that orients a community – originally a religious community – through the perception of its internal life and hence transcendence. It is a figure that has received increasing attention in recent years.[25] Indeed, it could be argued that understanding the power of the icon, and the limits of iconoclasm, has become crucial to understanding, perhaps even *appropriating*, the persistent, seemingly indestructible function of images as politico-religious agents. It is a frame of reference that seems unavoidable for the critical analysis of contemporary culture.

This is not to say that the scepticism towards the vitality of images that previously pervaded cultural discourse, and was essential to the anti-aesthetic tendency, does not continue to generate valuable analyses. However, its most important arguments – against the commodification and spectacularisation of the image, in art and across visual culture – now need to be brought into dialogue with a range of other approaches, approaches that open up other ways of thinking through how the aesthetic operates in art, but also beyond art, today. This cannot be achieved by reinstating traditional aesthetic categories, uncritically celebrating aesthetic experience or returning to beauty, nor by dissolving aesthetic concerns into social processes. Instead it involves, as a minimum, understanding how ethics and aesthetics are intertwined in the life of artworks and images: that they are no longer simply opposed is the key thought that permeates this volume. It is no longer sufficient to deny the life of images; we need to diagnose how they died, what it means for them to have lived, the forms of half-life they continue to possess, and the ways in which they inhabit our life-world. This is only part of what understanding the ethics of aesthetics might entail, but a necessary part nonetheless.

IN PRAISE OF PURE VIOLENCE (MATISSE'S WAR)

J M Bernstein

I   There is one moment in Elaine Scarry's otherwise exorbitant accounting of beauty as the sensuous lure and stand-in for all good things – for knowledge and truth, equality and justice – which, while on first impression reading as hopelessly sanguine as the rest, does seem phenomenologically true, indeed almost too obvious to mention, and, on reflection, suddenly gives her bright, Southern notion of beauty, all Provence and palms, a darkening aspect. After recounting the story of Odysseus being washed up on the shore to confront the astonishing gorgeousness of Nausicaa, Scarry bluntly contends that 'beauty is lifesaving .... Beauty quickens. It adrenalizes. It makes the heart beat faster. It makes life more vivid, animated, living, worth living.'[1] What holds for the experience of beauty, its animating character, is, according to Scarry, projected upon its objects: 'their being perceived as beautiful seemed to bring them to life or to make life-like. In some cases, maybe in all, this can be called a mimesis of life ....'[2]

In her first pass at documenting beauty's enlivening power, Scarry slides past the obvious, namely, that Odysseus' experience of beauty as life-saving only occurs in utter proximity to his near death. Later, as she attempts to provide beauty's enlivening power with a properly ethical force, she rushes past the darkness a second time: 'the more general manifestation of this same phenomenon is visible in the way one's daily unmindfulness of the aliveness of others is temporarily interrupted in the presence of a beautiful person.'[3] Our daily unmindfulness of the aliveness of others cannot be quite as simple as it sounds since Scarry has already shown that beauty is enlivening for the beholder, implying that in our unmindful state it is not just the object that is less than alive, because we have not been attending correctly, but that in our unmindfulness is our deadness, our not being fully alive, as if we were all normally like Odysseus but for the fact that we had not noticed we were drowning. In the astonishment that is the experience of beauty we discover we have been drowning all along.

II   What is bewildering about Scarry is her deflection of the question of what state of affairs it is from which we require to be saved, what the need for and fact of enlivening says, sotto voce, about our 'life', as if, benumbed and disoriented by beauty, she had failed to notice its worldly antecedents. Enlivening, coming to life, is indeed the moment in aesthetic experience that bears within itself an ethics and a politics, but not in the tidy idealist way Scarry supposes. Beauty is difficult, and enlivenment necessarily Janus-faced.

A more disturbing account of enlivening occurs in the opening paragraphs of the second part of Freud's 1915 'Reflections upon War and Death'. Freud begins by noting that prior to the war, while we were of course prepared to acknowledge that death was the natural and inevitable terminus of every life, we in fact behaved otherwise, displaying an 'unmistakable tendency to "shelve" death, to eliminate it from life.'[4] Our own death is unimaginable because each envisagement of it involves our survival as spectator. This is the premise behind the psychoanalytic thought that no one believes in his own death, that in the unconscious we are each convinced of our immortality. We keep death 'other' by *representing* it: death always happens to an other self as we look on. This naturally infects our relation to the death of actual others. In mourning and melancholy we mimetically adapt to the other's death, dying to life, while simultaneously and secretly being relieved (if not also appalled) by the fact that it is truly the other and not oneself who has died. This cycle of spectatorship and benumbed grief (itself a complex kind of spectatorship) is thus presented in a manner whereby, for all intents and purposes, conventional relations toward death are, in truth, forms of defence against it; but in defending ourselves against death we simultaneously insulate ourselves against life. It is just this routine state of being benumbed, half alive, alive without the vitality of life, alive without the caring appropriate to the fact of aliveness, that war sweeps away.

> It is evident that war is bound to sweep away this conventional treatment of death. Death will no longer be denied; we are forced to believe in it. People really die, and no longer one by one, but many, often tens of thousands, in a single day. And death is no longer a chance event ... Life has, in truth, become interesting again; it has regained its full significance.

Of course, the thought that with the radical proximity of death life becomes vital, enlivened, is not new with Freud—Homer grasped fully the brutal satisfactions of war. Freud is propounding two further thoughts: that perhaps *only* with the proximity of death can life be enlivened, full of significance; and, what keeps death distant is its always being the other's death rather than our own. Only when death can no longer be represented, which is to say, only when our relation to our mortality and the world is no longer one of spectating, can the experience of life as a mortal enterprise arise.

Less than nine months after writing 'Reflections on War and Death' Freud penned his little essay 'On Transience' ('Verganglichkeit' – literally 'Transitoriness'), in which he defends the idea that an object's transience, in particular beautiful objects, may have its worth increased by its fleetingness. The essay begins 'not long ago' as Freud is walking through a smiling countryside in the company of a taciturn friend and a young but famous poet. The young poet, disturbed by the thought of the extinction of the beauties all around him, was unable to enjoy the spreading scene. Freud then offers a blunt reminder: 'Limitation in the possibility of enjoyment raises the value of the enjoyment. It was incomprehensible ... that the thought of the transience of beauty should interfere with our joy in it ... The beauty of the human form and face vanish for ever in the course of our own lives, but their evanescence only lends them fresh charm.'[5] This fails to satisfy his interlocutors. On reflection, Freud surmises that the enjoyment of beauty was being spoiled in their minds by a revolt against mourning.

Freud's walk in the woods, his discussion with his friend and the young poet, his diagnosis of their revolt *against* mourning are but a stage for the essay's real time and concern as Freud records in the penultimate paragraph that this walk took place the summer before the war: 'A year later the war broke out and robbed the world of its beauties. It destroyed not only the beauty of the countryside through which it passed and the works of art which it met with on its path but it also shattered our pride in the achievements of our civilization, our admiration for many philosophers and artists and our hopes of a final triumph over the differences between nations and races.' The stakes of this essay are not simply the relation between beauty and transience, but the discovery that nothing, including the ideals that are the pride of civilisation, is permanent, that all things are transient. Hence, he raises the issue of whether, after the completion of our collective mourning, our high opinion of the riches of civilisation can be sustained under the pressure of the now unavoidable discovery of their fragility.

One senses that this essay ends one paragraph too soon. While Freud argues that transience, like rarity generally, can increase the value of an item, he needs to urge something stronger. If beauty is enlivening and the experience of beauty casts an animating visage upon its object, then would not transience be an internal rather than an external property of beauty? Can enlivening be detached from life, or life from the thought that what is alive must die? It would hence be unsurprising that in rejecting the object's transience the young poet failed to appreciate the beauty of the woodland scene. Only this fully licenses Freud's inference that it was a revolt against mourning that prohibited its enjoyment. Perhaps we must now say, what anyway directly relates the enlivening of war and the enlivening of beauty, that the shock of beauty, its enlivening, is a violent tearing of the self from out of benumbed half-living, that beauty like war makes vivid the proximity of death to the life lived, hence to the fleetingness and transience of life; and thus the experience of beauty is bound up with or is a form of mourning.

Or at least those conclusions define beauty in the new ontological setting that Freud believed the First World War entailed: after it we could not say any more that the immutable is truth, transitory is appearance. The mutual indifference of temporality and eternal ideas was no longer tenable.[6]

There is something about Freud's two essays that together feel like more than a rational argument. Sometimes I think of them as like two verses of a single poem, or, even better, as a diptych.

III   That war, its violence and sheer destructiveness, and beauty might be joined in a constellation around enlivement and transience is not the most immediate thought that occurs to one in reflecting about beauty. Yet when Barnett Newman, for example, recounts the development of modern art he begins with the troubled recognition of the impossibility of attaining the standard of perfection achieved by Michelangelo. Faced with the incomparability of that achievement, 'the impulse of modern art was [the] desire to destroy beauty'.[7] The beauty being destroyed is classical beauty, whose cold perfection is at one with its pretense to timelessness. In its place is to arise an experience connected with what Burke and Kant designate in terms of the violence of natural sublimity: an intensity of the pain and pleasure in the experience of the formless appearing of the overwhelmingly large and powerful. For them, we might say, the sublime brought what Freud took to be the black exaltation of war within the ambit of culture. But this excessive moment is not extraneous to the constitution of the aesthetic as such: the substitution of aesthetic experience, of the experience of enlivement before compelling sensuous particulars, in place of objective beauty is the beginning of the discovery that beauty's life-saving power is always for us the return of the repressed, a return of the conditioning of life by death, death's proximity, and hence indissolubly bound to the violence of the sublime, to the fracturing and fragmenting and tearing of form and proportion for the sake of aesthetic encounter. Perhaps we might say that the turn toward the aesthetic is implicitly a turn toward enlivement as art's governing orientation, that with modernity the question of art bends away from formal perfection and toward enlivement as what is at stake in the experience of beauty and hence what must be staked by a modern art.

Perhaps we could say that in order for modern art to become aesthetical it would need to go beyond mere representation and include within itself a moment of the sublime, a moment of the breaking from and the exceeding of limits, a moment of violence against good taste for the sake of enlivenment; in order for art to become modern and aesthetical, to continue mattering, it would need its own moment of war within itself. Perhaps we might say that the defining artistic practice of modernity, namely modernism, *just is war becoming art*, an art of pure violence.

IV

Gilles Deleuze opens *Francis Bacon: The Logic of Sensation* thus:

Francis Bacon's painting is of a very special violence. Bacon, to be sure, traffics in the violence of the depicted scene: spectacles of horror, crucifixions, prostheses and mutilations, monsters. But these are overly facile detours ... What directly interests him is a violence that is involved only with color and line: the violence of a sensation (and not of a representation), a static or potential violence, a violence of reaction and expression. (FB, x)[8]

The conundrum and ambition of Deleuze's Bacon book is, precisely, to differentiate pure violence, the violence of paint, from the violence of war, the violence constitutive of modernist painting from the representation of violent events, the violence of sensation from the violence of the sensational (mutilations, monsters, crucifixions, howls and screams). In carrying out this differentiation, it is essential that the violence of sensation be recognised as 'inseparable from its direct action on the nervous system, the levels through which it passes, the domains it traverses' (FB, 39).

Deleuze's Bacon book is intended as an analysis and defence of artistic modernism. Bacon, Deleuze contends, is resuming 'the entire problem of painting after Cézanne' (FB, xii); he is continuing the 'abandonment of simple figuration' that is a general fact of modern painting, a fact which, when seen aright, is the truth of painting altogether (FB, xiv). The truth of painting altogether is that the means for representing persons and things in traditional art, above all colour and line, are in fact the *source* of painting's power to claim at all, what makes painting a unique and irreducible form of interrogating experience and lodging a claim about it. Modernism is the series of painterly practices that liberates what had previously been the means of art, colour and line, into its subject matter; modernism is the self-presentation of painting.

But this claim about how paintings mean and claim presupposes a view about experience generally. Deleuze believes that the devices of modernism form a unique set of means for releasing for encounter aspects of objects and events that, in one way or another, are generally or have become blocked or repressed or veiled or excluded from ordinary (modern) experience. Painting matters generally because it secures access to a stratum or aspect of experience repressed by ordinary cognitive engagements; modernism is the form of painting that itself both reveals this truth about traditional painting and carries out more explicitly painting's interrogation of the sensory order. For Deleuze the general form of the blockage is representational form itself – the manner in which objects are opposed to representing subjects, so becoming something to be seen, a scene, and thereby removed from the kind of intimate exchange we entitle 'experience'.

This is the premise governing Deleuze's conception of sensation: representational form – the forms through which features of the world become identified and reidentified for instrumental and communicable purposes – excludes from our emphatic experience of objects and events just those material/sensuous features of them that make encounter between a material being with sensory powers and sensuously constituted material objects possible. Sensations in Deleuze's lexicon are what are experienced in the absence of representational forms. Hence modernist artworks, those objects designed for aesthetic encounter, designed to operate at the level of sensation, are for him simply materially connected sensations.

As Deleuze is explicitly aware, making Bacon the bearer of this argument is daunting since it is plain enough that he is some kind of figurative artist for whom there is a recurrent fascination with sensational imagery, the representation of violence. The orienting, critical gesture of Deleuze's analysis of Bacon is the contention that it is 'the confrontation of the Figure and the [monochromatic colour] field, the solitary wrestling in a *shallow depth*, that rips the painting away from all narrative but also from all symbolization' (FB, xiv) in order to produce the violence of sensation. Figure is Deleuze's term for what the representational image becomes in modernist painting; Figures are images that are not images of any object. The confrontation of the Figure and field provides for the general appearance of the bulk of Bacon's paintings. In light of this appearance, Deleuze comprehends the various devices of Bacon's art as so many means of achieving this appearance, and hence as the mechanisms for undoing narration and/or dis-figuring the representational image, for example, isolating the image through the removal of scene and background, and the corresponding use of cages and rings and round areas and veils; 'the great technique of local scrubbing … in which thickness is spread out over a non-figurative zone', thereby providing portions of images with a kind of painterly independence from the image of which they are a part (FB, 5);

the systematic occupation of the painting by 'large fields of bright, uniform, and motionless color' (FB, 5); finally, there is Bacon's reinvention of the triptych. For Deleuze the triptych achieves its effects by spreading the meaning of a painting across the discontinuous panels, thus dislocating the form and structure of the single easel painting into a discontinuous movement, a movement that rises and falls, is active or passive, systolic or diastolic across the three panels. In Bacon, painting the sensation means painting rhythm (FB, 72). Rhythm replaces form as the principle of composition.[9]

Deleuze states of the Baconian Figure that it is 'the body without organs (dismantle the organism in favor of the body, the face in favor of the head); the body without organs is flesh and nerve …' (FB, 45). The idea of a body without organs is best understood as a critique of the logic of the organism in which the parts of the organism are understood functionally in relation to the whole. This logic objectifies the body, turning it into a representational thing. Understood organically, the human figure is the upright subject. Deleuze thinks this objectifies or reifies the human body: one cannot think of the body as *having* organs – my arms and legs as ruled by my soul or singular self – while at the same time truly *living in* it. The body without organs is the lived body of Merleau-Ponty and Sartre in its passive, suffering, undergoing mode.[10]

A Baconian Figure is a body without organs, which ideally does not mean the representation of an actual body without organs – although there are plenty of them in Bacon: bodies deprived of the support of the skeleton, hence bodies that appear as mounds of flesh or with flesh hanging so desperately it is about to fall off or liquefy or melt into the canvas, or bodies in fact deprived of identifiable limbs or missing significant parts; and, pervasively, bodies that have lost their upright posture and their commanding frontal orientation. Despite this plethora of literally organless bodies, it is not primarily these that Deleuze means by the body without organs; rather, what he intends is the painterly departure from representational space as such, hence, broadly speaking, an image designed to produce radical experience; if images operate on us in this way they will incite and allow only a rhythmic response.[11] Images of bodies without organs are images of the human in which the self no longer directs and determines its environment; the body without organs is the body without will, hence the body that is moved internally by drives and needs, and externally by the forces acting on it: it is the suffering body, the body bearing the world, the body etched in the image of all that makes it that it cannot make in turn.

The violence of paint occurs through the transforming of colour and line. When colour loses its role of shading, modelling, contouring, when, that is, it is enabled to operate independently of its functional role in the provision of objects in space, it becomes a system 'of direct action on the nervous system … [Painting] liberates lines and colors from their representative function, but at the same time it also liberates the eye from its adherence to the organism … Painting gives us eyes all over: in the ear, in the stomach, in the lungs (the painting breathes …)' (FB, 52). Earlier on the same page Deleuze remarks that painting 'transmutes … cerebral pessimism into nervous optimism'. The violence of paint in disintegrating representational space for the sake of sensory encounter, gives us eyes all over. Even at its darkest, painting enlivens; such enlivenment is what eighteenth-century writers meant in their notion of pleasure in the pain of the sublime.

V   If Deleuze's argument about violence is to be vindicated, then it should operate where it seems least plausible, that is, where we are inclined to see nothing but painterly beauty without a hint of representational violence. And if there is any modernist painter who might be claimed to be a prophet of sensuous beauty it must be Matisse. It was he, after all, who infamously said: 'What I dream of is an art of balance, of purity and serenity, devoid of troubling subject matter, an art that could be … a soothing, calming influence on the mind, something like a good armchair that provides relaxation from fatigue;'[12] who intended in – some of – his works to create a luxurious world apart from the empirical world, a world of permanent pleasure and erotic absorption; who has been, thus, not groundlessly, indicted for his hedonism, for abandoning the austerity of the modernist quest.

That Matisse is the other great modernist painter of the twentieth century along with Picasso probably no longer needs arguing;[13] that his is an art of pure violence is perhaps less obvious. It is just this I will argue. Let me begin indirectly with the consideration of a National Gallery Degas, *La Coiffure* 1896; I take it as significant that this is a painting Matisse acquired – in 1918.[14] There is about this painting something wilful, unsettled, which is at one with its power. The fetishistic theme of hair combing is one that Degas had been exploiting for over a decade, but always in the past, in a line continuous with the bathers, for the purpose of observing the female subject at the precise moment when the position of her being a subject is abandoned for the sake of a quiet moment of animal self-absorption, a luxuriating in passivity, a moment in which the woman is captured feeling herself, feeling the body she is. Degas supposes that in order to present embodiment one must capture it at the moment when it feels itself rather than when it commands the world – Degas is coming to a version of the idea of the body without organs. Attending to the body – washing it, drying it, have one's hair combed – enables it to become simultaneously subject and object. If some of the bather pictures adopt the impressionist disregard for mimetic colours, nonetheless Degas had previously used his non-natural palette as a means for intensifying the flesh of his subjects: the echoing of the soft russet red that pervades the picture on the back of the women in *After the Bath* 1885 and *Woman Drying Herself c.*1888–92, or, even more emphatically, the same echoing structure but now in soft, pale blue, a chilled blue, that saturates *The Bath c.*1894. Maybe it was the shift from pastel to oil that encouraged him to push the issue further. Whatever the source, the innovation feels abrupt, a savage categorial violence: the radiant red, a red that seems to have been pressed through an orange dye, is no longer the descriptive means for rendering the scene but is the scene itself, as if the woman, hair, room were themselves vehicles for revealing the blinding redness, a redness that rather than reflecting light becomes a vibrating source of illumination. The reversal or inversion of the relation between substance and colour, colour becoming the substance, the object painted, the figures becoming the means or vehicle for structuring the display, contouring the colour so to speak, is accomplished while leaving the original representational scene fully in place. The balanced and therefore unresolved to –and fro between the representational scene and its red representing as itself the scene imagines an art of pure means, to use Fauvist language (Flam, 123), an art that liberates the means of representation into what art presents, so a shift from representation to presentation.

So Matisse doubtless must have, with a shock of recognition, experienced Degas' painting, as if it were the genealogical source, the perfect adumbration for his *The Red Studio* 1911 (fig.1), painted seven years before his purchase. In a sense, Matisse's painting is even more wilful and perverse in its inversions, making explicit the categorial inversions he was instituting. Here *all* the concrete material objects in the studio are rendered in light, thin yellow lines, as if they were slight, barely discernible modes of the red substance composing the room, as if the things were insignificant manifestations of red. What matters in the painting is its redness. Red is the substance of this paint world.

Matisse means this to be a form of categorial violence, a metaphysical contesting of the meaning of art. How radically he intends this can be gathered from the other perversion the painting enacts. If the material objects in the studio are skeletal creases in its red substance, the studio does have fully distinguishable attributes, namely, works of art themselves, Matissian paintings and sculptures, decorating it; the only exception, the only other objects represented, are the pencils on the desk – the means of Matisse's art. The paintings and sculptures really are merely decorative; decorative, Matisse is contending, in the derogatory sense in which his kind of painting had been accused of being merely decorative. But if we are capable of distinguishing between the red substance of the painting from the artworks decorating it, then, the argument of the painting urges, the presumptively merely decorative, secondary, negligible character of this red presentation, this merely aesthetic presence that abandons the representational world altogether to form a pure artworld, a world composed of art and the means of art, this red-world cannot be either merely secondary or decorative as supposed. The accuser cannot simultaneously condemn the painting's redness and its scattered artworks as being decorative in the same sense. The painting's redness does everything in the way of securing the canvas for perceptual attention that had previously been the prerogative of the representation of persons, events and objects.

Matisse means *The Red Studio*, I am suggesting, to be a kind of philosophical argument in paint, an argument about the meaning of art, about what makes an object capable and worthy of sustaining aesthetic attention, an argument then about the relation between substance and accident in the empirical world, and what art tells us about that metaphysical structure; and hence, finally, about how our naïve metaphysics of substance and predicates—colours just or only or merely secondary properties—generates a misbegotten value theory in which 'serious' art is on one side and the merely decorative is on the other. And, again, he carries out this demonstration through a violent inversion of the categorial roles of substance and accident, thing and property: red is transformed from descriptive means into the thing itself.

From this act of pure violence follows some of Matisse's most beautiful can-vases from *The Blue Window* of 1913 to *The Conservatory* in 1938, through to his colour extravaganzas of the final years like *Interior in Yellow and Blue* 1946, and his explicit reprise of *The Red Studio*, *Large Red Interior* of 1948, in which some of the objects—flowers, plants, vases—are allowed to maintain their real quality but 'as if preserved in redness'.[15]

VI Matisse was committed to a principle of overallness—every portion of the canvas was necessarily of equal weight and significance: 'For me,' he states, 'the subject of a picture and its background have the same value, or to put it more clearly, there is no principal feature, only the pattern is important' (Flam, 120). Now it might plausibly be argued that the acceptance of overallness is in fact nec-essary if extraction of the Figure from the figurative is to occur since, as Bacon's example shows, no matter how deformed, smeared, scrubbed the figure, in so far as it is isolated against a background it will take on representational/symbolic force. The figure/ground relation is, arguably, a transcendental component of the grammar of representation. Conversely, then, as Matisse fully recognised, a neces-sary condition for realising a painting whose meaning is irreducibly expressive

fig.1 Henri Matisse
The Red Studio. Issy-les-Moulineaux
1911, oil on canvas, 180.3 x 182.8 cm
The Museum of Modern Art, New York

(aesthetic) is that the surface of the canvas becomes, as Elderfield states it, 'the very locus of meaning. Only what existed there, and could never conceivably exist elsewhere, sufficed to recall external reality with all the urgency Matisse had experienced it. This led him to treat the surface … as something self-referential, in the sense that the images it displays show not the functioning of the structure of things, but rather what the process of painting had thrown up to reimagine their identities.'[16] The necessity for treating the surface as a self-referential locus of meaning is, of course, not a solution to Matisse's dilemma but a restatement of it – what overallness requires.

Achieving this self-referentiality will demand of Matisse a double movement: *a progressive disembodiment of the image combined with an increasing corporealisation of the picture surface as a whole.* Matisse's grammatical innovations are the means through which he carries out this double movement, which is itself equivalent to the extraction of the Figure from the figurative. Only a surface that is fully self-referential can be composed of Figures rather representations, or, better, only if a picture is self-referential in the designated sense does the very idea of a non-representing Figure become intelligible *überhaupt.*

This way of breaking from representation requires therefore also the dismantling of classical drawing. What happens to the line when its task is no longer to provide an outline or contour? Line can be detached from ideal form either through having the line's movement through space presume an enactment of movement through time, or through the speed and changing direction of the flat line; in the first case the line would appear to be the expression of an internal force, a drive or conatus, while in the latter case it would be responding to either internal or external forces. In either case, the line contains an uncanny expressive vitality of its own that secures its liberation from its traditional functional appropriations. The liberated line avoids its role of outline.

VII One can perceive directly the transformation from descriptive to pictorial line in Matisse's outlandish *Portrait of Mlle Yvonne Landsberg* 1914 (fig.2). While flattened, formal, and mask-like, the image of the young woman nonetheless might be thought to be a likeness. What makes Matisse's painting so riveting and bewildering, its breaking from being a likeness, are those extravagant sweeping heartlines that mysteriously emanate from her head, forehead, neck, shoulders, back and cleavage. One cannot help seeing those wild lines as bizarre embellishments, but yet they cannot be just embellishments since all the edgy, hard energy of the painting depends on them. Truly here drawing in its non-pictorial sense gives amplitude and life to the image, however supplementary, alternately compel-

fig. 2 Henri Matisse
Mademoiselle Yvonne Landsberg
1914, oil on canvas, 147.3 x 97.5
The Philadelphia Museum of Art

ling and excessive, those force-lines feel.

Matisse's use of the pictorial line was not new with this painting: it is already fully operative in the two great dance paintings of 1909–10. Here the bodies are themselves but parts of a circling movement that seems to enliven and pass through each body in turn, as if each were but a crystallised moment that exists for the sake of the movement that passes through them. Matisse recognised early on that in order to achieve this subordination of the descriptive to the pictorial he would have in a sense to make his figures faceless, anonymous (the face must not be a window onto the soul) and headless (the head cannot rule the body as the principle of its order but must be utterly continuous with it). For the sake of overallness, for the sake of a self-referential pictorial space, Matisse invents and reinvents the body without organs, a body that could be identical with the flow of lines inscribing it. If the faceless is routine in Matisse,[17] the headless becomes perspicuous if one contrasts the dance pictures with the late *The Dream* 1939–40, where the head becomes not much more than a pink wash and some black ripples within the sweeping white movement running from the dreamer's back through her non-articulated shoulder and arm. The force of this quiet, swelling movement is achieved through the way it presses along the right and left edges of the painting as if the canvas was inflated or held in suspension by it. If there is something powerfully animal about the dancers, there is something uncomfortably vegetable about the dreamer: if a plant could breathe, it would look like this.

Vegetable form is the clue to Matisse's dominant pictorial strategy with respect to the line. In the two *Nasturtiums with Dance* of 1912 Matisse seems to be recognising that pictorially the same suspension of classical drawing that he had carried out in the dance pictures is already carried out by nature in flowing vines and leaves, that that kind of vegetable form itself institutes a pictorial line. Dance expresses an 'impassioned impulse' (Flam, 210), not mere movement but movement that is musical, rhythmic; rhythm is the inner affinity between nature, movement and line. Matisse's term for lines rhythmically organised is 'arabesque'. Arabesque, he states, 'is musically organized' (ibid.). The arabesque is the paradigm for Matisse of a non-descriptive line, of the kind of endlessness and movement that Deleuze contends constitutes the Gothic line. If arabesque is thus a name for the non-descriptive line, *then matching the program of drawing in colour is the one of drawing in arabesque.*[18] Drawing in arabesque is a counter-drawing, drawing against drawing, drawing after drawing; drawing in arabesque makes drawing excessive, not for the sake of anything. But it is in not being for the sake of providing contour, outline, structure or scaffolding that drawing suddenly attains an uncanny liveliness.

Once Matisse perceives how the literal arabesque functions, he can extend the

fig. 3 Henri Matisse
Plum Blossoms, Green Background
1948, oil on canvas, 115.9 x 89
Pinacoteca Gianni e Marcella Agnelli, Turin, Italy

idea of the arabesque in two directions: first, toward a rhythmic form of pictorial organisation as a whole, and second toward the merely decorative line. Rhythmic organisation and solely decorative lines – all the kinds of lines and patterns (stripes, ribbons, leaves, petals, circles, diamonds (a favoured floor pattern), ripples, lattices, 3-shapes and palms) that can be found on wallpaper, carpets, screens, tablecloths, vases, hangings, clothing and Matissian paintings, as well as natural objects treated decoratively – join as means for disabling intellectual perception, the seeing of things by understanding them, conceptually grasping them. *In order to have eyes all over, the understanding eye must be blinded.* Arabesque in its expanded sense is, perhaps, Matisse's most incessant method for blinding vision for the sake of sensation. No work is more self-conscious about this, a statement of the strategy, than *Harmony in Red* 1908.

What is most obvious about this painting is the way in which its composition disallows the eye from finding an organising centre. Our eye is continually pulled away: by the scattered lemons, the green grass outside, and, above all, by the incomprehensible arabesque of the basket of blue flowers that appears indiscriminately, so to speak, on the back wall and on the table cloth. Our eyes dart and wander, glimpse, momentarily focus, and then move on: woman, lemons, arabesques, chair, tree and grass, red, green, yellow, black, woman, lemon ….

Arabesque, I am claiming, is the principle underlying Matisse's strategy of decoration. By decoration Matisse meant that everything counts equally. But he also meant that equalisation should be a form of blinding: the sheer piling up of elements and decorative lines spreads the painting across the surface of the canvas making each element, even prima facie descriptive forms, become images and Figures in a rhythmic whole, each element claiming visual attention, and each distracting our gaze from a visual claim arising elsewhere. In a decorative painting, what needs attending to is always elsewhere; in order to sustain this structure of distraction, the decorative requires structures of displacement and enjambment, decentring and dislocation. The decorative is thus an anti-descriptive device; in it elements relate to one another by affinity, rhyming, echoing, contrasting – rhythmically. This blindness of vision reaches a fever pitch in *Odalisque with Gray Culottes* 1926–7; the wild dislocation of foreground and background makes it impossible for us to concentrate, attend to the central figure: the half-naked woman lies there easily before us, yet we cannot rest our gaze upon her. Vision is being claimed everywhere and therefore, everywhere it is denied. In the act of looking, in the very activity claimed for looking, the cognitive act of seeing is denied. Beauty is blinding. That is the particular violence of pure painting.

VIII Matisse's creation of bodies without organs allows the possibility of a vision-less feeling response. Such a blinded experience of animation should, all things being equal, enable a sensing of the proximity of life to death since life is here not the life of an other, not something represented. But this is not quite how things go. Matisse's war, for of course this is what I have been getting at all along, his way of bringing the exaltation of war into the precincts of culture, his method of com-pounding enlivenment and loss, does not make death appear directly, does not make it appear as the immediate consequence of his dissolution of our spectato-rial relation to the world. Since the genius of pure violence is that it reverses the direction of real violence – isn't this exactly what it means to have an art of pure means? – permitting the means to (representing) life to become ends in them-selves, hence not killing but animating, then pure violence secures the proximity of life to death only indirectly and dialectically. The proximity is there in the only place it can be: in Matisse's modernist work against representation, in his dispos-ing of eyes and nose and mouth, in his creation of faceless and headless figures, and in his ecstatic recovery of expressiveness in the cold exuberance of his fields of red and blue and pink and green, and in the florid arabesques filling his canvas like those cramped patterns on old Persian carpets lying on our grandparents' parlour floor.[19]

All this turns on the movement into overallness, which I am contending is the constitutive feature of modernism's work against representation. Overallness is not or not primarily facingness, the acknowledgement of painting as paint-ing, although overallness as I am limning it does imply art's self-consciousness. Overallness as practiced by Matisse lives off the corporealisation of the canvas as a whole; but corporealisation is, again, the counter-movement, the other side of the progressive disembodiment of the image, the destruction of representational form which just is the fragmentation and destruction of the body. Overallness is the restitution of the claim of embodiment out of its social and art historical destitu-tion, the war upon its normative authority in urban, industrial society. Violence is paradigmatically the violation of the integrity of the body, its irrepressible claim to wholeness; violence as the violation of the intact body is always death-bearing. Yet it is through the mimetic violence of art, through overallness, that the body re-emerges as the form of all forms, what form imbricates and demands. With modernism, through its orienting overallness, form becomes – against the depre-dations of geometry, ideality and vision – what it always strove to be: *living* form. Matisse's transformations of colour and line are *compelled* by the discovery that representational form had lost its authority, which is equivalent to saying that the represented body no longer immediately lodged a claim to intactness, integrity.

The fate of form is always the history of the meaning of the human body. Matisse, discovering he was at war, that the scene of painting was a field of war, had to attack the very thing that one might have thought was painting's own: visuality. Overallness is the devisualisation of colour and the de-forming of line; only in blinding perception could the claims of colour and line be restituted, and with them, finally, the authority of the fragile and harassed human body.

Modernism is the movement through which enlivenment as the counter-thrust to the reifications of modernity becomes art's orientation, its desperate form of meaning. Enlivenment is possible only through conversion, only through losing the high and abstract ideals of equality and justice, and refinding and relocating them where the art of the West that began with Greek tragedy always placed them except in moments of great forgetfulness, namely, in the suffering body, the body without organs, that suddenly appears each time the stable world of known things collapses. Matisse, that most 'pretty' of painters, brings war into the precincts of culture. Matisse, that most 'pretty' of painters, makes of modernist painting a tragic art.

RESPONSE TO J M BERNSTEIN

Judith Butler

Jay Bernstein's 'In Praise of Pure Violence' opens by distinguishing two quite distinct accounts of the enlivening power of beauty. The first position, with which he disagrees, belongs to Elaine Scarry who argues that we are enlivened by virtue of our perception of beautiful objects as objects. Effectively, perception attributes beauty to objects that, in turn, incite and enliven us in some way. The second position, which might be said to be derived from Freud's reflections on war, suggests that loss and even devastation form the necessary background for being enlivened, if not astonished, by beauty. This last position accords with Wallace Stevens' well-known line that 'Death is the mother of beauty', a formulation that announces as well a distinctive entry into modernism. Death forms the necessary background for the enlivened response to beauty, but there is much that keeps us at a distance from death and, hence, from beauty as well. In Freud's view, there is a cycle of 'spectatorship and benumbed grief' – in Bernstein's view – that forms part of our defence against the idea of death, not only the death of the other, but most acutely, our own. Forms of *representing* death become the conventional means by which the experience of death is defended against. And in this benumbed state, we are also deadened to life. It thus follows, as Bernstein puts it, that 'perhaps *only* with the proximity of death can life be enlivened'. *(p. 39)*

Freud, of course, understood the paradoxical effect of war or, rather, the proximity of war, on the senses to the extent that war was able to import sublimity and exaltation into the sphere of culture. Where media-driven wars during our time can do the same is, of course, a serious and open question, though one we cannot pursue here. In any case, Bernstein takes Freud's analysis as his point of counter-departure (over and against Scarry) in order to make some significant and far-reaching claims about modern art. The conventional means for representing death produce an epistemological position rigidified as spectatorship and a con-stellation of the senses understood as benumbed grief or emotional deadness. In classical approaches to art, according to Bernstein, the ideals of objective beauty, relying on perfection, balance, form and proportion, are precisely what work against enlivenment. The assault, then, on ideas of formal perfection within modernism are precisely efforts to re-enliven or, indeed, to enliven for the first time our response to colour, line and the sensuous particulars of paint, in particular. This 'war' is necessary to secure the possibility for enlivenment. But in this last formulation, we see that what must 'die' is an expectation and measure of art that is classical in character, valuing perfection, composition, and order. And the reason this version of art must 'die' in this particular war, a war that will be said to be Matisse's war, among others, is that it composes one of those conventional responses to death and, hence, to life that make both death and life virtually impossible to feel.

Of course, the violence waged by paint is not the same as the violence of war. Proximity to war allows for an enlivened response to the world and to its sensuous particularity. Rote formulations, representations and conceptions are what work to deaden responsiveness. Hence, in waging a war against those conceptions, one is making a bid to feel the proximities of war and the possibilities for enlivenment. One is not asking for war, but rather, for a nearness to loss and devastation that brings out the astonishing qualities of what is and what remains.

Importantly, painting cannot at once be representational and also provide an occasion for enlivenment. The means for representing persons and things must exceed any mimetic or representational demand to portray them correctly, since the means is precisely the '*source* of painting's power to claim at all'. *(p.50)* What enlivens is the singular and non-transposable sensuous features of the painting that work upon the nervous system, belong to the here and now of the encounter and proceed from the particulars of the canvas. To the extent that the means of representation – paint and line, for instance – are what act upon the nervous sys-tem, enlivening it, they do so not only at the expense of representation itself, but explicitly *against* representation.

Our capacity for being responsive and enlivened depends upon our being a body, a body understood as a nervous system, and a body that is, in Deleuze's terms, 'without organs'. The importance of this formulation for Bernstein is clear: the body without organs is the body no longer figured as a set of organs, each of which has a functional purpose. Just as painting no longer serves the function of aiding and abetting a representational purpose, so the body reacts outside of any way that could be predicted or rationalised by any of its ordinary functions: work, reproduction, or any of the tasks of ordinary life. The body is, under these circumstances, a responsive terrain, and painting is precisely what acts upon it, enlivening what is otherwise deadened. Red in Matisse's paintings constitutes an assault on traditional representational art, and traditional representational art is itself an assault on enlivenment. This is, then, finally a war over life or, rather, conducted in the name of life.

In describing Matisse's war against aesthetics, Bernstein remarks that, 'Matisse means *The Red Studio* ... to be a kind of philosophical argument in paint, an argument about the meaning of art, about what makes on object worthy of sustaining aesthetic attention, an argument then about the relation between substance and accident in the empirical world, and what art tells us about that metaphysical structure.' *(p.47)*

This last strikes me as a very different aim from a direct action upon the nervous system, the position that Bernstein artfully derives from his reading of Deleuze. If redness is supposed to be an assault on representation, on conceptualisations and formulations that deny us a proximity to war, loss and devastation and, hence, of the astonishment of what appears as beautiful, then we have to ask, can redness also be having a philosophical argument, holding forth about metaphysics and engaging in aesthetic debates of this kind? If, as Bernstein argues, in Matisse 'red is transformed from descriptive means into the thing itself' *(p.47)*, can it really be possible that red is engaging in conceptual debates about metaphysics and the aims of art? Can it be both Deleuzian 'sensation' and 'a philosophical argument' or is this a place where Bernstein must, of necessity, depart from the Deleuzian account of painting if he is to sustain his thesis?

In his break with demands of representation, Matisse insists upon treating the surface as self-referential. *(p.49)* And Bernstein follows this insight with a very power-ful formulation of what happens to the body on that surface: 'a progressive disem-bodiment of the image [is] combined with an increasing corporealisation of the picture surface as a whole.' *(p.49)* If the image were embodied, it would be precisely the foregrounded and bounded image with mimetic ties to what it represents; the increased corporealisation of the canvas further destroys the image/background conceit that allows representational art to make its claim. Here we can see that a certain representational grammar is destroyed while the surface becomes perme-ated with expressive qualities. But does something else happen here as well?

After all, in the Deleuzian formulation, the 'body without organs' is clearly outside the frame and before the canvas, acted on at a distance, and responsive to colour and line that appear before it is released from its usual functional purposes. In the formulation of the body in Matisse, though, it would appear that the body is now absorbed into the canvas, surely not as a figure with representational status, but as a body without boundaries, corporealising the entirety of the canvas to produce 'overallness'. This last is central to Bernstein's argument, since it is the prin-cipal way that modernist painting wages its war against representation. But is there still a body before and outside the canvas? And do we need to presume and even safeguard that body before and outside the canvas in order to safeguard aliveness and enlivenment – the central aim of this essay? If the canvas is fully self-referential and the image is decorporealised as the canvas is fully corporealised, what hap-pens to the body without organs? Does corporeal responsiveness to the canvas become decorporealised as well? If not, and the body is corporealised in the face of the corporeal overallness on the canvas, then it would seem that some departure from Matisse's thesis about self-referentiality is needed. Although the body is not represented on the canvas, it is surely implicated by the canvas – and we need this last point to understand the ethical import of Bernstein's contribution.

Sometimes Bernstein seems to see this, but even in such moments, he seems to posit a radical continuity between Deleuze and Matisse and, correspondingly, a con-tinuity between canvas and body: 'Matisse invents and reinvents the body without organs, a body that could be identical with the flow of lines inscribing it.' *(p.51)* And we read that assertion of continuity again later: 'the body without organs that is the corporeal structure of some of Matisse's best paintings.' *(p.51)* But does there not have to be an ineradicable difference between the body that responds, enlivened, to the canvas, and the body virtually identical with the flow lines found there? Don't we need that incommensurability to know that this body, proximate to death, enlivened by what it sees, is never the same as what it does see? That structuring difference seems to be a precondition for responding to what one sees and becoming enlivened through that seeing. There is an 'over hereness' to the body that sees that can never be fully resolved into – or redeemed by – the corporealisation of the canvas.

For the canvas to act upon the nervous system, there must be a difference between the two and the possibility of the canvas working on the body 'from the outside'. If we close down this difference, we deny the difference between the body outside the frame and the one inside. If the 'corporealisation of the picture surface as a whole' is precisely necessary for a certain kind of bodily response to the picture, are we still equipped to make that argument? After all, if we were to accept Matisse's claim that the surface is completely self-referential, then we seem no longer to be able to refer to the body outside and before the surface that is reacting and responding to what it sees there. It may well be that we have done away with the benumbed spectator, but have we unwittingly jettisoned as well the very body without organs, responsiveness outside of all expected function? If we are to return to that body, it seems we must reject Matisse to return to Deleuze. But if the expressive features of the canvas overwhelm the claims of representation, then it is more important that the body becomes canvas, that there be a corporealisation of the canvas, than that the body, conceived as separate, becomes enlivening in relation to that canvas. It would be sad to choose, and I suspect Bernstein would share my alarm at the prospect of such a trade-off. After all, he is the one who says that Matisse's paintings can give us 'eyes all over'.

For the body to become canvas is surely a redemptive ideal, but if the body cannot become the other, then we are left with the conditions of seeing and responding – as well as with a certain experience of loss. This loss is precisely the loss of the redemptive possibilities of colour itself, since though colour may be overall and omnipresent on the canvas, it cannot save us from the moment when we have to look away to another landscape.

It is to this other landscape that I turn, then, in my final queries for Bernstein, whose fine language and acute descriptive capacities fascinate so effectively that I am at risk of losing my critical stance. The landscape to which we turn when we turn from the canvas is one that has lost its vitality. Why is this so? Is it the result of certain dominant representations taking hold? Is it the ideal of perfection that advocates of objective beauty defend? Is it the rote conventions about death in particular that regularly relieve us from proximity? Could it be that the life of the body – under certain conditions of labour or constituted within regulatory norms of sexuality or subjected to technologies that transform affect into lifeless function – is suffering from a deadness that is induced through an array of social and political actions upon the body? Is it by virtue of conceptualisations (of art or of death) or by other modes of being acted upon that the body's responsiveness is assumed to be dead, and that colour and line are rarely encountered outside their functional rationale? In the case of Matisse, according to Bernstein, painting pre-supposes catastrophe. It seems finally important to distinguish among these forces of deadening, since they are not all equivalent, and may work in different ways; does the body come to life differently depending on the cause of its deadening? And would we have this thesis about art, namely, that it enlivens, if there were not so much that threatens to deaden, if there were no horizon of loss and death? If some of these forms of deadening are socially contingent, if they emerge from the radical homogenisation of value under capitalism or by virtue of a media that keeps us infinitely remote from death, then to what extent are precisely these deadening agents required if we are to accept the enlivening task of art? Not all death follows from war, and not all deadening follows from representations alone. It would surely be self-defeating to require the deadening forces in order to articulate the task of art as enlivening. But perhaps it is enough to say that under these conditions of modernity, broadly defined, that loss, death and what deadens are too much with us, and that to feel the painting's impression on our skin is finally to receive the tactile at the limits of the visual – a triumph for what lives on despite the odds.

BEYOND SEDUCTION AND MORALITY: BENJAMIN'S EARLY AESTHETICS

Judith Butler

The early Walter Benjamin, an emerging critic and philosopher in his late twenties, penned his reflections on painting in a characteristically brief set of remarks.[1] Perhaps the first lines he wrote were about Kandinsky's pictures, and there he offers only a phrase: 'the simultaneous occurrence of conjuring and manifesting' (82). What is *conjured* would be what is invoked subjectively, brought forward, attributed, and what is *manifested* seems to emerge from the object itself. He goes on in an essay, 'Painting, or Signs and Marks', to define the picture *as a set of marks*. The mark, he tells us, is not to be confused with the sign. And though there are various kinds of marks, and various instances of signs, there is also something he will call 'the absolute sign' and 'the absolute mark'. These absolutes are not found separate from various particular marks and signs; they are, in his words, buried within them. Every sign contains within it the absolute sign, and every mark contains within it the absolute mark; and whereas the absolute sign is *magical* (83), the absolute mark is *mythical* (84). The mark is distinguished from the sign. A mark resembles nothing else in its manifestation. Indeed, a mark is a manifestation, and so Kandinsky's paintings, conjuring and manifesting, are composed of marks, marks that manifest without sustaining resemblance to anything else. The absolute sign is magical, not by virtue of what it represents, but precisely for the means of representation that it is, as well as the semblances it can and does maintain. The mark resembles nothing else. Moreover, marks take on a meaning first when they appear on living beings, and the examples he gives are the blush and the stigmata. On the other hand, he tells us that marks distinguish paintings.

As it will turn out, what defines the picture is also what links the picture to a realm of morality. Ultimately, Benjamin will argue that to see a picture is to reckon

fig. 1 Wassily Kandinsky
Improvisation 31: Sea Battle, 1913
National Gallery of Art, Washington

with seduction, beauty, life and guilt. And if we reckon well or, indeed, understand the picture with respect to its truth, we will understand the paradoxical necessity of averring seduction and attending to the lifeless aspects of what appears. This involves no less than a critical destruction of the work of art, one that entails a critique of law as well, specifically of retribution and revenge, in the name of a utopian possibility.

Although clearly a distinguishing feature of painting, the mark is also, for Benjamin, always moral, linked with innocence and guilt, with having been marked or even stained by a deed, an error or some guilt. Here he clearly references a theological past: the mark appears on the body of the person as a sign of sin or punishment, or even as a kind of confession of guilt. Blushing reveals something about the person, usually kept under wraps, perhaps considered shameful. The stigmata is such a traditional mark within theology, acquired through guilt, or functioning as a warning of guilt. If one is guilty, we are led to believe that one can only be relieved or assuaged of guilt through the act of atonement. But this causality, Benjamin tells us, is *magical* (and hence, belongs to what he calls the realm of the sign): 'Since the link between guilt and atonement is a temporal and magical one, this *temporal* magic appears in the mark in the sense that the resistance of the present between the past and the future is eliminated, and these, magically fused, descend together on the head of the sinner.' (84)

The mark thus has this archaic mythical meaning, indicating both guilt and atonement; it is a singular mark that resembles nothing else, individuating the living being who bears it. How are we to understand this mark as an archaic and individualising trace of guilt? Benjamin writes that it can be understood *only through painting*: 'As far as the realm of the mark in general is concerned, the only knowledge we can have of it in this respect will be described following our observations on painting … everything that can be said of the absolute mark is of great significance for the medium of the mark in general.' (85)

Painting turns out to be the way in which we might apprehend this mark, for it seems that, for Benjamin, painting is, in part, defined by its marks, and so all we must do is understand what painting actually is. He writes, 'painting is a medium, a mark, since it has neither background nor graphic line'. (85) He understands that this definition might not suffice, although he does not consider all the reasons that this might be so. The one reason he gives for its inadequacy is based on the logical circularity of the definition: 'if the picture were only a set of marks, it would be quite impossible to name it. The actual problem of painting can be discerned in the statement that a picture is indeed a set of marks.' (85) The logical problem seems to follow from the fact that marks exist in the picture, but the picture is also defined, in part, as a set of marks; the existence of a mark, however, is not sufficient to constitute a picture. To be a picture, the marks have to be organised in some way; they have to be given composition. Paradoxically, Benjamin solves this problem by claiming that what gives a unifying composition to a set of marks, and so designates them as a picture, is a kind of name: 'The picture may be connected with something that it is not – that is to say, something that is not a set of marks – and this happens by naming the picture.'(85)

At first, we might think that Benjamin is giving great weight to the *title* of the picture or, indeed, the painting. But the title is just a word, a sign, and not quite, on its own, the absolute sign, the one that alone has the power to unify the composition. That absolute sign is buried within every particular sign, even every particular title. The relation of the particular title to the more elusive name to which Benjamin refers is that of a loose resemblance, an affinity, even a kind of kinship. By virtue of this internal resemblance (or elective affinity), the title, as sign, is magical, conjuring, providing a unifying intention to a picture. Benjamin tells us that the picture has a relation to that after which it is named. That after which it is named signifies a higher power, something that transcends the marks and cannot itself be marked, and this something which operates as a name is at work in the creation of the composition; indeed, it is the creative or organising principle itself. What organizes the picture, however, is not the same as the marks that define it and are contained within it, since the name that organises through resemblance has as its content a set of marks that bear no resemblance to anything else. The name or the sign gives compositional organisation to a set of marks, but those marks are not signs, but rather *manifestations*.

The sign conjures; the mark manifests. 'Kandinsky's pictures: the simultaneous occurrence of conjuring and manifesting.' (82) The sign conjures through the resemblance at work between the particular word and the absolute sign to which it is related; the mark manifests, and this manifestation appears to be of a magical temporality that pertains to a moral universe of guilt and atonement.

The title is a graphic line, and Benjamin imagines titles as linked to the absolute sign that conjures a unity for the set of marks that define the pictorial. The sign and the mark work in tension with one another; the graphic line that is the title does not explode the mark, but makes its home there without destroying it. The graphic line, in his view, is higher than the mark, but the graphic line is not hostile to it. What he is describing, then, is the linguistic word that lodges in the medium of the language of painting, invisible as such and revealing itself only in the composition.

This notion of the linguistic word would take some time to explain. To understand what he means by this, it would be necessary to understand the ideality of the word as he discusses this in 'On Language as Such and on the Language of Man' and 'The Task of the Translator', two other pieces from this early period.

Of course, it is problematic that what Benjamin finds at the heart of painting is a linguistic word, though it may come as some consolation that it is not a word that can fully appear as such. 'The linguistic word' is a phrase he uses for what cannot be communicated or expressed in any language. (261) When he speaks during this period of a 'pure language' or 'ultimate essence', he is referring to a dimension of language that no longer expresses or means anything, what he will call the expressionless and creative word. (261) What Benjamin calls here the linguistic word is not *this* or *that* word, and certainly not just the title, but precisely an animating and organisational power that joins graphic line and the mark in a certain tension, the name for the exercise of compositional organisation itself.

In another short piece from 1919–20, 'Categories of Aesthetics', Benjamin distinguishes semblance from manifestation, revising his earlier distinction between signs that rely on resemblance and marks that constitute singular manifestations. A semblance is a mere appearance, something that takes place in myth and in the realm of the sign. We are apparently seduced by semblance: '*The seductive nature of beauty is based on the shamelessness, the nakedness, of the semblance that arms it.*' (221 italics in original) Semblance is linked with beauty, with beauty's armor, and with life. What it is armed against is death and, perhaps also, the loss of eros. To the extent that a work of art is living, it becomes semblance, but as semblance it loses its status as a work of art for Benjamin. The task of the work of art, at least at this point in Benjamin's career, is precisely to break through this semblance or, indeed, to petrify and still its life. Only through a certain violence against life is the work of art constituted, and so it is only through a certain violence that we might be able to see its organising principle and, hence, what is true about the work of art.

Benjamin distinguishes between forms of semblance in which something is being concealed, and others in which there is no concealment and no possibility for revelation. He gives the following example:

> A man is crossing the street when out of the clouds a coach with four horses appears, coming toward him. During a walk he hears a voice from the clouds, saying, 'You have left your cigarette case at home.' In our analysis of the two events, if we set aside the possibility of hallucination – that is, the possibility that this semblance has a subjective cause – we find, in the first case, it is conceivable that nothing lies behind the manifestation, but in the second case this is inconceivable. (223)

We are left to infer that something lies behind the voice, that some divine agent or speaking being makes possible the aural reminder that we hear, some voice that belongs to an agent who has watched our actions, whose perspective exceeds the one we have on ourselves. But the image of the chariot does not necessarily presuppose something behind it. It is, for this reason, a semblance. Paradoxically, the semblance in which nothing appears to lie behind the manifestation is the more potent one; it seduces us more forcefully, and this is conceivable, he argues, only in the visual realm.

Semblance makes a work of art seductive, believable and alive. In his words, it makes the work quiver with life. (224) Beyond semblance, though, is the sign that constitutes the organising intention of the work of art. The sign is not unlike that voice that maintains a perspective beyond our own. It never appears in singular form, but is only variously and indirectly indicated through its concrete appearances. This 'intention' or ideal can be understood as an essence that is distributed throughout its many appearances, partially illuminated by every individual sign that constitutes a fragment of an irretrievable and original whole. The relation between marks and semblance in the picture has a moral meaning, since marks are traces of guilt (in a sense we have yet to understand); and the semblance is its part in beauty. When we look at a picture, then, we are already negotiating seduction, beauty, life and guilt. Is there something in the picture that moves us beyond these vexed sensuous matters? For Benjamin, there is something else that works against *both* the mark and the semblance; in other words, something else in the work of art that works against its relation to guilt and to beauty. A perspective is conjured through various resemblances that is, significantly, not a human perspective. Importantly, neither semblance nor the mark are simply human creations, and they are most decidedly not expressions of a prior subjectivity – at least not for Benjamin. Both semblance and the mark bear upon the human, or the human figure, conjuring its beauty, manifesting its guilt. And they operate for us aesthetically to the extent that the human who is this semblance or bears such marks is a *living* substance.

Benjamin is intervening in art debates of his time in a complex way. Yves-Alain Bois remarks that Benjamin is refuting the avant-gardist contention that cubist 'art [is] completely estranged from its pictorial tradition'.[2] As Bois points out, Benjamin goes further to suggest that there is a distinctive vertical plane at work in painting, as opposed to drawing. And this vertical plain manifests and contains things – it does not work at the level of the sign. According to Bois, Benjamin opposes the cubist effort to 'horizontalize' painting, and we can see why. The loss of the vertical plane is the loss of the mark and, hence, a constitutive feature of painting itself. What is also lost, though, is the mark as the juncture of aesthetics and morality. The mark, like the stigmata, manifests; it does not signify. And this manifestation is precisely that appearance that bears its truth – its organising principle – through being compositionally organised along a vertical axis.

The paintings of Kandinsky and Klee and, to a lesser degree, Chagall, preoccupy Benjamin during this time. He refutes the presumptions of expressionism in both the literary and visual arts for its claim to ground artworks in subjective experience. For the work to be created is precisely not for it to emerge from, and express, the particulars of a single human subject. Creation precedes and exceeds both the subject and object of art. This work of creation can only be understood obliquely, through the affinities that are produced along the way. Thus, he proposes that the only way to apprehend the affinities that take place among works is through a practice of translation. Each work manifests or illuminates in fragmented form the ideal word, the absolute sign, or what he will also call the linguistic word. In 'The Task of the Translator' 1921, he refers to the creative Word as precisely *expressionless*; it does not convey information or express a subjective state: 'all information, all sense, and all intention finally encounter a stratum in which they are destined to become extinguished.' (261) Over and against those who would champion expressionism as the sudden revelation of a sequestered subjectivity, he once wrote, 'only a terrorist campaign will suffice to overcome that imitation of great painting that goes by the name of literary Expressionism.' (293) He speaks of the incapacity of literature to reach painting, insisting upon a distinction between the two (over and against, one would have to suppose, a form of collage, for instance, that would insist upon their mixing). His indictment is against expressionism in both its literary and visual forms. What is 'behind' the work of art cannot be a subjectivity in its singularity or its collectivity. And though he espouses no explicit plan of violence against this apparently debased construal of art, he affirms that only through a certain destruction of the most seductive dimensions of painting, for instance, can any of us discern the ideal, the creative and non-expressive word by which it is organised. The ideal works *against* its apparent beauty; only through the petrification of beauty does this ideal truth become available in fragmented form. 'The ideal of the problem … does not appear in a multiplicity of problems.' (334) Rather, it lies buried in a manifold of works, and its excavation is the business of critique. If the ideal appears at all, it is always partial and fragmented, putting the work of art at risk, and even mandating its critical destruction.

This ideal is linked with Benjamin's evolving notion of the divine name, one that he will associate with the Kabbalistic inquiries conducted by Gershom Scholem, and also with an ethic of radical forgiveness and a political utopianism, even an anarchism, that seeks to dissolve all state violence. But before he arrives at this conclusion in 'A Critique of Violence', he is interested in a different problem, namely, the original link he discerns between the work of art and morality. He writes:

> To the degree that a work breaks through the realm of art and becomes utopian perception,
> it is creation – meaning that it is subject to moral categories in relation not just to human

beings in the act of conception, but to man's existence in the sphere of perception. *The moral nature of creation gives the work the stamp of the expressionless.*
(222, my emphasis – written 1919–20)

Although it is not altogether clear what is meant by 'the moral nature of crea-tion', it will become clear, I think, when we consider the moral dimensions of time. In Benjamin's view, the work of art becomes alive through semblance, since semblance 'quickens the body' and 'communicates life'. This very life, however, must be dissolved for a work to achieve its completion. Indeed, a mere semblance is not the same as a work of art. He writes: 'I. Every living thing that is beautiful has semblance. II. Every artistic thing that is beautiful has semblance because it is alive in one sense or another. III. There remain only natural, dead things which can perhaps be beautiful without having semblance.' (283) The category of ex-pression does not work to describe this last occurrence, the beauty of those natural and dead things that is not associated with semblance or with life. These last are expressionless – they have a kind of beauty, but they are not alive, strictly speaking. A work of art must lose the beauty it acquires through semblance to become what he calls 'utopian perception' and to evince 'the moral nature of creation'. (222) Consider that, for Benjamin, when a work becomes mere semblance, it does so as a consequence of being completely alive. Precisely because it is a mere semblance, however, it does not qualify as a work of art. He writes, unequivocally, that what 'arrests this semblance is the expressionless (*das Ausdruckslose*)'. (221) Thus, for a work of art to become complete, it is required that semblance be arrested. This ar-rest takes place when the expressionless is stamped upon the work of art: it ceases to be alive and to work its seduction. In an important sense, the completion of the work of art is the destruction of its life. There is something in the work of art that destroys the work of art itself. When a work of art no longer works as semblance, it becomes paralysed as a kind of 'truth,' distinct from beauty and its life. Indeed, the expressionless is a curious sign of this truth, one that works against the seductive claims of beauty and life.

What is meant by this strange term, 'the expressionless'? Benjamin explains: the expressionless is the critical violence that, 'while unable to separate semblance from truth in art, prevents them from mingling'. This violence, described as 'a moral dictum' (224), holds truth separately from beauty. The 'expressionless' sepa-rates what is beautiful on the basis of semblance from what is beautiful on the basis of its petrifaction, understood as its death and arrest. The truth in art, to the extent that we can speak that way, is separate from its beauty. Truth, however, is on the side of the sublime, and of violence, and so he writes, 'In the expressionless, the sublime violence of the true appears …' (224). Only as dead, petrified and without life does the work of art shatter into the various fragments that illuminate (indirectly) the irretrievable ideal or intention that organises pictures and paintings. The expressionless completes the work of art by shattering it into fragments.

So how does this nearly Kabbalistic account of the destruction of the work of art relate to Benjamin's view of morality? I suggested earlier that we might not be able to understand what he means by the moral nature of creation without first understanding his account of time. What we know so far about the moral vocabulary that informs his approach to aesthetics might be summarised through the following points:

I   The marks of which a picture is composed are, in some sense, marks of guilt, related to the marks that signify guilt or warn against it, such as stigmata. These marks are borne by a living being. The marks of guilt are singularising: they stamp or brand a person in their individuality, and those marks are not like signs, and thus do not work through resemblance. Their force, we might say, is performative: they establish the guilty subject.

II   Guilt and atonement are linked through a magical temporality. The promise of atonement is that it will reverse the guilt that is its cause. The last will come into question in Benjamin's moral and political reflections, since time cannot be reversed, and deeds cannot be undone through new deeds. A way other than atonement is needed in order to expiate the guilty subject, and to establish another conception of time that does not seek to reverse the irreversible.

III Finally, painting is the way in which we might understand the mark; since the painterly mark, or the mark of drawing, is linked archaically with the moral mark of guilt. Correspondingly, it will turn out that the destruction of the work of art will be linked for Benjamin with the obliteration of the traces of guilt. And this obliteration not only constitutes an alternative to the model of atonement, but is made possible by a certain understanding of time.

In a 1921 essay, 'The Meaning of Time in the Moral Universe', Benjamin turns to a consideration of retribution, at which point we can see something of the critique of law that informs this aesthetic inquiry. He remarks upon how long the desire for retribution can endure. If the desire to exact a price from someone else for their misdeed is potentially infinite, and atonement is the means by which that other pays, atonement is as infinite as retribution, and each is the inverse of the other. He writes that the desire for retribution can in principle last forever, since no satisfaction from inflicting injury can reverse the course of the past. Benjamin considers the dominant way that the last judgement has been interpreted. He disagrees with the account of the last judgement that posits an end of time in which the postponement of revenge is no longer necessary, the day when retribution is given free reign. Over and against this view, Benjamin writes that it

> fails to understand the immeasurable significance of the Last Judgment, of that constantly postponed day which flees so determinedly into the future after the commission of every misdeed. This significance is revealed not in the world of law, where retribution rules, but only in the moral universe, where forgiveness comes out to meet it. In order to struggle against retribution, forgiveness finds its powerful ally in time. For time, in which Ate [moral blindness] pursues the evildoer, is not the lonely calm of fear but the tempestuous storm of forgiveness which precedes the onrush of the Last Judgment and against which she cannot advance. This storm is not only the voice in which the evildoer's cry of terror is drowned; it is also the hand that obliterates the traces of his misdeeds, even if it must lay waste to the world in the process. (286–7)

Forgiveness, which we might ordinarily understand as a capacity achieved upon reflection when passions have quieted, is here figured as a storm, a storm with a hand and a voice, and so a divine force, but *not* one that is based on retribution. Importantly, this storm of forgiveness constitutes a radical alternative to the closed economy of atonement *and* retribution. If we expect this notion of the divine to confirm a notion of the Jewish God as vengeful, we must consider that there is another Judaism at work here. This storm, with its hand and voice finally figures time itself, a time that is freed from the cycles of retribution, one that obliterates guilt and all its marks (a time, in other words, that will come to constitute an alternative account of the messianic). God's fury roars through history in the storm of forgiveness–this is not the vengeful God, but a *God who is seeking to destroy vengeance itself*. And if it is a God, it is in war against another, opposing the lightning bolts of divine wrath, preceding it, sweeping away the marks of misdeeds and so foiling the plots of revenge.

This figure of the divine is equivalent to time, a time that works its force with indifference to what humans happen to remember or forget. This version of time brings forgiveness only because it is not determined by the human experience of time. Indifferent to the human even as it subtends all human life, it is a time that is neither remembered (or remember-able) nor forgotten (or forgettable). Only that kind of time is expiative; it wields the power to extinguish the traces of all misdeeds, and in this way helps to complete the process of forgiveness. The past is forgiven because it is obliterated, but precisely *not* because it proves to be something that can be understood or resolved in some way. 'Time', according to Benjamin, 'helps, in ways that are wholly mysterious, to complete the process of forgiveness, though never of reconciliation'. (287) We can perhaps discern in this description of the completed process of forgiveness an echo of Benjamin's early remarks about the destruction of the work of art. In a sense, the time that is beyond remembering and forgetting is one that bears no reference to experiential time; it bears no human face; it is a time that is, strictly speaking, expressionless. Benjamin defines the expressionless as that which completes and destroys the work of art at once. The destruction that completes the work of art is thus related to the forgiveness that destroys all traces of guilt. The mark in painting is the point of departure for understanding the organisational or 'creative' work of the divine name, understood as purely ideal; and as ideal, this divine name and force is identical with the destruction of that sensuous appearance or semblance that alternatively seduces the subject and establishes his or her guilt. Since the expressionless separates semblance, the living and seductive dimension of the work of art, from its truth, it follows that only as petrified or dead phenomenon does the work of art evince its truth in fragmented form. But what does the expressionless do to the mark? As we know, the mark is a sign of guilt, and the mark brings the temporality of guilt and atonement into play. Benjamin wrote of the temporal magic that appears in the mark. This temporal magic is the one that is invoked by both atonement and retribution, the one that promises, impossibly, that a future event will redeem the past. The obliteration of the traces of misdeeds are, then, the obliterations of the marks of guilt, and so, at the level of the picture, the obliteration of marks. Actually, at the level of the picture, the mark undergoes its own effacement, expiating itself, as it were, of semblance, in the manifestation of this ideal truth. Thus, Benjamin is drawn to those pictures that enact this self-effacement of the mark in the name of the compositional unity that constitutes the partial and oblique force of a creative principle that is, at once, destructive—of both seductive semblance and its counterpart, guilt.

In this sense, the utopian perception that sometimes breaks through the realm of art is one in which a notion of time emerges that counters and destroys the time structured by retribution and atonement. It constitutes a form of forgiveness that offers no understanding of the guilty deed, but rather an obliteration of the mark of guilt itself. This power of obliteration constitutes a certain kind of violence, but it is important to understand that this is a violence mobilised against the conception of violence implied by retribution. Understood as 'a critical violence', it is mobilised *against* the logic of atonement and retribution alike. The destruction of that logic is linked with forgiveness, and this seems to constitute the critical violence of which Benjamin speaks, a violence, he claims, that is the consequence of a moral dictum. Although contemporary readers have understandably recoiled

fig. 2 Paul Klee
Zerstorung und Hoffnung (Destruction and Hope)
1916, lithograph and watercolour and graphite, 52.55 x 33.97 cm
Extended loan and promised gift of the Carl Djerassi Trust I to the San Francisco Museum of Modern Art

from Benjamin's injunction of violence, perhaps it is important here to understand more precisely what it opposes, and what it offers. The moral dictum that warrants critical violence is the injunction to forgiveness.

Does this happen through the work of art, or through its completion and fragmentation? If painting lets us consider the mark in a privileged way, and that mark is a performative effect of guilt or its premonition, then what sort of moral venue is painting for Benjamin? If the mark is effaced or, indeed, obliterated, and if the mark is understood as a necessary condition of painting, then it is clear that painting completes itself by destroying itself. And with this destruction of the reign of the mark, time is apprehended differently, no longer within the moral cycle of seduction, guilt, revenge and atonement. If, as Benjamin claims, the only knowledge we can have of the mark is through painting, and if painting comes to be understood as both semblance and marks, and if, further, the petrification of the work of art and its emergence as expressionless is the obliteration of semblance, then it would seem that what is left is the mark itself. But that would be merely to aver seduction in favour of guilt. Separated from semblance, the mark achieves a petrification in painting, a status as expressionless, something non-living; semblance is refused in the name of the mark, and the mark becomes obliterated in the name of a creative and destructive force, itself ideal. The work of art is destroyed in the sense that it falls into fragments that variously indicate an ideality that is captured by no mark. And painting can be said to conduct this process of destruction not simply by presenting semblance and marks, but by conveying the ideality of its creation and, hence, the destruction of the seduction and guilt inhering in its constituent elements.

What then is left for us to consider is this very ideality that is understood as creative and destructive at once. It constitutes, clearly, the theological background of Benjamin's early aesthetic writings. Apart from the vexed question of how to look at a picture in the way that Benjamin suggests we do, there remains the question of how the ideality that the picture indirectly evinces is linked to his moral understanding of time and forgiveness. Do pictures have a relation to forgiveness? What is the relationship between that ideality that is said to animate and organise the compositional unity of a picture and the forgiveness we have been considering in light of his moral theory and critique of revenge? Benjamin gives us figural descriptions of this divine force and ideality, but the figure of the storm is conceptually impossible: a storm with hands and voice – conceptualisable neither as a natural event nor a human figure, but only as uncoordinated fragments of both? The figure thwarts conceptualisation, and the question of God seems to arise at this juncture where figuration proves its impossibility. The divine cannot be represented, but can it be discerned in the non-signifying marks? The marks induce an apprehension of that modality of time that opposes and destroys the cycles of retribution and atonement that constitute human suffering. If the mark is originally associated with guilt, then it would seem that the obliteration of the traces of guilt would entail the erasure of the mark, or the subordination of the mark to the sense of time that it indirectly manifests. The painting becomes the site where beauty and seduction are eradicated and lost. We find in the deathly remainders a time that is equivalent to the end of retribution and atonement alike, one in which forgiveness takes hold, as it were, without expression.

If the moral nature of creation gives the work the stamp of the expressionless, then that stamp will have no human face, and will bear no semblance to the human. In the same way, the notion of time we are asked to consider is not one that is organised by human deeds and their consequences. This latter notion of time is importantly not a principle of life, but of what arrests life, one that obliterates the traces of misdeeds even if it must lay waste to the world in the process. It is this work of the expressionless that grounds the content of the work, and that also stops its life and facilitates its final fragmentation. It is at once a critical and sublime violence, even a divine violence.

Benjamin's conception of divine violence is most dramatically introduced in his essay, 'A Critique of Violence' (1921). There the term 'violence' takes on various meanings for Benjamin. Let's remember that he is making at least two sets of distinctions, one between law-founding and law-preserving violence, on the one hand, and then another, between mythic and divine violence. It is within the context of mythic violence, however, that we receive an account of law-founding and law-preserving violence, so let us look there first to understand what is at stake. Violence does not always mean physical violence for Benjamin, and this will become most true when he refers to the bloodless or non-violent violence of divine violence or destructiveness. Not all violence can be adjudicated by the law, since there is a violence in the founding of law itself, and that violence is, by definition, not yet within the adjudicative purview of the law; indeed, that violence is the condition of possibility for the adjudicative purview of the law. Violence brings a system of law into being, and this law-founding violence is precisely one that does not operate with justification. Indeed, the way Benjamin describes it, it happens by virtue of what he calls Fate.

When fate produces law, it does so in the first instance through simply manifesting the anger of the Gods, but that this anger takes form as law does not serve any particular end. To show this, Benjamin seeks recourse to the myth of Niobe. You may remember that Niobe's great mistake was to claim she, a mortal, was more fecund and greater than Leto, the Goddess of fertility. She offended Leto immensely, but also sought, through her speech act, to tear down the distinction between gods and humans. When Artemis and Apollo arrive on the scene to punish Niobe for her outrageous claim by taking away her children, these gods can be understood, in Benjamin's sense, to be establishing a law. But this law-making activity is not to be understood first and foremost as punishment or retribution for a crime committed against an existing law. Niobe's arrogance does not, in Benjamin's words, offend against the law; if it did, we would have to assume that the law was already in place. Through her hubristic speech act, she challenges or tempts fate. Artemis and Apollo thus act in the name of fate, or become the means through which fate is instituted. Fate wins this battle and, as a result, the triumph of fate is precisely the establishment of law itself.

In other words, the story of Niobe illustrates law-instating violence since the gods respond to an injury by establishing a law. The injury is not experienced first as an infraction against the law, but it becomes the precipitating condition for the establishment of law itself. Law is thus a specific consequence of an anger that responds to an injury, but neither that injury nor that anger are circumscribed in advance by law.

The anger works performatively to mark Niobe, and we can see here the convergence of the mark and the problem of paralysis that informed Benjamin's comments on pictorial art. In the picture, the mark manifests – it does not work by semblance. The mark is, moreover, mythical, whereas the sign operates through magic and conjuring. The mark is the mark of guilt, establishing the guilty subject, taking form as the petrified rock, arresting life in the moment of guilt.

And though Niobe herself lives, she is also paralysed or cauterised within that living, since she becomes permanently guilty and, hence, partially petrified into rock. She constitutes a petrification performed by the mark, and the retribution that the gods take upon her is apparently infinite, as is her atonement. In a way, she represents the economy of infinite retribution and atonement that belongs to the sphere of myth. She is partially rigidified, and hardened in and by guilt, yet full of sorrow, crying endlessly from that petrified well-spring; and so the form her punishment takes comes to represent the subject bound by law, accountable, punishable and punished. She would be fully deadened by guilt if it were not for that sorrow, those tears, and it is those tears to which Benjamin returns, we might conjecture, when he considers what is released through the expiation of guilt. Her guilt is at first externally imposed. She does not herself murder her children, and yet she assumes responsibility for this murder only as a consequence of the blow dealt by the gods. The blow effects a magical causality whereby the afflicted assume causal responsibility for the affliction. It would appear, then, that the transformation of Niobe into a legal subject involves the magical – and illegitimate – transformation of a violence dealt by Fate into a violence that follows from her action, and for which she, as a subject, assumes direct responsibility.

Interestingly enough, Fate characterises the establishment of law, but it does not account for the destruction of law or legal coercion in particular. On the contrary, Fate establishes the coercive conditions of law; it binds the law to the person, steeping the subject in a guilt-ridden form of accountability, and Fate also accounts for the perennial sorrow that emerges from such a subject. Fate, however, cannot be the name that describes the effort to abolish those conditions of coercion. To understand the latter, one must move from Fate to the God, or from myth, the sphere to which Fate belongs, to the divine, the sphere in which a certain non-violent destruction belongs.[3]

It is important to remember that divine power not only destroys mythical power, but that divine power *expiates. This suggests that divine power acts upon guilt.* Divine violence acts upon law-making and the entire realm of myth, seeking to expiate those marks of misdeeds in the name of a forgiveness that assumes no human expression. Divine power thus does its act, its destructive act, and can only do its act, if mythic power and its capacity to mark and constitute a subject as guilty are already in place and have already produced the punishable offense along with a system of punishment that mandates perennial retribution along with a perennial atonement and sorrow.

Guilt, unexpiated, seems to lead to this nearly death-like state, the rock-like condition of Niobe, paralysed by and through guilt with her endless tears. Yet, it is in the name of life that expiation would be visited upon Niobe, which raises the question of whether the expiation of guilt is somehow a motivation for the revolt against legal violence. The desire to release life from a guilt secured through legal contract with the state – this would be a desire that gives rise to a violence against violence, one that seeks to release life from a death contract with the law, a death of the living soul by the hardening force of guilt. This is the divine violence that moves, like a storm, over humanity to obliterate all traces of guilt, a divine expiative force, one that anticipates and thwarts the divine rage that would exercise its punishments.

Earlier, we referred to the paradoxical centrality of the 'word' to Benjamin's understanding of painting and the pictorial in general. That 'word' was absolute, creative, and wielded the power to organise the composition of the painting. In this way it is like the 'word of God' that constitutes the commandment. Significantly, for Benjamin, the commandment does not establish human guilt, and it does not mark those for whom it is intended. The voice of the commandment cannot be figured by any semblance, so there is a bar against any representation of the divine that would establish its resemblance to any human or sentient figure. The linguistic word, the creative name, is thus neither mark nor semblance, neither guilt nor beauty, neither retribution nor atonement, and it can only be received, as it were, to the extent that a certain resistance to both beauty and morality is successful. In the example of mythic law, the punishment instills guilt and fear, and Niobe herself becomes an example of the punishment that lays in wait for any who might compare him or herself to the gods. She comes to represent guilt; she is the mark in his earlier sense, and she is also partially frozen in sculpture, and so a visual semblance of the state of guilt. Benjamin's commandment, on the other hand, is some kind of word that is delivered, but that does not wait around to enforce the actions it requires. It is as if what the commandment commands is nothing more or less than struggle with the commandment itself. Rather than a criterion for judgement, the commandment functions as a guideline (*Richtschnur des Handelns*). And what is mandated by the commandment is a struggle with the commandment whose final form cannot be determined in advance.

In Benjamin, the divine is allied with what is revolutionary and anarchistic, with that which is beyond or outside of principle. We saw this anarchistic moment already when the solitary person is conjured as wrestling, without model or reason, with the commandment. It is an anarchistic wrestle, one that happens without recourse to principle, that takes place between the commandment and the one who must act in relation to it. No reason links the two. And so we can discern the non-necessity that forms the legal order in which the subject is shackled coercively, and where guilt and accountability, in these circumstances, lead to an uncritical acceptance of the status quo.

When Benjamin writes about the 'destruction' of law that the general strike can entail, it would seem that he is writing against legal coercion in the name of some other organisation of life. And yet, he provides no view of what another life might be, or how life itself finally figures in his critique of law.[4] The anarchism or destruction to which Benjamin refers should not be understood as an aim of social and political life, that is, a condition that should be striven for and instated. Rather, the anarchism and destruction constantly recurs as the condition of positive law and as its necessary limit. He is pointing toward the non-thematisable conditions of law, the non-necessity that grounds its coercive force.

'Destruction' is thus a term used for the critical purpose of calling into question a given operation of positive law, but also the economy of guilt that would reduce all human suffering to moral misdeed. In this sense, destruction can be found in the anarchistic moment in which the appropriation of the commandment takes place, the strike against the positive legal system that shackles its subjects in lifeless guilt, as well as the moment when a work of art completes itself.

In the 'Critique of Violence', the word is the commandment, the commandment not to kill, but this commandment can only be received, paradoxically, once life itself has been stilled. Is this also what the painting finally says? Does it obliterate beauty and guilt by becoming a work of art, in Benjamin's sense, only to speak a truth that would refuse the moral and legal violence against life, including the death penalty, that sign of legal violence *par excellence*? If this 'destruction' yields another time, one beyond legal violence, is this a non-violent destruction? Does the painting release us from the sufferings induced by morality and law? And does it open us to the sufferings that pertain to human transience, inducing a perspective that is emphatically non-human, expressionless? And is it this movement beyond the marks of guilt that opens us to the utopian possibility of a time beyond coercion and revenge? And if this is not a time to be achieved, an end to history, as it were, is it nevertheless there precisely in the possibility of those historical ruptures that leave behind those conditions that once seemed necessary and fatal?

RESPONSE TO JUDITH BUTLER

J M Bernstein

In her essay, Judith Butler approaches Walter Benjamin's early metaphysical aesthetics with an almost disorienting empathic identification. Immediately after completing my first reading of this exquisite essay—an exquisiteness that I shall need to critically arm myself against—I gave it a new title: 'Niobe's Tears.' Those terrible tears of eternal mourning—hence a mourning that is akin to melancholy—are already a departure from the cycle of revenge and retribution that are the terms of law, positive and moral. Butler's generosity is to imagine the terms of the completion of that departure and conversion: the critical violence that enables forgiveness and thereby a transformed relation to others. It is hence natural that she should turn to another form of ethical relation, wrestling with the commandment 'thou shall not kill', in order to exemplify what this counter-violence comes to. My question, when it arrives, will be whether what she thinks this wrestling amounts to really is continuous with what Benjamin imagines?

When faced with the extravagances of Benjamin's early thought, Theodor W. Adorno adopted a more critical approach than Butler: to transform neo-Kantian theology into neo-Marxist materiality—a process that contains a violence of its own. So, for example, while for Benjamin the idea of the name inherits the authority of Platonic form, designating a 'higher power' that gives a 'compositional organization to a set of marks' (p.64) that are not signs but manifestations, for Adorno the approach operates in the opposite direction: through decomposition, the illusion of organic form is dissolved in the direction of the artwork's material – medium-bound – conditions of possibility: 'Music as a whole rescues the intentions, not by diluting them in a more abstract, higher intention, but by readying itself, in the instant in which it crystallizes, to summon the intentionless.'[1] 'Intentionless' is Adorno's term for Benjamin's 'expressionless'. For Adorno, modernist art practices are designed, against the seductions of beauty and semblance, for the sake of finally encountering 'a stratum in which' all intention 'is destined to become extinguished' (p.70). That extinguishing of intention occurs when, through the decomposed constellation of the material elements of a medium – sounds in music, line and colour in painting – we encounter a suggestion of meaning beyond and independent of anything we could intend to mean; a work, thus, 'draws the name closer, through the unfolded totality, the constellation of all its moments'.[2]

Now the point here is that in making these adjustments, Adorno was exploring how modernist artworks refashioned that relation between concept and intuition, universal and particular that had governed the moral metaphysics of modernity – the violence of the suppression of unique particulars beneath indifferent universality. And this does go directly to the ambition of locating in art the possibility of 'a politics beyond the cycles of revenge and guilt' (p.73) since for Adorno those cycles are dependent upon the repeated and perpetual *sacrifice* of particular to universal. The great power of Adorno's program is that his various accounts of artworks, the essay, the fragment, and the notion of constellation, by focusing on the minimal elements of cognition – concept and intuition – secure a non-metaphysical meaning for Benjamin's leading ideas. Although the demonstration would be complex, I would argue that at this level of analysis Adorno discovers plausible conceptual translations for Benjamin's enigmatic ideas.

Nonetheless, Butler could object here that even if the cycles of revenge and guilt depend on the sacrificial logic of particular to universal, Adorno's translation manual does nothing to show what a politics or ethics that broke from that logic would look like. Of the two, Benjamin was the more determined and luminous political thinker, and Butler thus has more than sufficient reason to linger with his difficult formulations.

That said, I nonetheless think the route to salvaging Benjamin's thought is through some kind of conceptual translation. In this respect, Butler's paper surprised me, for what is strangely missing from it is any mention of Hegel's conception of recognition – a notion she has, better than anyone, creatively refashioned for us again and again. To my ear, Benjamin's telling of the fable of Niobe conceptually replicates, exactly, Hegel's critique of Kantian morality and positive law in 'The Spirit of Christianity and its Fate'. On Benjamin's account, what is terrible in Leto's vengeance is that through it Niobe becomes 'permanently guilty and guilt turns the subject who bears it to rock' (p.78). This says metaphorically what Hegel struggles to spell out conceptually.

Hegel construes criminal justice as Kantian moral justice writ large: criminal justice makes explicit and formal, that is, gives institutional shape to, what transpires informally in routine occurrences of immorality since, formally, both are structures of law. Hegel's negative thesis is that criminal justice has only one response to trespass: punishment – which for him is but vengeance by another name. In a sense, Hegel considers the punishments rendered by penal justice a tortured concession by law that there is *nothing* it can humanly do to respond to trespass, that punishment is not so much a human response to transgression, but what we do when no further human response is possible. Punishment is the form of response to trespass that is the severing of response. Why? At the centre of the puzzle is the absolute separation between the universality of the law, its eternal authority, and the action that defies it. Formally, these two belong to distinct domains: law belongs forever to the intelligible, ought-ish, world of reason, while the criminal act belongs to the sense world of particularity that is. Act and law are connected to one another – the act breaks the law, denies it – and yet separate. Hegel's contention is that all that punishment accomplishes is the solidification of the separation of the criminal from the law: his imprisonment or death makes factual the separation that the criminal act itself announced. Because the criminal has negated the rights of all others, then until his claim to right is cancelled, the affront remains. Hegel's bald thesis here is that, for this dualist logic, nothing less than cancelling the criminal's position as active-legislator will, in actuality, restore the authority of the law itself. Every act that emphatically breaks the law necessarily undermines lawfulness as such by cancelling its authority. Hence, 'if there is no way of making the action undone, if its reality is eternal [in supplanting the law], then no reconciliation is possible, not even through suffering punishment.'[3] *Suffering* punishment does nothing with respect to the cancellation of the law involved in the offence. Only the removal of the legislative authority of the criminal, the authority rightfully possessed only through obedience, can restore the authority of the law. The death penalty is not one option among others; it belongs to the very being of law. This is the violence and moralism of judgement, what makes moral judgement a moralism: every moral judgement says 'Guilty!' forever, and in so saying announces the penalty of death.

In place of the logic of law, Hegel places a living coming to terms with fate: recognising what one has done, feeling contrition, confessing, and the other forgiving. Where Benjamin seems to be seeking to surmount the logic of vengeance with something higher, divine violence, Hegel seeks for something mundane and lower, the messy everyday business of sorting out our ongoing relations with one another. Now I hear just this messy business in Butler's description of what wrestling with the commandment 'though shall not kill!' involves since what makes this a commandment and not a law is that it is nothing but an expression of what is indeterminately experienced in the recognition that I am here and now confronted by another living, human being. Not killing, the heroic non-act, is, one might say, simply the minimum form that an affirmative recognition of this fact takes; but there is a wrestling here precisely because there is no law, that we are in a sense continually improvising our responses to one another in order that we might discover what is fitting, what will allow this relation to continue in a non-self-defeating manner; hence that what we call moral laws and principles are, in truth, only shorthand mnemonics for these discoveries about what makes for suitable relations, what allows us to keep going on with one another in a shared world.

All this might sound remote from questions of art, and the problem of violence. But there is a connection. The complex, irreducibly messy business of improvising a response to another, recognising her, follows a rigorous aesthetic logic. To experience a work as a beautiful semblance falsifies it because its authority as a work of art does not derive from likeness; the authority of works depends on their internal order, their composition, and likeness with its glittering life must hence be destroyed for the sake of this. Now this thesis is itself compatible with two opposing views: messianic rationalism and transcendental empiricism. In the messianic view the work's speechless truth imbricates what Benjamin calls in the essay on Romantic criticism, indifferently, either the Absolute or the Idea. From the perspective of transcendental empiricism, the work has a *name* that exceeds it because the composition does not follow and cannot follow from an antecedent plan, hence a universal. What makes works unique is their irreducible singularity, their order *without law*. But this discovery of the idea of order without law is precisely the discovery of modernist art. There is an order that is more than the mere aggregation of the parts but yet there is nothing behind that coherence. Order without law is of course the utopian ideal of anarchism, which is to acknowledge that anarchism, like the idea of a general strike, is an aestheticising of the political. Because any work of art once complete becomes a precedent, a law, then to create another work *after* involves the necessary critical violence of negating the authority of the precedent in order that something new, a new law, may arise. Isn't this the pattern necessitated by what I called above recognition and the improvising of ethical life? Isn't this the necessary violence that destroys without violating the soul of the living? If there is to be new life, will we not need to forgive those that destroy the old? Isn't this, near as damn, what is involved in wrestling with the commandment 'thou shall not kill'?

Butler would object even here: does not the proposed logic simply presume, impossibly, the displacement of positive law? Isn't this what is implied by her suggestion that the anarchism or destruction that Benjamin is referring to 'cannot be understood as another state or an alternative to positive law, but that it constantly recurs as the condition of positive law and as its necessary limit' (p.80)? Hence her suggestion that 'destruction is at once the anarchistic moment in which the appropriation of the command ["Do not kill!"] takes place, and the strike against the positive legal system that shackles its subjects in lifeless guilt' (p.80). What is the reference here? I imagine it as the moment in which our fellow citizens are lined up with the police standing opposite them with their batons raised, their guns to the ready, their dogs with teeth bared growling, ready to attack, a moment when only a logic of kill or be killed seems operative; and yet in the midst of this these citizens do not kill, but gently lock arms one with another and, wholly implausibly, anarchically, break into song – 'We shall overcome...'.

ART
AND
ALIENATION

Noël Carroll

I   Introduction

The topic of this volume, art and ethics, conjoins two concepts whose close association would have been utterly unobjectionable philosophically for almost every
major Western thinker from Plato to Hume. In his Preface to Shakespeare's Plays,
Samuel Johnson asserts that 'the end of poetry is to instruct by pleasing', where the
instruction he has in mind is, first and foremost, moral instruction.

In what might be labelled the pre-modern period,[1] traditional art was an in-
tegral part of its cultural milieu, transmitting, but also in the process shaping, the
shared ethos of its intended audience – conveying and clarifying, refining, reinforcing and galvanising the religious, ethical, political and otherwise cultural values of
those it addressed. Art tutored peoples in pertinent norms of interpersonal relations, in their societal obligations and expectations; it imparted information about
folk psychology, and especially about moral psychology with respect to virtue, vice,
the connection between motives and action, and so forth. Art showcased the customs of the relevant groups, illustrating models of desirable and undesirable character traits, concretising society's conceptions of duty, and advancing the preferred
attitudes toward historical and contemporary events and even eschatological ones.
Art also functioned as a site for pointers about correct manners and carriage, and
endorsed ideas about personal style in general, including suggestions about one's
style of movement, mode of gesture, deportment, and so much more.

Pre-modern art, in short, functioned as one of the – if not the most – powerful disseminators of the ethos of a people and it was widely recognised to possess
this capacity. Art was a comprehensive source of enculturation in the sense that it
very frequently engaged the whole person – simultaneously setting in motion one's
mind and one's body (one's senses, emotions, desires, and pleasures). Furthermore,

precisely due to this comprehensive appeal to the multiple aspects of the whole person – its potential to function as a sensuous universal – art was a particularly effective means for instilling the mores of a culture in every fibre of the very being of its citizenry.

Virtually no one denied this for two thousand years in the West. Indeed, it is probably true that much art in our own time still performs this role. However, since the eighteenth century, it has become at least controversial to suppose that moral instruction, even broadly construed, is the mission of art properly so-called. Mass art, it might be conceded, may still traffic in morality – projecting exemplars of virtue and vice (as does the recent Chinese film *Hero*) – but the qualification will quickly be voiced that such is not the legitimate ambition of serious art (otherwise known as genuine art). That is, at least since the mid-eighteenth century, the seemingly untroubled conjunction of art and ethics has been problematised in ways that continue to incite fierce debate even in these allegedly post-modern times in which categorical boundaries everywhere are supposedly evaporating.

The purpose of this essay is to diagnose how we have arrived at a point at which for many a link between art and ethics seems anomalous. To that end, I will sketch what I take to be parallel developments in the artworld, on the one hand, and in the philosophy of art on the other, which have resulted in the modern – or perhaps more aptly the modernist – prejudice that art and ethics are irretrievably twain. I will also attempt to undermine the presuppositions and the reasoning that recommend the separation of art and ethics. And I will conclude with some programmatic advice about what artists and philosophers of art might do at the present conjuncture.

Although the relevant developments in artistic practice and philosophical theory intersect – both historically and conceptually – in various ways, it is also the case that the artworld figures and philosophers who share a mutual suspicion of the legitimacy of connecting art and ethics could have arrived at their conclusions by independent routes without in any way availing themselves of the considerations that energise their allies in the other estate (respectively the artworld and philosophy). Thus, in what follows, I will begin with an admittedly broad outline of what disposed the artworld to abandon the pre-modern conviction of an obvious linkage between art and ethics, and then I will go on to review philosophy's case against the connection. Though there are points of tangency between these briefs, they also, as might be expected, often rest upon different concerns. Since the artworld case for the separation of art and ethics is in many ways practical, I will limn its shortcomings by underscoring the unhappy consequences this policy has had for the relevant artworld practices. But in so far as the philosophical position in favour of a categorical separation between art properly so-called and ethics is theoretical, it will require a philosophical refutation. Indeed, just because the philosophical conviction is theoretical, it may be more difficult to dislodge than the artworld prejudices in question. But I shall try, before concluding with some broad prognostications about how artists and philosophers might profitably negotiate the relation between art and ethics in the future.

II   The Artworld Declares its Independence

The disposition to deny any intimate bond between art and ethics is the consequence of a larger artworld endeavour to hive off art from other social practices and to establish art as an autonomous realm unto itself. That is, if the artworld is a domain independent from the external concerns of any other social institution, then it straightforwardly follows that art is something distinct from ethics and certainly not beholden to it.

As modernisation took hold in the eighteenth century, processes of specialisation began to accelerate. Among other divisions, the Weberian triplet contrasting rationality (theoretical reason and knowledge acquisition), instrumental and practical reason, and aesthetics evolved, enshrined in such intellectual monuments as Kant's three critiques.[2] Within the context of a changing society, the artworld found itself, or, at least, imagined itself, to be embattled on several, sometimes overlapping, fronts of which each, in turn, called for damage control, if the reputation of art was to survive in the way the friends of art desired in the emerging division of labour. In each case, the defensive strategy that attracted the artworld involved issuing a declaration of autonomy – an affirmation of the independence of art from other sorts of interests – in an effort to insulate art from the claims of other, putatively encroaching, social initiatives.[3]

These defensive manoeuvres included, among other things, the assertion of the separation of art from utility. On the one hand, utility could be construed as a euphemism for the crude mercantile inclination of an emerging bourgeoisie to reduce all value to market value. To affirm that artistic value was something else – something categorically different to market value – not only claimed autonomy for art but did so in the name of acknowledging that there was more value to be had in the world than one could find summarised on a price tag.

However, the declaration of the separation of art from utility could not only serve as code for the animus against vulgar materialism. It also affirmed the independence of art from social utility in general. Art was no longer to be demoted to the status of an instrument in the service of religion and/or politics and/or any other larger social project. The artist was becoming a free agent in the same marketplace he suspected, and what he had to sell was his own vision unencumbered by the commissions of patrons such as the church and the state. With employers like that, art had been expected to discharge social functions, often in the form of moral instruction. But the artist as a free market agent declared himself liberated from any obligation to be socially useful. Where what was on sale was self-expression, the artist agitated for deregulation. Art, its advocates clamoured, had to be free to pursue its own purposes, sui generis purposes on a par with, if not more important than, those of neighbouring social practices.

But what were the purposes of art? In pre-modern times there had not been the notion of art with a capital A – Art as a concept that defined a certain cluster of practices including painting, sculpture, music, poetry, drama and architecture. Rather 'art' connoted a skill; it was a term that signified mastery in doing something. Thus, one spoke of an art of this or that – an art of painting as the skill of painting and an art of war as skill in battle. In this context, it was the object of the preposition in the formulation 'the art of ——' that gave the phrase its content.

But in the eighteenth century, a subset of the arts – the so-called fine arts or beaux arts – were gathered together in an alleged system.[4] This presented the lovers of fine art with the task of establishing the criteria for membership in the newly anointed institution of the beaux arts. At first, undoubtedly extrapolating freely from Aristotle, representation or, more specifically, the representation of the beautiful in nature was proposed as the litmus test for citizenship in the republic of the arts. But with the rise of absolute music – pure orchestral music – representation became a scarcely credible requirement for the status of art properly so called. Something else had to be found to credential a candidate as art. And the alternative that still commands wide acceptance is that a genuine artwork is something produced with the intention that it facilitate disinterested contemplation. Disinterested contemplation of what? Of the artwork itself, usually in terms of its design or form for its own sake.

This conception of the artwork corresponded with the growing use of art by the developing bourgeoisie as a means of enriching through connoisseurship the leisure time that was increasingly at their disposal. Whereas previously art was most frequently encountered incorporated in the serious business of culture – for example, in the form of civic or religious statues of moral exemplars at the appropriate institutional sites or in the form of music, song and pageant as parts of political or spiritual rituals – art became re-oriented as a form of play, contemplative play free of social interests and needs. The purpose of art – the feature that won something entry into the modern system of the arts – was said to be precisely that it was not essentially useful for anything other than the exercise of the free (that is to say disinterested) play of one's contemplative powers.[5]

Ironically, this enabled art to function as a sign of conspicuous consumption – a badge of social distinction for the bourgeois consumer – at the same time that the severance of art from utility was supposedly a gesture of resistance against crass materialism. And yet it provided the nouveau riche with the wherewithal to don aristocratic airs.

But, in any event, a direct consequence of the conception of art as a locus of distinterested contemplation (especially of form) was to remove art from the domain of ethics, since the very notion of disinterested contemplation was itself a pleonasm[6] that came to signal the exclusion of financial, political, religious and, of course, ethical purposes with respect to an art object properly so called.

The artwork was to be contemplated as an artistic design for its own sake, not as moral instruction. Its purpose was to be, not to do – not even to do good. To assess the artwork in terms of ulterior social purposes, such as moral edification, was tantamount – on the evolving construal – to a category error.

Furthermore, by asserting that art is its own socially autonomous realm of value, the artworld not only claimed cultural capital for itself; it also attempted to fortify itself against censorship. When officials of the church or the state mobilised to squash art they believed to be offensive – generally morally offensive – the artworld could respond, at least rhetorically, that art as such is not in the service of morality, even if that is how it appeared in pre-modern times. Indeed, art was immune to the claims of morality in so far as it sustained a distinctive sort of value peculiar unto itself. Attempts to police art morally were categorically out of bounds. Admittedly, this rhetoric was not always successful in the past. However, it has gradually come to influence the law and has in fact begun to serve as a firebreak against censorship, as in the Mapplethorpe case in Cincinnati.

Lastly, in addition to serving as a defence against the perceived threats of market materialism, utilitarianism and moralism, the assertion of the autonomy of art also removed art from competition with science. When art was conceptualised as representation, it was natural to think of it as engaged in an activity comparable to science – that of describing the world. But from the seventeenth century onwards, art seemed to be a less and less likely peer to science in terms of the discovery of facts. Quite simply, science appeared to outclass art as a source of the acquisition of objective knowledge. If the arts were thought to be engaged in the same enterprise as the sciences, art undoubtedly would appear to be the weaker vessel. So within these circumstances, clearly an advisable gambit was to withdraw from the field of competition and to declare that one's contribution lay elsewhere. Where? In providing opportunities for disinterested contemplation, which experiences, in turn, were said to be valuable for their own sake. That is, art was not valuable for the knowledge it could supply, as one might have wrongly supposed with respect to genres like historical painting, but for the experiences, primarily of formal design, art afforded – experiences alleged to be valuable in and of themselves.

It perhaps goes without saying that this withdrawal from the field of knowledge also severed the relation of art and ethics. For in a culture where it was commonly believed that objective moral knowledge was not only available but that it could be taught, taking art out altogether of the knowledge game – a.k.a. science, broadly conceived – was, in effect, to surrender one of art's primary claims upon society's attention. Plato had envied Homer's reputation as the educator of the Greeks where the education in question was primarily moral. Plato attempted to erode Homer's standing by arguing that in as much as Homer and the poets had no knowledge, they had nothing to teach. Those who celebrate the autonomy of art in terms of its independence from cognitive pursuits thereby grant Plato's point without a fight; but in abdicating all claims to knowledge whatsoever they relinquish any prerogative to educate the populace ethically and thus forgo their former place of pride at the nerve centre of the culture at large. By claiming autonomy and disavowing service to broader social projects, art ironically loses its authority in society instead of establishing it on a firm footing.

In order to defend the arts from materialism, utilitarianism, censorship and an invidious competition with science, along with perhaps the desire on the part of the artist as free market agent to sell without constraint his wares – notably, self-expression with the onset of Romanticism – the artworld asserted its autonomy from the rest of society and its purposes. This tendency is manifested historically in the nineteenth century in slogans like 'art for art's sake', which apparently arose via Benjamin Constant through a misunderstanding of Kant's third critique,[7] and then gained wider currency through movements such as aestheticism which enlisted followers such as James Whistler, Walter Pater and, of course, Oscar Wilde.

Moreover, at the same time that the artworld declared its independence polemically, it was also changing itself physically in ways that reinforced the notion of art's autonomy. Whereas pre-modern music accompanied rituals of power and faith, absolute or pure music in the modern era was composed for a newly invented institutional site, the concert hall, which was a machine for concentrating contemplation upon musical form apart from distracting social purposes, like religious commemoration.[8]

Likewise, the art museum, another emerging institution, was a way of abstracting artworks from contexts in which they performed social, political and/or religious functions so that their form rather than their social meaning became the most salient thing about them. The Louvre, for example, assembled the politically charged paintings and statues of the ancien régime from the locations in which they symbolised Bourbon power for the express purpose of defanging these representations – placing them instead in a museum setting where they would no longer perform their intended social function but would become merely decontextualised objects for contemplative appreciation.[9] The museum and the galleries modelled upon it have a decontextualising and, therefore, desocialising tendency, which, among other things, can cause anxiety when photographs, such as those of the Abu Ghraib atrocities, are displayed on the whitened walls of galleries where their form glows forth as opposed to what strikes us when we find them in newspapers where they are juxtaposed to suitably accusatory headlines.

If the architecture of the artworld under the dispensation of art's autonomy seems almost cathedral-like, it is an echo of the religiously derived language of the self-sufficiency of art and of its value for its own sake – terminology originally coined by Plato and Plotinus to characterise the absolute and later appropriated by the Catholic Church to speak of God.[10] It is almost as if after centuries of using art as an instrument of worship, people became so accustomed to praying before religious paintings and statues that they came to take the artworks themselves as the objects of adoration and began to worship them. How else would one make sense of the curious conviction of certain modern aesthetes that art could save the world?

The aestheticism of the nineteenth century turned into the formalism of the twentieth, capably defended by polemicists like Clive Bell and Roger Fry who tutored generations in the appreciation, understood as the disinterested contemplation, of a species of pictorial value, called significant form, which was allegedly independent of any social concerns, perhaps most obviously ethical ones. To attend to the moral content of a picture – its political or religious significance – was to be looking in the wrong direction: at the world, and, therefore, away from what one should be looking at, viz. the picture and its structure. In other words, it was to be focused wrongly on those Spaniards being massacred by the French firing-squad and not on the painting by Goya.

Likewise modernism, à la Clement Greenberg, continued the theme of the autonomy of art, reinterpreting the notion of art for art's sake epistemologically – asserting that genuine art was about art in the sense that its task was to reveal and acknowledge its own nature, specifically the nature of painting as a two-dimensional thing. By making self-reflection the goal of art, the modernists sustained the separation of art from other social practices initiated in the late Enlightenment and early Romantic period, the notion of reflexivity translating into the contemporary variant of the idea of art for art's sake. Moreover, this framework for conceptualising ambitious art-making continued to be unquestionably the hegemonic one through Minimalism which, despite Greenberg's disapproval, used the model of critique he had fashioned as its primary means of self-understanding.

Consequently, it was still the case as late as the 1970s that the assertion of the autonomy of art was a generally accepted article of faith across much of the artworld, including its most powerful domains.

However, there is a serious question about whether the separation of art from the rest of the culture, including the ethical realm, achieved the desired effect or whether it was the victim of what Hegel called the cunning of reason (better known as history). If my abstract characterisations of the various artworld motives behind its declaration of independence are correct, the notion of the autonomy of art was intended to bolster the prestige of the artworld, and to raise it to an equal, if not greater, status than adjacent social enterprises. But, in the long run, this strategy appears to have failed.[11] Ambitious art has become marginal to the life of the culture. The artist has made great strides in winning his/her freedom, at least in principle, from moralism, commercialism, utilitarianism and so forth by flying the flag of autonomy. But the other side of the coin of that autonomy has been a corresponding degree of alienation from the wider society. For in as much as the artist spurns engagement with broader social interests, such as enculturation, the surrounding society loses interest in the activities of artists. Only those with highly specialised concerns take an interest in art for art's sake. Once artists remove themselves from the ongoing concerns of the culture, the culture predictably loses interest in the arts, except on those occasions where the artworld provokes some scandal, the sensation momentarily commandeering the public spotlight.

The cost of the kind of freedom the artworld has aspired to in the name of autonomy has been an ever-accelerating diminution of attention toward ambitious art-making, even among the educated elite. It is no accident that alienation—especially alienation from everyday society—has been the recurring theme of the stories about the artist in the era of the autonomy of art. It symbolises—through the particular—the plight of an artworld that demands freedom from society on its own terms. The alienation of the artworld, in other words, is largely self-inflicted, and the abandonment of the role of transmitter of the ethos of its intended audience is arguably the deepest wound the artworld has perpetrated upon itself.

If this diagnosis is convincing, then it seems obvious that the separation of art from ethics, however well-intentioned way back when, has been a self-destructive policy on the part of the artworld. In order to reverse the alienation of the artworld, the artworld needs to reclaim its function as a source of promoting—both critically and sympathetically—the ethos of the people it intends to address. The novel, even in our own times, has consistently proven itself to be a resilient force in the life of the culture. As new segments of society empower themselves—persons of colour, women, gays, post-colonial peoples—the novel serves as a vehicle for articulating their concerns and values and for celebrating while also constructing their emerging ethos. The literature of these groups, like the literature of the Jews and the Irish before them, encourages attention for being engaged in the community, not by standing outside the community and declaring itself a community of interest unto itself. The challenge for the fine arts, it seems to me, is to discover its own way of reinserting itself into the social process.

In Philadelphia, for example, there is a thriving mural arts program. Begun in 1984 as a way of combating graffiti, the program now comprises more than 2400 indoor and outdoor murals. These murals celebrate local neighbourhood heroes, values and activities. Some of them commemorate victims of crime and express the desire that such will never occur again. Some sketch the ethnic history of the people in the community. Others symbolise the hope that different neighbouring ethnic groups can reconcile and tolerate diversity. Some picture pastoral scenes, providing a glimpse of serenity in the midst of the bustle of urban life. But all address what the adjacent communities value, including ethically value, and for that reason are much beloved, are objects of comment and discussion, and part of the life of the streets they emblazon.[12]

For instance, the mural on Fabric Row includes the image of an elderly couple showing a child – perhaps their grandchild – a piece of cloth. They are talking about it. One presumes they are telling the infant what it is and how it is made, while also expressing their pride in their trade and its ethos. Such murals are embraced by the people of Philadelphia because they are integrated into the pulse of the community as emblems of the everyday life and values of the neighborhoods whose history, aspirations, tragedies, folkways and values they enshrine. These artworks are not, after the fashion of much performance art, merely symbols of the continuity of art and daily living. These artworks are embedded in the ebb and flow of the culture in ways that might be instructive to the reigning artworld that has imprisoned itself behind the blindingly white walls of the gallery and museum.

Before turning to the reasons that philosophy has separated art from ethics, let me briefly review three objections that might be leveled at the very sketchy account that I have just offered of the alienation of the artworld. The first observes that my characterisation of the influence that the notion of the autonomy of art has exerted over the artworld for the last two centuries is vastly exaggerated, even if we narrow our purview to avant-garde art. For in opposition to the lineage that extends from the proponents of art for its own sake through the Greenbergian modernists there is an alternative tradition that has sought to dissolve, as they say, the boundaries between art and life. Here one may have in mind Dada and its heritage, including Conceptual art, Fluxus, early post-modern dance, Joseph Beuys, happenings, readymades, and so on. How can I say that the artworld has separated itself from society when these highly visible gestures against the autonomy of art have been undertaken expressly in order to reunite art with the everyday life of the culture?

My answer is simply that these movements, which I think are both fascinating and important, nevertheless are essentially part of an internal debate within the artworld. A dance composed of ordinary movement may symbolise a continuity between everyday life and art, but it does not influence everyday life outside the concert hall. It engages an artworld dialectic, albeit on behalf of the heteronomy of art, but it does not intersect with any more concrete social issues. If it projects egalitarianism, it does so in the most etiolated fashion, and, if it claims for itself the property of being ordinary movement, then it is self-refuting, since ordinary movement is not intended to symbolise a dissolution between art and life. Such dance requires an artworld atmosphere in order to live; it does not live in the wider culture.

A second objection to my account is to recall that the assertion that art is autonomous need not be understood as a denial of ethical or political significance. The affirmation of the autonomy of art is itself a political or ethical act – an act of defiance in the face of the reductive tendencies of instrumental reason, on the one hand, and the all-devouring market on the other. Such is broadly the view of some of the leading figures of the Frankfurt School of Critical Theory.

However, this, like the not unrelated polemics of Dada and its progeny, is largely an in-house debate within the artworld. The autonomy of art becomes a political symbol or allegory for those who know how to decipher it – which is to say predominantly denizens of the avant-garde artworld. This is not to suggest that this is not a legitimate activity or to deny that it is a worthwhile debate to enter. But neither can it be regarded as an avenue for reconciling art with society, since, of course, it regards the alienation of art from society as a moral badge of courage. It conceives the ethos of existing society to be too utterly fallen to be worthy to enlist the services of art. Art is not only conceptually opposed to other social practices; it must be politically and morally opposed as well. Yet this stance, even if it were intellectually defensible, would hardly relieve the alienation of art nor would it restore a role for art in the everyday ethical life of society.

Finally, I anticipate that many will reject my diagnosis on the grounds that it is obsolete. Though the idea of the autonomy of art may have been ascendant through the Minimalist moment, with the arrival of politicised post-modernism in the late 1970s and its consolidation in subsequent decades, it will be proposed, faith in the autonomy of art has become an artifact of the past. Art is no longer regarded as autonomous, nor is the ambitious art of the present self-alienated from the rest of the culture. It is patently engaged, primarily in social criticism.

Here I want to make two brief comments. Though there is a great deal of politicised post-modernist art on offer, including the work of Barbara Kruger, Jenny Holzer and Mary Kelly, it has not neutralised the effect of two centuries in which the ideology of the autonomy of art held sway. For that reason, the appearance of politicised art in the venues where ambitious art is exhibited is still controversial. Influential critics continue to wonder aloud whether artists have lost their way and rail that they have forgotten about pleasure and beauty and other formal qualities. The notion of the autonomy of art has not been banished by any means. It remains in constant reserve. Only time will tell whether it or politicised post-modernism will win the hearts and minds of prospective artists. That is, the future of the artworld is still up for grabs.

Second, politicised post-modernism and autonomism both appear to have one thing in common: an adversarial relation to the rest of the culture. The autonomist declares art to be separate from everything else and categorically contrasts artistic value to other sorts, sometimes even suggesting that it is superior. Politicised post-modernism does not place art completely outside of the culture, but it does assume that the artist occupies a privileged position, namely that of social critic.

Indeed, in debates about government funding of the arts, artworld advocates often claim that it is the essential role of the artist to be a social critic and that this is what warrants government funding. But not only is this claim completely without any historical warrant—was even one medieval master builder a social critic, or, for that matter, was Leni Riefensthal?—but it also reiterates the idea of the art as somehow distanced from the rest of the culture, a stance that is guaranteed to perpetuate the alienation of art if it is pursued as the exclusive vocation of ambitious art.

My point here is not to suggest that art should not engage in social criticism. That is one thing that art should do. That is one way in which the artworld needs to reclaim its connection to ethics. But social criticism is only one aspect of the ethical role of art. Ambitious art also needs to get back into the activity of articulating, transmitting and celebrating that which is positive in the ethos of its audience. Artists cannot simply stand above the rest of the culture and rain down admonitions like Old Testament prophets. If its only relation to society at large is negative, this will have the practical effect of its marginalisation as a scold. Art must engender a more intimate relationship with its viewers by creating symbols of the positive ethical values of the culture that people find worthwhile as guides to and ways of making sense of their lives.[13] In that way, social criticism will be recognised to hail from within a wellspring of the society and not from an unelected position on high.

III
Philosophy and the Autonomy of Art

Like the artworld, philosophy has also defended the thesis that art is autonomous from other cultural endeavours, most notably, ethical instruction and leadership. Philosophy's sometimes subconscious acceptance of the notion of the autonomy of art, moreover, has blinkered philosophical research into the arts, proscribing entire areas of inquiry – including the relation of art to the broader society, politics, morals, personal relations, and to knowledge and even to philosophy itself. Philosophy's espousal of autonomy has not only reinforced the alienation of art from a theoretical perspective, it has also marginalised the philosophy of art. For if philosophical theory reconfirms the sentiment that art is of no interest outside the artworld, then why should philosophical aesthetics attract anything more than insider interest?

However, whereas the artworld's affirmation of autonomy arose, one hypothesises, as a solution to the perception of various practical predicaments, philosophy, at least in part, is drawn to the autonomy thesis for reasons having to do with a certain conception of the nature of the project of the analytical philosophy of art.

That philosophy parallels or echoes certain dominant artworld themes is not surprising. Some, of a Hegelian bent, will maintain that philosophy is predictably always the reflection of a form of life (such as the artworld), while those who like their Hegel spiced with Marx will claim that both the artworld and its philosophy are merely converging reflections of deeper economic forces.Correspondingly, those of a more Anglophone persuasion are apt to argue that in as much as the philosophy of anything aspires to be the rational reconstruction of the conceptual frameworks and modes of reasoning of whatever practice it is the philosophy of, needless to say, the philosophy of art will tend to rehearse the presuppositions of the artworld. I think that each of these conjectures has a great deal of plausibility and adds to the explanation of why the philosophy of art gravitates so readily toward the autonomy thesis and, thus, in its own way, contributes to the alienation of art. Nevertheless, I also believe that there is a further motive operating here that makes the notion of the autonomy of art particularly seductive to philosophers of art, especially those of an analytic disposition.

Earlier I noted that the so-called modern system of the arts only emerged in the eighteenth century. Before that it was just as 'natural' to classify music with mathematics, while painters could belong to the same guild as chemists, since both ground pigments. But in the eighteenth century, the practices we now find gathered together on the arts quad of the campus became a canonical grouping. And this provoked a conceptual or theoretical question, namely: What criterion or criteria must be satisfied in order to qualify for membership in this system? Or, in other words: What is art?

Answering this question became the philosopher's task; specifically, it was the job of the philosopher of art. This project was conceived as the enterprise of discovering the essence of art–that property or combination of properties that any art form would have to possess for any instance of that art form to count as an artwork and not as something else. Note that this construal of the goal calls for the disclosure of something that all artworks properly so called possess necessarily, but which is not possessed by non-artworks. The search for an essence of art–let us call it essentialism–dictates the kind of answer that will be attractive to philosophers. Furthermore, I suspect that it is the very kind of answer that this brand of essentialism anticipates that makes the notion of the autonomy of art enduringly attractive to philosophers of art. That is, the notion of the autonomy of art is compelling to philosophers of art for reasons internal to their theoretical project, given their essentialist leanings.

Why? Because if one can demonstrate that art has some generic value that is by definition different from and in contrast to every other sort of value–including every other sort of personal and/or social value–then one will have located a necessary feature of art sufficient to differentiate at a stroke art from everything else. If one can isolate an autonomous value for art–one separate from and even contrary to every other kind of value–then one has the conceptual resources adequate to demarcating virtually automatically the border between art and artworks and every other social practice and its products.

Essentialism and the thesis of the autonomy of art have, I want to say, a natural affinity. This is not to imply that an essentialist with respect to art must accept the autonomy thesis, but that, for the reasons just given, the autonomy thesis is a permanently fatal attraction for philosophers of art of this ilk. And yielding to this temptation, of course, is a major factor, among others, that accounts for the scant interest said philosophers have shown concerning the intersection of art and ethics, not to mention other social practices, throughout the twentieth century.

Needless to say, it is not enough for the philosopher of art to assert that art has autonomous value and to leave it at that. Nor can he defend this view by advertising that it solves his problems ever so conveniently. The philosopher must specify the allegedly necessary property of art that grounds the unique sort of value that, in turn, differentiates and categorically separates art from everything else. Moreover, one must characterise that feature in such a way that it is evident why both that property or set of properties and its associated value is distinctive of all and only art.

Historically, the feature that it seems to me philosophers smitten by the autonomy thesis return to again and again is that of form valued for its own sake and not for the sake of anything else.[14] That is, it is the form as such of the religious statue

and not the form of the statue as a means of promoting reverence that we appreciate when we appreciate the statue as art, or qua art (to revert to the standard way
of speaking in discussions like these). Essentially valuing form for its own sake, it
is thought, distinguishes art from everything else, just because in every other realm
of value, we value things for their consequences. For example, however much we
may be said to admire knowledge for its own sake, we also value the enterprise of
knowledge acquisition for its proven pragmatic potential.

But when it comes to art, it is hypothesised that we value art qua art solely for
its affordance of the disinterested contemplation of form for its own sake – something that, by definition, is separate from (or autonomous from) the concerns of
every other social practice. This kind of philosophical formalism, of course, need
not deny that historically art has been dragooned into the service of other social
practices, like moral instruction, but only maintains that these supposedly ulterior
functions are at best irrelevant to art's distinctive value as art – though at worst,
these entanglements are lethal distractions.

Yet why believe that form valued for its own sake is the one and only value to be
heeded when approaching art qua art? The argument is an essentialist one; it goes
like this. What does everything we call art have in common? Some artworks are
political, some are religious. Some engage in moral instruction, but others simply
abet experiences of delight, and apprehensions of beauty. Some artworks raise terror, others soothe. And so on. The local purposes of artworks, styles, movements
and genres are various. Artists undertake many briefs. But is there something they
have in common? Yes, suggests the formalist: ex hypothesi, they all aspire, no matter their medium or genre, to find a form appropriate to the point or purpose of
the work in question.

As an artist, one is a maker. Artists are makers with skills in manipulating and
organising the means that belong to their media and genres – makers who find
forms that suit whatever the artwork is about, whether it be the salvation of humanity or, maybe less exaltedly, the provocation of visual pleasure. Artists, in the
sense relevant to the modern system of the arts, are always the creators of form, and
when we attend to their creations qua art we attend to the forms they have invented
as forms and not as the means to something else. For that is their distinctive contribution; they are at the very least artificers of form, if nothing else.

That is, what we value in art qua art are the forms the artists have made for their
own sake. Why? Because this is what the artist qua artist has done; she has created
forms. We admire their ingenuity, coherence and elegance, and not their contribution to, for example, social or psychological knowledge or to ethical insight or
education. Those achievements do not putatively belong essentially to the artist.
Indeed, the formalist may claim that other sorts of experts are better at securing

those ends. The artist is an expert in the creation of form and, for that reason, we should contemplate his designs as designs–inspect them from the inside, so to speak, and not in terms of the ostensibly external purposes they may serve. What any artist achieves qua artist is the form or structure that embodies the point or purpose of the work. It is not the point or purpose of the work that is artistically significant or valuable but the way in which it is made manifest formally.

Furthermore, the friend of formalism adds, there is no feature other than form that obtains with comparable generality across the practices and objects we call all and only art. Admittedly, other practices evince form, but only in the realm of art properly so called is the sole locus of worthiness form itself irrespective of the purposes, if any, that it might serve. Only artistic form is autonomously valuable.

Put succinctly, the argument begins with a question: what qua art, in the sense relevant to the modern system of the arts, is it that artists (all artists) do? Supposedly, the only feasible answer is: they create forms. No other property reaches so generally across the arts. Thus, the exhibition of form for its own sake must be the value of art, since beyond the universal creation of form, the aims of artworks are too diverse and, indeed, often too conflicting to provide a comprehensive and consistent source of value. This conclusion, moreover, fits nicely with the view that art affords the opportunity for disinterested contemplation, since it specifies, in a way that makes the notion of disinterested contemplation concretely intelligible and operational, that upon which one should focus–the form of the artwork on its own terms or for its own sake. Furthermore, in so far as one is to attend to the form for its own sake, thinking about the object disinterestedly comes to seem natural, since we are to concentrate on the form independently of its purpose. For little effort would appear required to contemplate the object disinterestedly if what we are tracking is the form of the work in isolation from its allegedly non-aesthetic purposes.

Given what I hope are obvious reasons, we can call this the common-denominator argument. It is very compelling, particularly for anyone committed to the kind of essentialism I have characterised so far. However, the argument is not irresistible.

One thing to notice about this argument is the way in which it presupposes that art and artistry can be informatively and exclusively identified and assessed independently of the context and content of the art in question. As observed previously, prior to the advent of the modern system of the arts, art was simply the skill of x, where x, say medicine or sculpture, and the aims thereof, informed one of the values and standards of excellence that pertained to the activity in question. To modify a saying of Gombrich's, there were arts; there was no art as such.[15] But in the eighteenth century, the notion of a category that incorporated certain arts under a single, uniform concept won wide acceptance. And formalism, as the most enticing variant of the autonomy of art thesis, gained traction as that subsection of the arts were hypostasised as ART. Formalism performed the service of rationalising this collection of the arts as a system, by proposing that the kind of thing that Art (with a capital A) is is the exhibition of form for its own sake.

But even granting that there is something so abstract, called Art, and that the discovery of appropriate forms is a concern of every practitioner who belongs to this enterprise, it should also be clear that practitioners of the various art forms, genres, styles and movements who are citizens of this republic may have further commitments, given the kinds of artists they are, in addition to the creation of form. In other words, due to the particular type of artist one is, one may be responsible qua that sort of artistry for more than the creation of form. The formalist asserts that one must appreciate an artwork on its own terms, but he wrongly assumes that the terms of a given artwork must be specified exclusively in terms that are common to every artwork – namely, just formal terms. However, artworks belong to specific kinds which possess their own terms that are more pertinent to the appreciation of the specific artwork qua artwork – that is, qua the kind of artwork it essentially is – than are generic considerations of form. To be truly respectful of the artwork on its own terms, then, requires acknowledging the kind of work it is. And the kind of artwork it is may demand that one attend to it as something other than a sui generis formal design.

For example, a realist novelist, given the nature of the realist novel, is not merely expected to create a coherent novelistic form. She is also typically expected to be a penetrating and accurate observer of society, or, at least, of the social milieu she describes. She is expected to distill these observations into, among other things, characters that readers can use in a way that is analogous to how concepts function in order to comprehend social conditions.[16] This is not an extraneous or dispensable responsibility for the category of realist novelist. It is a constitutory element of what it is to be a realist novelist. It is part of the art of the realist novel. The realist novelist, as the kind of artist she is, not only creates a consistent, probable, narrative-dramatic structure, but also strives to provide astute and clarifying commentary about the society she depicts. It would be simply ad hoc to protest, as the formalist might, that that aspect of creating realist novels is merely journalism or reportage, whereas the genuinely artistic part is the way in which the variety of characters and actions are unified formally or colligated by an overarching concept or theme.

To split in half in this way the role of the realist novelist qua the kind of artist she is falsifies the way in which this form of art is understood both by those who write novels in this genre and those who read them. Neither side of this relationship regards the social commentary as nothing but a pretext for formal invention. That is why aspiring novelists of this sort are told to develop their skill (the art) of observation. Both sides of the exchange – both readers and writers – believe that the art of the realist novel as such aspires to the illumination of social reality, which elucidation may include the promotion of a moral perspective – perhaps original with the author – concerning the state of affairs represented in the story.

Moreover, such novelists are not only expected to be social observers. They are encouraged by the tradition of their practice to be psychologists as well. When in *House of Mirth*, Edith Wharton surmises, on the basis of a carefully crafted character study, that 'it is less mortifying to believe oneself unpopular than insignificant and vanity prefers to assume that indifference is a latent form of unfriendliness',[17] she is discharging a central function of the realist novelist – the revelation of psychic scenarios and syndromes that govern everyday life. The task of the realist novelist is not simply to exhibit in a formally perspicuous fashion the findings of others, but to discover, illustrate and explain what makes people tick. And this includes the keeping track of new personality types, interpersonal strategems, anxieties, virtues and vices as they emerge and mutate with changing times. We admire novelists because of their ability to distill the scripts that determine and explain behaviour. This, as well as finding a suitable formal design, is part of the charge of the novelist. Indeed, in many cases we are willing to overlook the formal lapses of a novelist if her social and/or psychological and/or moral insights are estimable. Moreover, we count these observations as part of her achievement as a novelist and not as something else.

It is not clear that the task of social and/or psychological and/or moral exploration is of a secondary or inessential interest to the reader or the writer of the realist novel, since both may in fact regard the purpose of the form of a novel to be justifiably subservient to advancing as forcefully as possible the novel's social and psychological insights, and/or its moral perspective. That is, even if form is a concern of every artist qua artist, there is no reason to suppose that in any individual artwork, given the kind of thing it is, that it is form for its own sake that is of central importance to it for either the artist or the audience as both are informed by the practice. Think, for example, how we talk about Dostoyevsky.

Also, the form of a tribal mask designed to terrify outsiders is something that occupies the native artist, but not so that interlopers savour it for its own sake. Were they to do that, the mask would be self-defeating, since it is not intended to transfix foreigners in aesthetic ecstasy but to send them off in flight. Likewise, the visions of hell in our own culture – such as those by Bosch and Breughel – were not designed to encourage contemplation for its own sake. They are meant to frighten the viewer – to call her back to the straight and narrow path out of fear of eternal damnation. These spectacles are not intended to be consumed disinterestedly. Nor is it the case that the viewer regards her terror of hellfire as valuable for its own sake; it is valuable for the way in which it encourages pious living. In these examples, it is quite evident that though the artist is concerned with the form of the work, the form for its own sake is neither the mandated focus of the work, nor the focus for the intended audience.

At best, the common-denominator argument might establish that in general artists are concerned with form – that a commitment to formal invention is a general feature of art. But this falls far short of what the autonomy thesis requires and for two reasons. First, it is logically consistent with the assertion that a formal dimension is a necessary condition of all artworks, that artworks have other, non-extraneous dimensions, given the kinds of things they are, which may be purposive and contentful and, furthermore, these dimensions may be equally or even more essential than the formal dimension with respect to the type of art at hand.

Second, even if we agree that every artwork has a formal dimension, there is no reason to imagine that it is the formal dimension for its own sake that should qua artwork preoccupy us. For with respect to certain sorts of artworks, form may be merely a transparent gateway, albeit an indispensable one, for facilitating the audience's absorption in a larger point or purpose (such as social, psychological, and moral insight as in the case of the typical realist novel). This is not to say that there are not artworks for which the contemplation of form for its own sake is not apposite, but only that, even if appropriate or suitable form were aimed at by every artwork, it does not follow that it is the intended focus of every artwork. Moreover, the realist novel is not the only art form where this is so. Similar points with respect to the visual arts might be made regarding the genre of caricature. Hogarth, Daumier and Grosz are surely as, if not more, esteemed for their discernment, both social and moral, as they are for their formal prowess.

Philosophical formalism is the best hope for the thesis that the art is autonomous, for it lights upon a feature of art that appears to be not only arguably generic but detachable from other realms of social value, namely, form for its own sake. However, as we have seen, it is not form for its own sake that is of general concern across the arts in the modern system but just form, often for the sake of something else, and, in any event, in a way that is consistent with artworks possessing other aims, such as ethical instruction, that are as artistically essential to the kinds of artistic practices they instantiate as is the commitment to formal efficacy.

Without formalism, the strongest case for the philosophical endorsement of the autonomy thesis founders. For formalism gives the philosopher something positive that art is about, namely form for its own sake. Without that, the thesis becomes simply negative and hollow in a way that is ultimately uninformative and, therefore, intellectually unsatisfying. But without the common-denominator argument, it is hard to see how to get formalism off the ground.

That, of course, will not stop philosophers from trying, since the notion of the autonomy of art fits so neatly with their essentialist ambitions. However, here it must be emphasised that essentialism at the level of Art with a capital A is purchased at the price of ignoring the natures of many of the art forms, genres, movements and styles that fall under that umbrella concept but which, due to their own essential aims, are inextricably and heteronymously enmeshed in such enterprises as the discovery of knowledge (psychological, social and moral); the promotion of insight and understanding (personal, political, ethical, religious); the clarification and dissemination of the ethos of a culture or subculture; and so on. Autonomism for the sake of essentialism about Art with a capital A obscures getting clear about the natures of the arts (beginning with a minor case a and ending with a small s). It is an instance of the philosophy of art standing in the way of the philosophies of the arts.[18]

The autonomy thesis in the philosophy of art has served to alienate philosophical inquiry into the relation of art from other social practices in a way that parallels the withdrawal of modern art, under the aegis of autonomism, from the life of the broader culture. In the philosophy of art, this has resulted in an unduly constricted, even distorted, view of art, one that has been virtually blind to many of the dimensions, such as its ethical address, that make art important. But in addition to the violence done to the data, this approach has also inflicted damage to the field of the philosophy of art. It has turned it into an area of barely marginal interest. For in allegedly discovering that art serves no interests but its own – a.k.a. form for its own sake – philosophy 'proves' that no one outside the artworld need take any interest in it. By embracing the autonomy thesis, the philosophy of art alienates both art and itself from the wider culture.

Of course, in philosophy, untoward practical consequences alone do not refute a thesis. But given the long history of art, the burden of proof belongs to the autonomy theorist.[19] Apparently his best argument is the common-denominator argument. Therefore, if it fails, as I hope I have shown it does, we are free to reopen the kind of inquiries about the arts that Plato and Aristotle initiated, inquiries that attempt to ascertain the intimate relation of the arts to the emotions, morals, politics and so forth of the communities they serve.

IV

Conclusion

For nearly two centuries, the artworld and the philosophy of art have to a surprising degree defended the viewpoint that art is autonomous from other social practices. An immediate consequence of this has been a decoupling of art and ethics, despite their long-standing affiliation heretofore. The hegemonic trend of ambitious art through much of the modern period has been to stress the independence of art from morals not only as a hedge against censorship, but also as a way of removing self-perceived constraints upon the self-expression of the artist. The serious artist through most of this period has not respected moral instruction and exploration as a worthwhile vocation, but as topics that belong to children's authors, to the creators of animated cartoons and maybe the producers of soap operas. However, the cost of the self-alienation of art from the broader culture has been the pervasive marginalisation of ambitious art that is only sporadically relieved on the heels of some or another scandal.

The marginalisation of serious art is a practical problem that I believe flows from the artworld's continued affirmation of autonomy and the policies that stem from it. The antidote, broadly stated, is that artists once again have to become involved in the life of the culture, taking up many of the responsibilities that modern art has shed under the sign of the autonomy of art. This includes re-entering the ethical realm, not only, I stress, in the role of social critic, but also as transmitter and shaper of that which is positive in the ethos of their audience. The ambitious artists present will undoubtedly challenge me to say how this is to be done. I do not know exactly; and anyway, it is their job to figure this one out. But let me suggest that they might start by thinking about the Constructivists.

The philosophy of art is lured toward the autonomy thesis for theoretical rather than practical reasons. The influence of the autonomy thesis, even where it is not explicitly embraced, is everywhere apparent in the philosophy of art as currently practised. That is why so few of the textbooks in the analytic tradition have sections devoted to the relation of art to society, to politics, to national identity, to racism, to morality and so on. For under the presupposition that art qua art is autonomous and that the philosopher of art examines only that which is essential to his object of study, such relations are not on his radar screen.

This myopia has not only reduced the extent to which the philosophy of art is taken seriously–how important or pressing can the study of something that is connected to nothing else really be?–but it has skewed philosophical research in its obliviousness to the fact that most art–such as mass art–even today (even if you want to deny that it is ambitious art) has been and is involved with ongoing social concerns. Thus, by abandoning the commitment, both explicitly and implicitly, to the autonomy thesis and by attending to art's involvement in society, politics and ethics, the philosophy of art could not only provide a truer account of its object of study, but it will begin to reverse the opinion, shared even among other philosophers, that it is as useless and extraneous as it has attempted to demonstrate, wrongly to my mind, that art is.[20]

RESPONSE
TO
NOËL
CARROLL

Adrian Piper

Noël Carroll mounts a double-barrelled critique of contemporary art practice as alienated from the rest of social life. One antidote, he argues, is for artists
to celebrate in their work what is positive and constructive in their audience's
ethos. A second antidote is for philosophers of art to abandon the essentialist,
common-denominator conception of art for a plurality of such conceptions, each
of which is anchored in a particular context and set of practices. I share Carroll's
concerns about the relation of art practice and art theory to the rest of social life,
so the following remarks should be understood within a broader context of general agreement. My comments target the first antidote because I believe it speaks
more directly to philosophers of art than it does to artists.

Carroll works from a conception of artistic practice that, he argues, had legitimacy in the past but no longer does:

Art tutored peoples in pertinent norms of interpersonal relations, in their
societal obligations and expectations; it imparted information about folk psychology, and especially about moral psychology with respect to virtue, vice, the
connection between motives and action, and so forth. Art showcased the customs

of the relevant groups, illustrating models of desirable and undesirable character traits, concretising society's conceptions of duty, and advancing the preferred attitudes toward historical and contemporary events and even eschatological ones. Art also functioned as a site for pointers about correct manners and carriage, and endorsed ideas about personal style in general, including suggestions about one's style of movement, mode of gesture, deportment, and so much more. [...] Pre-modern art, in short, functioned as one of the – if not the most – powerful disseminators of the ethos of a people and it was widely recognised to possess this capacity. (p.90)[1]

But this characterisation of pre-modern Euroethnic art relies on an ambiguity between intentional and consequentialist characterisations of art. While art may well have visually represented certain ideals of interpersonal relations, ethics and virtues, and thereby tutored and imparted information about them to its audience, it would be very hard to prove that these efforts – assuming artists deliberately made them – were normatively effective. If such ideals were already normatively effective in the culture through other methods of socialisation, works of art representing the relevant content and preoccupations could have just as easily reflected and condoned rather than instilled them. Alternatively, if the audience to such work viewed it the way we view advertainment media attempts to tutor and inform us about such ethical ideals, the case for its normative effectiveness would become even harder to make. Nor was the social content of pre-modern Euroethnic art restricted to the morally inspirational, as David and Goya demonstrate. Carroll rightly calls attention to the importance of social content in pre-modern Euroethnic art. But he does not convince me of its effective didactic function.

Carroll argues that this function was undermined and finally destroyed by the consequences of industrial modernisation, which, by encouraging labour specialisation in virtually every area of endeavour, forced art into a defensive posture. By asserting the autonomy of art and its independence from other social, instructional, religiously and morally inspirational practices with which it had formerly been associated, he argues, art was able to defend its own territory from the encroachment of others that threatened to render it obsolete. While on the one hand this freed artists to be 'free market agents' agitating for the 'deregulation' of their own self-expression as market commodities, on the other it divorced art—and by impli-cation artists—from engagement with ethical and social issues of daily life. (p.93)

Carroll's hypothesised explanation raises several questions. First, he treats the 'art-for-art's-sake' fetal curl as a consequence of industrial specialisation that in turn resulted in a disconnection between art and ethics. I question the validity of this proposed causal chain. Industrial specialisation was one of many expressions of the development of capitalism, which by itself severs the natural link between art and ethics and replaces that link with one between art as a rarified commodity and the economic profit that is its final goal. Once economic profit takes prec-edence over ethical and social concerns, the disengagement of art profiteers from ethics follows automatically, and position papers on the so-called autonomy of art are merely face-saving apologia with no independent causal role.

But second, Carroll's narrative does not distinguish between the critics and aestheticians who were writing those position papers, and the artists whose out-put those position papers were trying to influence. He does not consider how the enormous social and economic revolution capitalism represented affected actual artistic practice: whether artists wanted to be 'free market agents' or were forced into it by economic circumstance; whether artists conceived themselves as putting their self-expression up for sale; whether or not they were required to conceive themselves differently in this regard under capitalism than they had been in pre-industrial Euroethnic society; and to what extent and in what specific ways these forces affected the content of their work. For example, Carroll claims that 'art be-came reoriented as a form of play, contemplative play free of social interests and needs. The purpose of art—the feature that won something entry into the modern system of the arts—was said to be precisely that it was not essentially useful for anything other than the exercise of the free (that is to say disinterested) play of one's contemplative powers.' (p.93) But he clearly does not mean to thereby describe actual artistic practice, which was in neither epoch for the artist merely 'a form of play, contemplative play free of social interests and needs'; and for the artist certainly was useful for earning a living, attracting patrons and commissions, and expressing personal obsessions. The turbulent careers of Vincent Van Gogh, Paul Gauguin, Mary Cassatt and the Salon des Refusés offer clear counter-examples to Carroll's claim.

Later in his discussion, (pp.101–102) Carroll rightly attributes this view specifically to philosophers of art who meant to prescribe how viewers ought to respond to works of art under the new post-industrial regime. But his hypothesised causal chain linking industrialisation, specialisation and the rise of an autonomous realm for art only works by conflating the distinction between critic and artist at the outset. Art has never been independent of social concerns for the artists who depend on producing it in order to make a living, or who depend on somehow making a living in order to produce it. And the labour-intensive physical process of actually funding and producing art, regardless of the type of art in question, is not well served by the description of it as 'contemplative play free of social interests and needs'. Whether or not its content can be described in this way depends entirely on who is viewing it.

Similarly, when Carroll argues that 'a direct consequence of the conception of art as a locus of disinterested contemplation (especially of form) was to remove art from the domain of ethics, since the very notion of disinterested contemplation was itself a pleonasm that came to signal the exclusion of financial, political, religious and, of course, ethical purposes with respect to an art object properly so called,' (p.94) he cannot be understood to suggest that artists or actual artistic practice had been 'remove[d] from the domain of ethics'; or that either involved 'disinterested contemplation'; or that either 'signal[led] the exclusion of financial, political, religious, and, of course, ethical purposes with respect to an art object properly so called'. Artists famously are always confronted by hard ethical and social choices – not to mention financial ones – in their ongoing struggle to get their work done. It is not possible to have a career as an artist without navigating all of these issues; and artists are driven by all sorts of purposes to do their work.

Nor can Carroll be understood to be describing a particular trajectory in the historical development of art's actual content. Abstract content conjoined with deeply embedded normative social and cultural function can be found in African,

Native American and Australian Aboriginal art, whereas realistic social content conjoined with minimal or normatively impotent social and cultural function can be found in Euroethnic art from the Renaissance onward. Although Carroll is certainly right to argue that the rise of industrialisation generally determined a new social role for works of art, it is not possible to link the rise of abstraction with the onset of industrialisation, as one might be tempted to do in interpreting Carroll's hypothesis.

Instead, the passages just discussed strongly suggest that Carroll's hypothesis about the social and historical origin of art for art's sake is in fact an account of the origin of a certain philosophical conception of art; not an account of art's own changing function in society at all. That critics and aestheticians came to regard works of art independently of their social function does not imply that those works had no social function, regardless of where they were viewed. Similarly, when Carroll describes concert halls and museums as institutional devices for abstracting and decontextualising works of art from any social purpose and focusing it on disinterested contemplation, (pp.95–96) he is at best describing architectural structures aimed at promoting a certain way of viewing art – not structures in the function of which artists themselves were necessarily complicit. Again: that works of art were decontextualised from their social function by being exhibited in museums and concert halls does not imply that such works had no social function; quite the opposite. Thus Carroll is describing a new way of conceiving art in general, not the way particular works actually function for those who view it. Any artist whose work has been rejected by a museum because of its political content knows that such institutions are effective in 'decontextualising' only those works of art that do not actually require such delousing in order to be acceptable for exhibition there in the first place.

But if this analysis of Carroll's hypothesis is correct, and it is true that his animadversions are in fact directed against a certain way of conceiving art rather than against any particular kind of art itself, then his suggested antidote – that '[i]n order to reverse the alienation of the art world, the art world needs to reclaim its function as a source of promoting – both critically and sympathetically – the ethos of the people it intends to address' (p.97) – is not an appropriate prescription to address specifically to artists; and his reservations about the success quotient of some artists who have directly addressed political issues in their work are irrelevant.[2] The problem he has dissected lies not with the work of art itself, or its content or its form, but rather with the way it is taken up into the culture by viewers, critics, aestheticians and art institutions.

Carroll then goes on to admonish artists to take their lesson from literature thus: 'The novel, even in our own times, has consistently proven itself to be a resilient force in the life of the culture. As new segments of the society empower themselves – persons of colour, women, gays, post-colonial peoples – the novel serves as a vehicle for articulating their concerns and values and for celebrating while also constructing their emerging ethos.' (p.97) But it is of course the uneducated viewer, into whose awareness these 'new' segments of the society 'emerge', who is required to 'construct the ethos' – often expressive of quite ancient civilisations that were intellectually and culturally advanced at a time when Euroethnics were still living in caves – of these 'new segments of the society'. Here again Carroll projects onto artists an approach to the work typical of an art critic or aesthetician. Whereas he earlier projected onto Euroethnic artists a way of conceiving the work that was to be found primarily in the arbiters of its art-critical elite, now he projects onto artists from other backgrounds an attitude toward this work that at best needs to be confronted by the uninformed audience that is privileged to finally view it. The 'segments of the society' from which these artists come are new or emerging only to those who had no prior awareness of them; and the 'ethos' their work expresses must be constructed only by those who had no prior understanding of it.

However, the meat of Carroll's advice for artists is that we should celebrate our community values rather than disengaging from and critiquing them: 'The literature of these groups, like the literature of the Jews and the Irish before them, encourages attention for being engaged in the community, not by standing outside the community and declaring itself a community of interest unto itself. The challenge for the fine arts, it seems to me, is to discover its own way of reinserting itself into the social process.' (p.98) Now I do not think Carroll can find a work of art that 'declares itself a community of interest unto itself', although this is precisely what Euroethnic art critics and aestheticians who propound the art-for-art's-sake thesis do declare in their approach to the artwork they view, regardless of its content; and even though it is false that they themselves constitute such a community. In fact, Carroll does not say what he means by 'the community', and I do not think it would be appropriate to exhort an artist to celebrate community values if the artist comes from a community, such as our own, in which there is so little to celebrate and so much to criticise. But the example he discusses – the mural arts program in Philadelphia – suggests that he equates community with neighborhood, with ethnicity, and/or with urban location. All of these are rather limited conceptions of community relative to which it is easy for anyone – any artist, any critic, any viewer – to stand outside any or all of them at a particular time or period. I doubt that Carroll can give an example of a work of art that 'stands outside the community' in the broader sense in which we as contributors to and readers of this volume are equally members of the same community that also includes inner cities, neighbourhoods, and other subcultures and ethnic groups. That community, increasingly as the globe grows smaller, is the one in which historically esoteric Euroethnic elites will need to be able to find their appropriate place. When they do, they will have something to celebrate.

Thus it is not art that needs to be 'reinserted into the social process', nor artists that need to thus 'reinsert their work', for neither art nor artists were ever divorced from the social process in the first place. Rather, those viewers of art who are, for their own reasons, tempted to try to disconnect the works of art they view from their producers, from the conditions of their production, from their social and economic meaning or from their institutional context need to re-educate themselves as to what they are viewing, what it means, who they themselves are, and in what their own political relation to the work consists. They need to consider the possibility that it is not the work that is disengaged from these coordinates, but they themselves.

Carroll's positive thesis regarding the kind of art artists ought to make is that '[a]rt must engender a more intimate relationship with its viewers by creating symbols of the positive ethical values of the culture that people find worthwhile as guides to and ways of making sense of their lives'.(p.100) As an artist I instinctively resist being told what to do by other people who don't do it themselves, so I find these prescriptions difficult to swallow on grounds of form alone. Nevertheless I enjoy giving free advice at least as much as Carroll does, if not more, and so am sympathetic to the wellsprings from which such suggestions may arise. So I would like to close merely by pointing out a difficulty in implementing this worthy program in a society as fully defined by unregulated free-market capitalism as ours is at this historical moment. The difficulty is that if such art does not sell, it will not have the desired inspirational effect; whereas if it does sell, it cannot have the desired inspirational effect. If it lacks market viability, this will foreclose the pro-motional advertainment media campaigns necessary to give it measurable social impact. On the other hand, if it does sell, then regardless of what other 'positive ethical values of the culture that people find worthwhile as guides to and ways of making sense of their lives' it may contain, these will have been subordinated to the demands of profitability. The work will have been reconfigured in order to maximise demand and minimise market downturn. There may well be some 'symbols of the positive ethical values of the culture' out there that can survive such a packaging campaign intact, but I have yet to see one.

POLITICAL ART AND THE PARADIGM OF INNOVATION

Adrian Piper

Post-modernism claimed that originality is no longer possible, and that the artist is merely a scavenger who rearranges prefabricated materials, images and ideas – call this the anti-originality thesis. This thesis was itself original, and therefore
self-defeating. But quite aside from its self-contradiction, the anti-originality thesis was objectionable for several reasons. First, it rationalised the long-standing
mainstream Euroethnic practice of using without attribution and exploiting for
personal profit the creative products of marginalised cultures, while those marginalised cultures themselves continued to labour under conditions of obscurity
and deprivation. Second, the creative products of marginalised cultures express
meanings that can only be understood by understanding the culture in question.
The anti-originality thesis decontextualised and resituated them in such a way as
to discourage cross-cultural communication and reinforce mainstream tendencies to ignorance and self-congratulation. Third, the anti-originality thesis began
to gain currency in the United States in the late 1980s – at the very moment when,
as the result of the increasing popularity of the concept of 'otherness' bequeathed
us by post-structuralist anthropology, the innovative contributions of artists from
those marginalised cultures began to gain recognition. The anti-originality thesis
enabled mainstream artists, who had risen to prominence on the basis of aesthetic
innovation now clearly familiar from the work of formerly unacknowledged minority artists, to dismiss the value of originality in any case – thereby cementing
the art-historical significance of the mainstream group while denying it to those
on the margins. The anti-originality thesis thus served an urgent function at an

important historical moment. It was an ideological fiction that provided an institutional bulwark against the marginalised outsiders who were beginning to storm the barricades.

A further shortcoming of the anti-originality thesis was the shallow conception of originality it presupposed. According to this conception, true originality does not depend on materials, images or ideas already present in the culture at large, but rather contributes entirely novel ones. It does not synthesise or reconfigure any such previously existing elements, but rather creates new ones from scratch – as though these were mutually exclusive alternatives; and as though any entirely novel entity could be cognised in the first place. In order to speak to us, a work of art must use languages we can recognise.

If works of art in any field really had to expunge all familiar images, ideas, media and materials in order to meet such criteria of originality, none of the major art-historical figures we consensually recognise as original would pass the test. Should we then have gone back and re-evaluated whether Picasso made too great a use of African art to count as innovative according to this criterion? And if so, should we then have valorised Picasso's cubism even more highly because of its unoriginality? And should we now valorise more highly works of art that are more derivative, and disparage works that are insufficiently derivative? These are some of the reductio ad absurda to which the anti-originality thesis leads.

Finally, the impotence of the anti-originality thesis was demonstrated by the long-standing art world practices of selecting, exhibiting, marketing and canonising modern art. Regardless of conflicting opinions about quality, all parties to these practices converge on the essentials of how to bring work to the attention of a larger audience and how to keep it there. Whether the audience in question is the artist who first makes the work, the dealer who first shows it, the viewer who first sees it, the critic who first writes about it, the collector who first buys it, or the institution that first legitimates it, the language of innovation functions in the same way. It frames the work as 'cutting edge', as something that, in some important respect, has not been done before: as breaking new ground, pushing the envelope, challenging received notions, framing the debate in a new way, rejecting cherished principles, violating conventional thinking, and so on. Most of us have been deploying these familiar clichés to suit our art professional promotional roles since the onset of industrialisation. And sometimes they are even warranted by the work in question. For all of these reasons, it is very difficult to take the anti-originality thesis seriously, as original as it originally seemed to be.

Indeed, the promotional fervour with which the concept of originality is invoked to market and canonise modern art finds its parallel in the fervour with which the anti-originality thesis itself was marketed as original. The enthusiasm that greeted this novel thesis when it first appeared, the heat with which its advocates elaborated upon and proselytised about it, and the seriousness with which it was taken up in extended discussion – all were sound indicators of its originality. Then began the gradual process of dogmatic hardening by which this new idea became old – its canonisation in the art-critical literature, the creation of academic chairs for its proponents, the generations of graduate students pressed into service to spread the gospel, the incorporation of this gospel into academic syllabi, and finally the new generations of graduate students who sought to meet the requirement of dissertation originality by calling the anti-originality thesis itself into question. This cyclical, essentially self-cannibalising process – it's new, it's old, it's new because it's old, it's old because it's new, etc. – characterises the historical shelf-life of the anti-originality thesis as well as that of modern art.

But this process is not confined to art or academia. It typifies a culture that more generally perpetuates itself by creating desires for 'new and improved' commodities, consuming them, digesting them, spitting them out, and moving on to the next ones – i.e. the culture of unrestrained free-market capitalism. The following observations are based in my experience of American culture and politics. But to the extent that you permit the globalisation of American culture to invade your own, you may find them relevant there as well.

The culture of unrestrained free-market capitalism feeds on the shared and foundational experience of incompleteness, inferiority – of generalised insufficiency, or want. The experience of generalised want is created by media fabulations of a fantasy world of perpetual happiness that sharply contrasts with our complex and often painful social reality, plus the promise that this fantasy world can be realised through the acquisition of those material goods that serve as props within it. For those who have the wealth to acquire such props, this promise is broken on a daily basis, and the hollow dissatisfaction at the core of perpetual acquisition is a constant reminder that something is missing. Unfortunately, this dissatisfaction only rarely leads to interrogating the basic premise of the fantasy itself – i.e. that the acquisition of material props can realise it in the first place. Usually the conclusion is, rather, that more props are needed to do the trick.

This is the function of the globalised advertainment industry. Based in the American myth of acquisition and consumption, it offers tantalising desire-satisfaction events as palliatives to the agonies of conscience caused by America's historical crimes against humanity and their present consequences. And it is nourished internationally by comparable agonies in other countries: The fall of the Austro-Hungarian Empire, of the British Empire, the Second World War in Germany and Japan, the Soviet regime in Russia, the Cultural Revolution in China, to name only a few. The globalised advertainment industry exploits our shared need to escape from the morally unbearable present of those consequences, by producing 'new and improved' goods and services that deaden their pain and divert our attention. And it expends enormous resources convincing us to want them. That is, the advertainment industry creates interminable and insatiable desire for the new that narcotises the ugly realities and moral self-dislike inherited from our past atrocities; and promises an end to that self-dislike in repetitive infusions of desire-satisfaction. The enduring themes of originality and innovation that characterise the discourse of modern art – indeed, contemporary culture more generally – is merely one example of that dynamic.

However, as for other such examples, there are limits on the extent of acceptable innovation in modern art. I have already suggested that no art object can be original in every respect, if it hopes to gain cognitive recognition from its viewers. A concrete particular that is not recognisable relative to the pre-existing concepts and categories by which we make sense of experience can form no part of that experience. But the limits of acceptability are much narrower than this. Unrestrained free-market capitalism depends on the rhetoric of innovation to drive consumption of the objects, events and services that perpetuate it. To the extent that a work of art undermines such consumption itself, it sacrifices acceptability, approval and status within that economy, no matter how innovative it may be in other respects; and is marginalised accordingly.

A work of art can innovate in many ways that thus conflict with the foundations of unrestrained free-market capitalism. Here are a few of them, in no particular order:

First, it can critique irrationally unequal distributions of power and resources that impede the level playing field democratic social institutions theoretically presuppose. Art that critiques racism, sexism, homophobia, anti-Semitism and other forms of xenophobia would exemplify such work.

Second, it can interrogate the commodity production that is the currency of unrestrained free-market capitalism. Art that, through its form or its content calls into question the value of material embodiment, of refined techniques of production or of the use of expensive materials would exemplify such work.

Third, it can call attention to the exchange relations among agents that drive an unrestrained free-market economy. Art that examines the transactions between artist and critic, dealer and collector, art and exhibition venue, promotional visibility and sales or profitability and institutional canonisation would exemplify such work.

Fourth, it can subvert the act or process of consumption itself. Art that disintegrates, or rots, or self-destructs, or evaporates after a fixed period of time, or that, through viewer participation, continually alters and expands its own form, or that elicits distancing, or self-critique, or intellectual reflection, or anger, or disgust rather than desire, or that rejects materiality thwarts the normal process of commodity consumption that links such objects with desire-satisfaction.

Fifth, it can call into question the fundamental values of consumption. Art that satirises desire or sexuality or wealth or technology, or that calls attention to alternative value systems that oppose or reject these, or that requires criteria of aesthetic evaluation that are incompatible with them, or that invokes utopian social ideals of fairness and equality would exemplify such work.

These brief descriptions identify some of the kinds of work we typically call 'avant-garde', or 'cutting edge'. They are only a few of the ways in which a work of art can come into conflict with the conditions required by the smooth functioning of an unrestrained free-market economy. Such works have in common a genesis in culturally transgressive ideas or concepts that drive artists to actualise them, despite their incompatibility with the norms and ideology of capitalism. By resisting conformity to the social and economic status quo, they function primarily as paradigms of artistic self-expression. Thus two concepts – avant-garde or cutting-edge art on the one hand, and self-expression on the other – are linked in art that defies the cultural conventions of unrestrained free-market capitalism, by expressing a part of the self that exists beyond the limiting boundaries of desire. Cutting-edge paradigms of self-expression, in turn, frustrate the conventional economic function of art as a high-end currency of exchange in an unrestrained free market.

This kind of art thus embodies a tension between two central ideas assumed to be entwined in most modern democracies: free expression and free-market consumption. Capitalism typically defends free-market consumption as the most meaningful exercise of free expression in a modern democracy: to quote a particularly compelling recent ad, 'I want to break free-e-e!' – while drinking Coke. In this paradigm, freedom of expression equals freedom to consume, to satisfy desire. Hence freedom of the self, in this narrative, is in fact equivalent to enslavement by desire; and non-equivalent to autonomous self-regulation. Rather than being moved by principled internal dispositions that define and structure the self independently of the external influences on it, the self under unrestrained free-market capitalism is driven by its pursuit of objects external to it. Rather than controlling its desires and deferring their gratification in light of such principles, the self is controlled and defined by its desires, and so is at the mercy of the external stimuli that drive it. Unrestrained free-market consumption thus transforms the self into a marionette jerked here and there by the strings that attach it to external sources of self-gratification. Unrestrained free-market capitalism's version of freedom of expression thus presupposes what Kant would call a heteronymous self that is defined by the external objects it appropriates and digests. This is precisely the opposite of the originality and innovation that unrestrained free-market capitalism claims to nurture. Commodities that actually satisfy these desiderata would thus seem to stunt their growth in those who consume them.

Cutting-edge art of the kind described earlier demonstrates that there is no necessary connection between freedom of expression and free-market consumption. The two are antithetical where freedom of expression transgresses the habitual desires that market consumption inculcates. Such work serves to remind us that there are other capacities within the self – curiosity, wonder, intellect, reason, self-awareness, for example – and may even awaken those capacities within some viewers. By stimulating alternative capacities within the self and eliciting alternative responses that outcompete the demands of desire, such work also may inspire new possibilities of creative self-expression in its viewers. If it can be dismissed by the incurious with the comment that 'I could do that if I tried', it can also be embraced by the curious with exactly the same thought.

To the extent that such work frustrates market exchange and consumption, it tends to exist at the margins of an unrestrained free-market economy, if at all. And it receives less of the financial support or institutional legitimation than does work which functions more smoothly within the constraints of free-market capitalism. It denies such work an audience at any or all levels of entry into the nerve centre of contemporary art: dealers decline to make studio visits to see it, or decline to show it on grounds of its unmarketability; or, should the work pass that hurdle, critics, mindful of the conservative publishing interests that ultimately ensure their own marketability, decline to write about it; or, should the work pass that hurdle, curators, mindful of the conservative administrative interests that ultimately determine museum policy (including staff hiring), decline to accord it the stamp of institutional canonisation; or, should the work pass that hurdle, conservative institutions and collectors, mindful of the contradiction to their own values such work expresses, decline to purchase it. In direct proportion to the threat to such values that this type of cutting-edge art represents, it is immediately or gradually eliminated from public awareness and from the historical record by those conservative capitalist interests themselves. Cutting-edge art thereby exposes the ideological deception by which unrestrained capitalism claims the mantle of freedom for purposes of self-legitimation. Unrestrained free-market capitalism in fact restricts quite narrowly the freedom to express oneself in works of art that subvert the market transactions through which such works are supposed to be consumed.

By excluding from institutional legitimation those works of art that thus call into question the foundations of this system, the system of free-market capitalism itself thereby ensures a permanent supply of innovative but perpetually marginalised artworks that do, in fact, 'break new ground', 'push the envelope', 'challenge received notions', 'frame the debate in a new way', 'reject cherished principles' or 'violate conventional thinking' – to the detriment of their creators' livelihoods. Typically, these judgements are applied approvingly to those innovations that respect the highly circumscribed limits of unrestrained free-market capitalism: the rhetoric of the margin is most effectively manipulated by those most firmly ensconced at the centre. But they are withheld from innovations that actually do most strongly interrogate or subvert market forces. Instead, such art typically receives either heavy blasts of unfocused hostility, or little if any recognition at all. Because such work destabilises the power relations constitutive of unrestrained free-market capitalism, I shall bring all of it under the rubric of explicitly political art.

By contrast, implicitly political art is often preoccupied with abstraction, or pure form, or perception, or beauty. Its content avoids topical, politically divisive subject matter; and its form extends and celebrates accepted materials, techniques and modes of production. It may serve to inspire or delight us, or provide an escape or asylum from the painful social realities that surround us. As such, implicitly political art is no less culturally necessary, significant or valuable than explicitly political art. A healthy and well-functioning society makes room for both. Most artists who produce implicitly political art are extremely fortunate to have the luxury of an inner, creative sanctuary in which the drive to produce such work can be nurtured. They are fortunate to be spared the necessity of grappling consciously and always, at all levels of their being, with the urgent social problems that often drive explicitly political art. Most producers of implicitly political art have reason to be grateful for the creative solace from such problems they are privileged to enjoy.

However, some who produce implicitly political art do not escape such problems, but rather are ensnared by them. Motivated by self-censorship, and by the strategic understanding that making explicitly political art lessens the chances and the magnitude of professional success, this kind of implicitly political art is an expression of imprisonment within the bounds of political conflict, rather than an escape from it. These artists make a reasoned decision that voluntarily cramping their own scope of self-expression and confining their investigations within free-market capitalist conventions is well worth the trade-off in professional success. They thereby sacrifice freedom of expression for the material rewards of institutional legitimacy. They knowingly subordinate the self-expressive function of their work to its function as a currency of market exchange; and – like artists and writers in the former eastern European countries under Communism – exchange clarity for 'subtlety', forthrightness for 'understatement', and political protest for 'irony'. The authoritarian extremes of capitalism and socialism thus dovetail in the artistic evasions and self-protective camouflage they force professionally ambitious artists to adopt.

Regardless of the background determinants of implicitly political art, it qualifies as political because – like all events, actions and choices embedded in a social context – it has political preconditions and political consequences. Whatever its other benefits – and there are many – implicitly political art reinforces and exploits the conditions required by unrestrained free-market capitalism. Implicitly political art tacitly endorses the status quo by taking advantage of it, presupposing it, and declining to interrogate it. This would include art that purports to contain no political content, or contains political content so masked and subdued under layers of irony, esoteric allusions and insider jokes that it is perceptually invisible; or art that requires the expensive and sophisticated production techniques of any high-end commodity; or that diverts the viewer's attention away from her own compromised location within the matrix of power relations that constitute a free-market economy; or that celebrates or reinforces the addictive habits of commodity consumption and desire-satisfaction themselves. A healthy market economy, embedded within the constraints of a stable and well-functioning democracy, would accommodate both art that celebrates it and art that interrogates it.

Obviously all of these different characteristics identify a multi-dimensional sliding scale of degrees according to which a work of art may be explicitly or implicitly political. No work of art is well served by all-or-nothing judgements at either extreme, and to call a work either implicitly or explicitly political is not to pass judgement on its quality or value. Nevertheless, these two possibilities, together with the continuum of degrees between them, are exhaustive. The concept of 'non-political art' – i.e. art that is political neither in its content, nor its form, nor its social or economic presuppositions, is another ideological fiction of unrestrained free-market capitalism that has been used for propaganda purposes just as effectively as explicitly political art has.

To see why explicitly political art is systematically marginalised in an unrestrained free-market capitalist art world, consider the instrumentalising function that transforms all objects, events and relationships into tools of desire-satisfaction in an unrestrained free-market economy more generally. This function consists in a disposition to view all such objects, events and relationships as potential instruments of personal profit, and to appraise and rank them accordingly. Here the archetypal question is, 'How much mileage can I get out of this?' The question can be posed of any object, event, relationship or condition. It is in essence a question as to how the maximum possible personal profit, i.e. satisfaction of personal desire, can be wrung from it. Unrestrained free-market capitalism thus subordinates all such states of affairs to the satisfaction of personal desire. I describe it as unrestrained because it imposes no constraints of custom, policy or principle on the pursuit of desire-satisfaction.

For among the states of affairs thus subordinated are, of course, political relationships. After all, the 'free' in 'free-market' refers to a market unregulated and unrestrained by government interference. Advocates of free-market capitalism like to claim that government interference is unnecessary to a society in which all consumers are rational profit-seekers whose patterns of individual consumption conduce to the well-being of all. But this sunny view ignores the instrumentalising function that defines unrestrained free-market capitalism, which encourages forming temporary alliances and monopolies that maximise profit by reducing competition. It also encourages unethical free riding when this is an effective means to the same end. It now seems clear that the combination of monopoly with free rider corporate practices is a lethal one that demands governmental regulation rather than refutes the need for it; and that such monopolies are incapable of policing themselves.

However, the drive for personal profit and desire-satisfaction is at odds with political regulation designed to secure the stability of all transactions within a society. Social stability requires three basic conditions. First, it requires mutual trust, and so an embedded convention of honouring contracts, or promise-keeping. Second, it requires a fair distribution of economic resources, so as to minimise conflict over those resources. These two conditions, in turn, require a third: an enforcement mechanism that distributes rewards for honouring contracts and economic fairness, and punishments for violating them. The machinery of government – of legislation, administration and adjudication – is predicated on these basic social requirements.

In a healthy and well-functioning society, individual odysseys of desire-satisfaction are constrained by these requirements. Those that conflict with them are systematically discouraged by the society's entrenched customs, as well as by its penal system. In such a society, government functions not only as a constraint but also as a counterweight to the pull of uncontrolled profit-seeking. Such a government consistently protects the rights of free speech when these are in jeopardy. It consistently inflicts punishments for criminal behaviour. It passes and consistently enforces policies, procedures and regulations that ensure fairness in all contractual transactions, even where these policies may thwart individual advantage. And it consistently advocates on behalf of the powerless, in order that their voices and their claims receive the same attention as those of the powerful or eloquent. However, we have already seen that in an unregulated free-market capitalist society, government performs none of these functions consistently because it is, in reality, a subordinate instrument of capital accumulation that acts only when and where it serves corporate interests to allow this.

A society driven by unregulated free-market capitalism is unhealthy and dysfunctional because in it, the basic structural requirement of social stability itself is subordinated to individual odysseys of desire-satisfaction, rather than the other way around. Unregulated free-market capitalism satisfies the conditions of social stability–i.e. trust and fairness–only to the extent that these are compatible with the accumulation of personal instruments of desire-satisfaction. Thus contracts are honoured only if it is profitable to do so, but violated if this would be more cost-effective. Resources are distributed fairly only when inequitable but self-aggrandising distributions would be too costly–for example, when the risk of public disclosure, potential social disruption, expensive litigation, falling revenues or stock prices, a tarnished reputation and the like would be too high. More generally, in an unregulated capitalist society, social stability is a worthwhile investment only to the extent that one's gated and guarded residential community cannot be sufficiently fortified against the danger of riots outside it; or to the extent that financial resources cannot be protected in anonymous off-shore bank accounts.

However, unregulated free-market capitalism does not merely subordinate transactional stability to maximising personal desire-satisfaction at the tactical level. It ensures the compliance of those whose job it is to secure social stability itself–i.e. the legislative, executive and judicial branches of government–by purchasing their allegiance to personal profitability instead. By rewarding government officials with gifts, bribes, campaign contributions, personal favours, capital resources, high-status official appointments and high-paying jobs in the private sector, corporations condition those officials to reciprocate by creating and implementing public policies that are advantageous to corporate goals. In a society overtaken entirely by unregulated free-market capitalism, what may look from the outside–and, indeed, even to a naïve insider–like a serendipitous partnership between business and government is in fact a corporate business relationship between an employer and the government officials employed to protect and promote the corporation's best interests. Government is thereby similarly instrumentalised as a tool by which the powerful may maximise desire-satisfaction and personal profit.

For example, the American Republican party enacted a hostile takeover of the 2000 Presidential election through its five corporate employees on the Supreme Court. Their decision to hand the Presidency to a candidate who had lost the popular vote flaunted their power in the face of a politically disabled electorate, and irreparably defiled the legitimacy and judicial authority of the Supreme Court itself. These five Supreme Court Justices were more than willing to trade their personal integrity, moral authority, the dignity of their office and the very idea of a democratically elected President for personal gain. Once these salaried rewards of capital are established conventions of governance, the desire for justice or a commitment to the ideals of democracy and freedom become irrelevant to the function of political office. Corporate profit and political profit become mutually reinforcing variants on the same theme.

And once the bond of trust between a citizenry and its government is decisively broken by this kind of corruption, that government can no longer motivate the democratic participation of its citizenry, because its claims to embody democratic values and represent fairly its citizens' best interests are no longer credible. However, at this stage such a government does not need the democratic participation of its citizenry to survive. On the contrary: its survival is secured by the same corporate profits it is now reconfigured to protect, and the democratic participation of its citizenry is little more than an irritant and an obstacle to that goal. The society's best interests that government now cynically purports to represent in staged and scripted public relations events are at best an afterthought.

Then the best hope for such a citizenry is simply to wait for the inevitable squabbles over power and resources to develop into wars between the major players in business and government, and wait for them to turn back to the citizenry to forge alliances that can leverage their respective positions relative to their enemies'. But an informed and sophisticated citizenry in such a society will not mistake such transient, tactical alliances of power for the relations of fair representation that identify a true democracy. Nor will it depend on that government to represent fairly citizens' best interests where they can offer government no incentives of power or profit to do so. So, for example, a community or subculture that is powerful neither in numbers nor in capital resources should not expect acts of magnanimity from its elected representatives, even where these are required by considerations of fairness. In unregulated free-market capitalism, political representation is just another instrument for maximising personal profit, and is as transient and unstable as the desires that profit satisfies. Talk of fairness is cause for mockery.

Now we can see more easily why, in a society driven by unregulated free-market capitalism, explicitly political art that undermines its foundations is relegated to the margins, while implicitly political art that depends on and reinforces those foundations is rewarded. Those of us in whom the acculturated commitment to democracy runs deep may naturally think that free exchange in Mill's marketplace of ideas is far more essential to a well-functioning democracy than unregulated exchange in the marketplace of goods and services; and therefore that artistic expression is a paradigm of democracy rather than of consumption. However, in an unregulated free-market society, expression itself is nothing more than a subordinate instrument of profit and desire-satisfaction. Speech, including artistic production, is a tool for achieving a desired end, whether or not its content refers to any matter of fact. A person who says what he thinks you want to hear rather than what he believes; or makes statements that are at odds with her actions; or deliberately misrepresents policies or matters of political fact; or uses speech to threaten, intimidate or deceive, or fill valuable air time, or placate his constituents or 'spin' a publicity disaster is a familiar spectacle in American political life, as well as outside it.

Only the gullible take such instrumentalised speech seriously. An audience that recognises such speech as the tool of manipulation and self-aggrandisement it is simply tunes out. A public figure who engages in instrumentalised speech, knowing that no one believes it, knowingly uses such speech as a cynical and arrogant display of force that taunts its audiences with its inability to fight back; and debases it by the force-feeding of lies. Thus, reminding a disenfranchised citizenry of its powerlessness to set rational and honest terms of public dialogue is the demoralising role of an advertainment media industry under unregulated capitalism.

Under these circumstances, cutting-edge artistic self-expression can find no protection, because it violates the instrumentalisation of speech on which unregulated capitalism feeds. On the contrary: such self-expression is a threat to its smooth functioning that must be marginalised and disabled as efficiently as possible; and so is, under these circumstances, a form of self-endangerment, indeed career suicide, for its creator. Where government is merely an instrument of capital accumulation, there can be no genuine alternative economic support system to sustain and encourage works of art that contribute to public dialogue by interrogating, criticising or undermining the political status quo in the ways earlier described. There can be no deeply embedded social arrangements relative to which interrogation, criticism or the presentation of alternatives can be publicly acknowledged as valuable; and no social framework within which these values can find consistent and concerted defence. That is, such a society has no room for a 'loyal opposition'–of the sort that the BBC, for example, frequently provides to the British government–and no incentive to supply the basic social preconditions in which art as a paradigm of self-expression can flourish. All it can be–all it is permitted to be–is an instrumental, high-end currency of market transaction.

Consider an actual case. In the 1990s in the United States, the Philip Morris corporation (now renamed Altria) backed both reactionary politicians who opposed governmental funding for avant-garde art, and also artists and major art institutions that exhibited it. On the surface, it seemed inconsistent to support both political representatives such as Senator Jesse Helms who opposed such work on the one hand, and also art institutions that encouraged it on the other. But at a deeper level there was no inconsistency. Since Philip Morris sells drug addiction and death for profit, it was and remains clearly very vulnerable to political and moral criticism. And, as both Philip Morris and Senator Jesse Helms were fully aware, avant-garde art can be an extremely powerful and potent voice of moral criticism and political protest. So it was in Philip Morris's interests to control the content of such art, to restrict it to the critically innocuous and politically inoffensive. It attempted to accomplish this, first, by helping Senator Helms eliminate public funding for avant-garde art. Second, Philip Morris simultaneously established itself as the major source of private corporate funding in the arts. Thus in essence, artworks and exhibitions could receive funding either from Philip Morris and corporations like it, or not at all.

By refusing to fund explicitly political art that criticised, protested or undermined its corporate interests, and choking off alternative sources of funding in the public sector, Philip Morris successfully discouraged the making, exhibiting and performance of such work. Having already bought the complicity of elected representatives in eliminating government support for works of contemporary art, it then bought the silence both of artists who wanted those professional opportunities, and also of the art institutions that otherwise would have offered them. Both censored themselves, and subordinated contemporary art to the demands of unregulated free-market capitalism, by producing and exhibiting commodities it could easily digest.

This example illustrates the truism that in a society in which government is a tool of business interests, we can hardly expect it to be a beacon of democracy in the arts. In such a society, adherence to the ideology of unregulated free-market capitalism is a primary objective of content programming in the advertainment industry, as well as of acculturation throughout the society more generally. Such ideological adherence is strictly incompatible with an unconditional commitment to freedom of expression. So, far from being celebrated as an expression of the democratic exchange of ideas, artwork that interrogates, criticises or offers alternatives is discouraged by the withholding of political as well as financial support. Through such negative reinforcement consistently applied, the scope of thought and imagination themselves are diminished to minor variations on the actual – at the same time that desire, consumption and impulse shopping are magnified into fantasy retreats from it; and we gradually lose the capacity to conceive a world in which our lives, our experiences and our selves can be any better or any different than they are now. This is how a purportedly democratic form of government can be complicit in the suppression of reason when this conflicts with the profit motive.

Now one very great achievement of explicitly political art is to demonstrate, at a concrete perceptual level, what alternatives to the status quo actually look like. That is why it often makes its viewers so viscerally uncomfortable. Explicitly political art does not always, or necessarily, present its viewers with alternatives to the status quo that are genuine improvements on it: explicitly political art can be politically reactionary as well. Nevertheless, some explicitly political art does give form and reality to dreams of betterment – of more humane attitudes towards others who are different, more considerate treatment of natural resources and materials, more judicious forms of social organisation, or more reflective and sophisticated approaches to our own psychological dispositions – and may stand as a back-handed reproach to the excesses of unregulated free-market capitalism for this reason alone. Seen from within the framework of such a society, explicitly political art may well seem to push the envelope a bit too far; to violate so many cherished assumptions and break so much new ground that the ground itself may seem to tremble beneath our feet. In these cases, explicitly political art may well transgress currently acceptable norms of innovation. But it does not violate the demands of human progress.

RESPONSE TO ADRIAN PIPER

Noël Carroll

I think that Adrian Piper and I are in broad agreement on several basic issues. We share a moral repulsion from excessive consumerism both because it diverts resources from those in need and because it harms the obsessive consumers themselves by undermining their understanding of self-realisation. Though I concur with Prof. Piper that what she neatly calls 'advertainment' sometimes functions as a palliative for guilt, I would add that it also operates as a distraction from social concerns and as an addiction whose relentless insatiability keeps consumerism in perpetual motion. I don't think that Adrian would reject these observations.

Neither Adrian nor I are fans of the existing capitalist economy, although I, like Adrian, would scarcely call anything a free market that relies on the support of governments that were bought out by business interests long ago. In the United States, the two dominant political parties are both beholden to the corporate interests that bankroll them. And the media, in search of greater profits, sells the competition between the Democrats and the Republicans as a never-ending sporting spectacular—like a horse race or the world series—thereby stoking the passions of the red and blue states as they root for their favourite players. It is just not as lucrative to analyse seriously the political ideas and programs of the candidates as it is to portray luridly the slugfest as the two parties—to mix metaphors—stagger suspensefully toward the finish line. That which Plato bewailed as the effect of tragedy is more accurately an essential feature of news 24/7. Money has utterly corrupted the American political system. That is probably something else on which Adrian and I concur.

However, I have the impression that we may not be in synch in terms of the way in which we would map the terrain of the artworld. Though I may be mistaken, I interpret Adrian as dividing contemporary art practice into two major precincts: explicit political art—which may be progressive or reactionary—and implicit political art which, by not interrogating either the art market or the larger capitalist system/consumer culture, 'tacitly endorses the status quo'. As I understand her, Adrian sees these two poles as opposite ends of a single continuum.

But I am very uneasy with this way of portraying the artworld, even for political purposes. It tracks art along a single dimension with opposed alternatives at either end. Yet I worry that this scheme is not complicated enough to do justice to the situation, even from an exclusively political standpoint. Put bluntly, Adrian's proposal strikes me as too Manichean—too much of an 'either you're part of the solution or you're part of the problem' or, as they used to say, 'you're either for history or against it'.

But the lay of the artworld, it seems to me, is more aptly characterised as being more complex, as involving more than one dimension, which dimensions, in turn, are not necessarily interrelated, oppositionally or otherwise. That is, I suspect that some art-making exists off Adrian's grid, if not logically, then, at least, effectively. My map of the artworld is more fragmented than Adrian's is.

For instance, my wife and I had our portraits done by Barbara Westman. We, of course, paid her for her work, though the money was modest and no gallery was involved. These portraits did not interrogate or criticise the art market or capitalism at large. So I infer that they fall into Adrian's category of implicit political art which, then, further entails that they tacitly endorse the status quo – if for no other reason than that money changed hands without any criticism of capitalism, consumerism or advertainment being voiced. But is that really sufficient to warrant the charge of endorsement? On this view, doesn't an oppressed peasant who sells his harvest rather than giving it away endorse capitalism in this sense despite the fact that he resents what he recognises as exploitation? Surely this is more a matter of suffering the existence of capitalism because practical, alternative modes of living are not feasibly available.

Some artists may be indifferent to the continuance of the capitalist system but nevertheless enter into relations of market exchange not because they endorse it but because there is no other modus vivendi in sight. As Hume argued, living within the boundaries of a certain social system does not mandate one's endorsement of its policies. Adrian would appear to maintain that participating uncritically in the economic system of the artworld and the capitalist system beyond supports these institutions and, thus, endorses them. But doesn't this make the notion of endorsement too thin? My tax money goes to all sorts of programs that I do not endorse in any robust moral sense. If one insists that anything that supports the persistence of x ipso facto endorses it, then the concept of endorsement appears to have been drained of existential seriousness.

Though the issue of complicity with some demonstrably corrupt practices of the artworld may arise genuinely with respect to some art, and, though it may be that an artist's compromises with the system justifies the accusation that he has implicitly endorsed it, I do not believe that it is useful to propose, as I think Adrian does, a model in which every time an artist sells an artwork that does not criticize the status quo she is selling out. Though the struggle against the market may be of profound importance, it is not the only project for the contemporary artist. Nor does the pursuit of these alternative projects seem automatically contemptible politically. Barbara Westman's portraiture, celebrating, as it does, the lives of couples, can be pursued without endorsing the market; indeed, it is, for all intents and purposes, indifferent to the market. After all, were there some alternative system of exchange, I am sure that Barbara Westman would be equally happy, if not more happy, to employ that one in capitalism's stead.

Basically, I have been pushing for a category of non-political art. I think that for Adrian this is an ideological fiction. Art that declines to criticise the market endorses it. Yet this presumes an unexplained imperative that art should always be criticising the status quo and, as well, it assumes, without argument, that artists may not legitimately have other fish to fry. This stance seems to me to serve no useful philosophical or political end. It fails to capture comprehensively the place of art in human life. And instead comes off as excessively draconian. It permits no space for joyous celebration. No political aim is well served by being dour with respect to what is, practically speaking, innocent pleasure.

So one anxiety that I have about Adrian's approach is that it appears to attempt to dragoon all art into a gigantic struggle for and against the status quo. But I am willing to bet that there is a substantial body of art which in effect stands outside this face-off. Some of it is simply decorative, but some of it may also address the modality of personal experience and feeling, apart from the social system.

Another fear that I have about Adrian's view is that even within the domain of explicitly political art, her characterisation of the options available to the artist are too narrow. Adrian assigns the artist an exclusively critical role – she can criticise, interrogate, unmask and subvert the status quo, while also projecting alternatives to it. The posture of the explicit political artist is implacably adversarial. Undoubtedly, this is an important, and at times, like our own, an indispensable social function for some artists to take up. But I doubt that it is ever the only function or even the only political function legitimately open to artists.

For art may also be justifiably expected to promote and to communicate what is positive in the ongoing political and moral culture that it inhabits. In my essay in this volume, I mentioned the murals of Philadelphia which honour local heroes and the virtues that make their neighbourhoods thrive, which commemorate the history of the people that comprise the community and their culture and values, and which

portray natural beauty as a symbol of the order the populace aspires to and cher-
ishes. This art ministers the needs and seeds the dreams of its audience without
necessarily engaging in criticism of the status quo. This seems to be an authentic
avenue of political art-making, though it is not necessarily explicitly critical of anything. Likewise, the twin giant mains of light raised on the ruins of the World Trade
Centre after 9/11 expressed a communal resolve to hold onto and to articulate
that space – to turn oblivion into a commitment and a show of strength. They were
genuine, progressive political symbols, but they were not critical of the status quo.

The positive political contribution of art need not be restricted to upbraiding
both the artworld and/or the rest of the culture, though that often seems to be the
unexamined prejudice of a great deal of serious art-making and criticism nowadays.
Art may also have a political and a moral role to play as one of the primary vehicles
for purveying and clarifying what is admirable, fine and wise about the ethos of the
culture to its members. The only reason to challenge this would be to suppose that
the culture in question is so disreputable that it or, at least, no part of it offers anything worth saving and celebrating. But the prospect that any moderately functioning society is so fallen appears so remote that such a stance toward society borders
upon a degree of perfectionism that may be puritanical.

Also, I think that I probably do not understand the terms of the scenario that
Adrian suggests concerning the market and critical art. On her view, critical artistic
voices are marginalised by the system. The market has no interest in being chal-
lenged by dissenting voices, so it shunts them aside. This schema makes a certain
amount of sense in the abstract. But does it obtain empirically? Offhand, I would
say that it does not, since a great many artists and art critics who have criticised the
art market are lionised by the artworld. Hans Haacke and Douglas Crimp come to
mind as examples. But perhaps I do not really get what Adrian thinks genuine criticism of the market or marginalisation by the market comes to.

Lastly, to return to some points upon which Adrian and I agree, I think that her
reservations about the anti-originality thesis and her suggestions concerning what
is involved in a sensible conception of originality are all well taken. I would even
grant that artistic resistance to the market is a paradigm of free self-expression,
though I would hasten to add that there are other paradigms as well, including ones
where the relation to the marketplace is not at all urgent and where the absence of
resistance thereto is without stigma.

DO ARTISTS SPEAK ON BEHALF OF ALL OF US?

Thierry de Duve

I propose to engage the debate with Howard Caygill on one potential common ground, that of Kant's *Critique of aesthetic judgement*. It is my conviction that when it comes to understanding what is at stake when we utter aesthetic judgements, Kant basically 'got it right'; yet that historical changes since Kant's time have made some shifts of emphasis necessary in our reading of the *Critique of Judgement*. One aspect of these changes is the crisis of representation synonymous with modernity, one of the major aspects of which is the crisis of representativity affecting the legitimacy of artists to speak on behalf of all of us. Focusing on Kant's idea of the sensus communis, I shall argue that, in spite of this crisis, the notion of artists speaking on behalf of all of us is essential to art, as art; and that its legitimacy does not hinge on the artist's purportedly universal mandate but rather on the artwork's universal address.

Ms A and Mr B quarrel over a rose

The first point that needs to be argued is that Kant 'got it right'. I mean that Kant's account of what humans do when they experience the world aesthetically, and of what this means and implies for them, is the best ever given. I'll try to explain it in the simplest words. Here is a rose. Ms A says: *Oh what a beautiful rose*. Mr B replies: *Are you out of your mind? I've never seen a rose so ugly*. Kant witnesses the scene, while looking at the rose himself. As it happens, he agrees with Ms A – and thus you would think his conclusion would be: Ms A is right, Mr B is wrong. But that's not what he concludes. Reflecting on his own pleasure, as well as the fact that Ms A and Mr B disagree, he notes that beauty is not an objective property of the rose but rather a subjective feeling. Now you would expect him to conclude: Ms A and Mr B are both wrong in ascribing beauty or ugliness to the rose as if it were a fact. They should have said: I like, or I dislike, this rose. But that's not what he concludes either. He concludes that Ms A and Mr B are both right in claiming so-called objective validity for their judgements. Why is that? What the phrase 'this rose is beautiful' (or ugly) actually does is not ascribe objective beauty (or ugliness) to the rose; rather, it imputes to the other the same feeling of pleasure (or pain) that one feels in oneself. Whether it is Ms A claiming that the rose is beautiful, or Mr B claiming that it is ugly, their disagreement amounts to shouting at each other – even if they do it politely: *you ought to feel the way I feel. You ought to agree with me.* To say that Ms A and Mr B are both right is to say that this call on the other's capacity for agreeing by dint of feeling is legitimate. This is what Kant understood better than anyone before or anyone since.

Three things are worth emphasising here. The first is that every aesthetic judgement, in Kant's terms, every pure judgement of taste, contains an ought, addressed to someone. This is not the case with judgements about what Kant calls 'the agreeable', which deal with merely personal preferences, and where disagreements are not an issue. Ms A addresses Mr B and vice versa. Obviously, they don't only address each other. They would have had the same aesthetic experience in front of the rose if there had been nobody present. They would not have expressed it out loud, but they would still have addressed their silent 'this rose is beautiful' (or ugly) to an implicit 'you'. The phrase is not addressed to anyone in particular, but it has an addressee. Let's say that the grammatical structure of an aesthetic judgement is something like: 'this is beautiful, isn't it?' The 'you' is indeterminate, and thus universal. It refers to anyone and everyone. Conclusion 1: *aesthetic judgements imply a universal address.* The second thing worth emphasising is that aesthetic judgements are not logical; they are based on feeling. Feelings are subjective and involuntary – you might say: egotistic and automatic. Egotistic: I know my feeling from it being mine. Automatic: I can't help but feel what I feel. Pleasure and pain certainly correspond to, and perhaps epitomise, this general definition of feelings. Both agreeableness and beauty yield pleasure. The former is content with being merely egotistic whereas the latter claims universal assent. And it does so automatically, i.e. involuntarily. Conclusion 2: *a true or pure aesthetic judgement is a call for agreement by dint of feeling involuntarily addressed to all.* The third thing worth emphasising is that this call for agreement holds true for both Ms A and for Mr B, despite their disagreement. Ugliness, too, claims universal assent. When Mr B claims the rose is ugly, he invokes his dissatisfaction, displeasure or pain in looking at the rose, in the name of what he thinks is his superior taste in roses; he nevertheless claims that Ms A, or indeed anyone and everyone, ought to agree with him: Ms A should know better and not derive pleasure from such a mediocre example. Conclusion 3: *what is ultimately at stake in an aesthetic judgement is neither the rose's beauty nor the feeling it arouses; it is the agreement.* The faculty of taste is not important in itself. It is important in as much as it testifies to a universally shared faculty of agreeing, which Kant calls sensus communis.

Sensus communis

Kant's *sensus communis* is not ordinary common sense, it is common sentiment. Shared or shareable feeling, and the faculty thereof. A common ability for having feelings in common. A communality or communicability of sentiment, implying a definition of humankind as a community united by a universally shared ability for sharing feelings. There is no proof that sensus communis exists as a fact, though. What exists as a fact is that we say such things as 'this rose is beautiful', that we say such things by dint of feeling, and that we claim universal assent for these feelings, whether we know it or not. Of course, humanity as a whole will never agree on the rose's beauty. Witness Mr B. But that's not required for the phrase 'this rose is beautiful' to be legitimate (I'm not saying true, I'm saying legitimate). All I need is make the supposition that my feeling is shareable by all. And that's what I do suppose. That's what we all suppose, Ms A, Mr B, you and me, everyone, when we make aesthetic judgements. The implied 'you ought to feel the way I feel' is what justifies me in my claim, you in yours, and all our fellow human beings in theirs, even though there is not a hope in the world for universal agreement among us. War is the rule, peace and love the exception. But Kant feels it is his duty as a phi-losopher to grant all humans the faculty of agreeing, and to theorise it correctly. Either taste *is* this faculty, or *signals* it. Kant hesitates between these two theorisa-tions, but in the end he decides it doesn't matter. What matters is that regardless of whether *sensus communis* exists as a fact, we ought to suppose that it does. The standard reading of the third *Critique* sees the theoretical necessity of this supposition clearly, but in my view pays insufficient attention to the quasi-moral obligation that makes us 'require from everyone *as a duty*, as it were, the feel-ing contained in a judgement of taste'. The reading I propose underlines Kant's scepticism as to whether *sensus communis* is a natural endowment of the human species – say, an instinct – or whether it is merely an idea, but one we cannot do without. I cite chapter and verse:

> This indeterminate norm of a common sense is actually presupposed by us, as is shown by
> our claim to lay down judgements of taste. Whether there is in fact such a common sense, as
> a constitutive principle of the possibility of experience, or whether a higher principle of rea-
> son makes it only into a regulative principle for producing in us a common sense for higher
> purposes; whether, therefore, taste is an original and natural faculty or only the idea of an
> artificial one yet to be acquired, so that a judgement of taste with its assumption of a univer-
> sal assent in fact is only a requirement of reason for producing such agreement of sentiment;

whether the ought, i.e. the objective necessity of the confluence of the feeling of any one man with that of every other, only signifies the possibility of arriving at this agreement, and the judgement of taste only affords an example of the application of this principle – these questions we have neither the wish nor the power to investigate as yet.[2]

This is from § 22. When, in § 38, Kant finally returns to the postponed questions, his deduction of the judgement of taste (and in Kant *deduction* means legitimation without proof) is itself a reflexive and regulative use of judgement, which is why Kant, apparently to his own surprise, finds it easy:

This deduction is thus easy, because it has no need to justify the objective reality of any concept, for beauty is not a concept of the object and the judgement of taste is not cognitive. It only maintains that we are justified in presupposing universally in every man those subjective conditions of the judgement which we find in ourselves.[3]

I read this passage as the best indication that it is the claim to universality that signals disinterestedness, the free play of the faculties, or purposiveness without purpose, and not vice versa. This finds confirmation in aesthetic experience. Not in a special pleasure that would distinguish the feeling of the beautiful from the 'mere' feeling of the agreeable and that would indeed be shareable by all, but in the fact that we feel strongly about the so-called objectivity – the claim to shareability – of our aesthetic judgements. Such feelings show themselves best, sometimes violently, in cases of aesthetic disagreement with someone we love or respect. Children are good guides; they sometimes break a friendship over their favourite colour. As adults, we have learned that colours are a matter of the agreeable, and we rarely fight over the beauty of a rose. But when it comes to art... Just check with your feelings when you tour the galleries: with the intensity of your enthusiasm and the sorrow you feel when your enthusiasm is not shared; with your fear of the judgement of others concerning your taste, when they are people whose judgement you respect; with your embarrassment, shame or despair when you listen to a gallery owner praise a work you find despicable; with the way a truly innovative work, for which you are not yet ready, throws your very sense of what art is off balance. Check for yourself, and you'll see what I mean. Kant has once and for all fathomed the depth of aesthetic disagreements among humans: they amount to nothing less than denying the other his or her humanity. Hence his scepticism about *sensus communis* – ultimately the faculty of living in peace with our fellow men – and his conviction that it nevertheless ought to be postulated, even in the absence of theoretically demonstrable empathy in the human species. The amazing thing is that he grasped that an issue of such magnitude – are we capable of living in peace? – was at stake in a sentence so anodyne as 'this rose is beautiful'. When replaced by 'this thing is art', the real depth of his thinking on aesthetics comes to the fore.

The 'Kant after Duchamp' approach

This leads me to my second point, the historical changes since Kant's time. The replacement of 'this is beautiful' with 'this is art' is not mine. Nor is the replacement of a rose (a natural object) with a thing (a human artefact). Both were forced on us by the historical development of modernity in all domains, including the scientific, the political and the artistic. Beauty in nature was in Kant's day *the* place where hope in the ethical destiny of the human species was put to the test. It no longer is, for reasons too complex to go into here. Art (I'm not saying beauty in art, I'm saying art period) is now this place. To testify that humans ought to be living in peace with each other, when everyday life demonstrates that they can't, such is the social function of art – if art has a function, and if it can be called social. Imagine Ms A and Mr B quarrelling, not over the beauty of a rose, but over some controversial piece of contemporary art – for example, Carl Andre's *Equivalent VIII*, the famous 120 bricks bought some years ago by the Tate Gallery for a sum Fleet Street deemed to take an extravagant and scandalous toll on the taxpayer's money. Ms. A says, admiringly, 'Ah! this is art.' Mr B counters: 'You're out of your mind, this is trash.' Their verdicts are cast in the binary form that has become paradigmatic whenever a work of art, such as Marcel Duchamp's *Fountain*, rather than begging viewers to appreciate its qualities within the conventions of a medium, asks them to decide on its sheer admissibility into the domain of art altogether. Need I recall that Carl Andre's *Equivalent VIII* is made of *ready-made* bricks? That the bricks are simply laid down in rows and columns without mortar or anything else that would assemble them into a unitary and finished whole? And that this particular arrangement is just one combination out of several, all said to be of equal value?

Carl Andre is a sculptor, not an 'artist-at-large'. Yet his art is as much a part of the reception history of Duchamp's readymades in the 1960s as it is an expansion on the tradition initiated by Brancusi. Mr B is familiar with Brancusi, in whose work he perceives beauty. But he sees neither beauty, nor talent, nor even craftsmanship in a pile of bricks. 'This is not a piece of sculpture', such is his verdict. Given that it is not a painting, a poem or a piece of music either, then it is not art. You might say that Mr B is insufficiently informed, that he hasn't followed recent trends in art, or that he has yet to acknowledge receipt of Duchamp's readymades. A crash course in the art of the 1960s might change his mind. Mr B is infuriated by such paternalism. There are rooms at Tate Modern that he visits with pleasure. It is not that he is ill-informed; he flatly refuses to acknowledge receipt of Duchamp's readymades, on behalf of what he is convinced is his superior taste. In his view, being a public gallery funded with taxpayers' money, the Tate ought to exhibit only works worthy of the name – things conveying a sense of the human in art with which he can empathise. Things eliciting universally shareable feelings rather than conjuring intellectual speculations on the limits of art which only snobs enjoy. Mr B wants art to call on *sensus communis*.

Ms A is neither a snob, nor an intellectual who enjoys speculating on the limits of art. Nor does she identify art worthy of the name with 'superior taste', which she regards as the taste of people who think *they* are superior. She too has her favourite rooms at the Tate. She is proud that British museums are free. She feels that some of her taxes are being given back to her as pleasure – and not just pleasure: some of the works really stretch the limit, she thinks. She likes the fact that they are thought-provoking. Some are ugly or even verge on the disgusting, but she forces herself to persist beyond her negative gut feelings. She never thought these works pronounced a taboo on other works' more traditional aesthetic qualities. She loves Brancusi, and senses the beauty of his work. She doesn't know that Carl Andre once claimed to have laid Brancusi's *Endless Column* flat on the ground, but she instinctively feels the relevance of sculpture renouncing verticality. Ms A is interested in the time she lives in; it is a time that has little place for idealistic élans, and should be ashamed of monuments that rush skywards. She appreciates the humble, everyday quality of Andre's piece, its simpleness and lack of craftsmanship. She even chuckles at the thought that she could have made it herself. Ms A is a democrat, and she too wants art to call on *sensus communis*.

Is it not clear that everything said above concerning judgements of beauty remains when art is at stake rather than *beauty*? Kant's account of aesthetic experience, and its consequences for *sensus communis*, remain as valid as ever. We need look no further for an adequate aesthetic 'theory'. Still, the shift from beauty – whether in nature or art – to art, period, has made a new reading of the third *Critique* necessary. The shift in question may be summarised by saying that the naked phrase, 'this thing is art', has replaced 'this painting (statue, poem, piece of music, etc.), is beautiful (good, great, fantastic, super, groovy)' what have you, as the canonical expression of the *modern* aesthetic judgement, when it pronounces on the liminal admissibility of candidates to the name of art. Taking stock of this replacement and investigating its consequences is what I call the 'Kant after Duchamp' approach to aesthetics.[*] Some 125 years separate Kant's *Critique of*

Judgement from Duchamp's first readymades, and somewhere in the middle – say, with Courbet and Manet – the phenomenon known as modernism or the avant-garde came into being. It took some fifty more years after Duchamp's first ready-mades for the latest trends in modernist or avant-garde art to acknowledge receipt of them. Then new questions arose: are we still modernists? Has the avant-garde not failed?

Formalism versus multiculturalism

Modernism has often been associated with formalism, especially in the writings of Clement Greenberg. Post-modernism, in part born out of a radical critique of those writings, has by now spawned a number of interpretations. One of them is its association with multiculturalism. Modernism and formalism are tied to the claim of universality built into aesthetic judgements. Post-modernism and multiculturalism do away with it, and are declaratively anti-Kantian. It will certainly come as no surprise to anyone familiar with current art criticism that universality in art is a vexed question, mortgaged by the strongest doubts – politically motivated doubts, and rightly so – about the legitimacy of artists to represent humanity as a whole and to speak in its name. Such preposterous claims are hegemonic, ethnocentric, colonial, sexist, and entail the same abuse of power that is encountered whenever the Western, white, male, heterosexual worldview seeks to prevail in the name of 'mankind'. Granted. For some time now, multiculturalism has seemed to be the best alternative to universalism in art and art politics. But most advocates of multiculturalism shy away from denying artists any right to represent a community at all. Even the most radical relativists in matters of art and culture are careful not to lapse into total subjectivism. Words such as *identity* and *representation* – words that had been largely deconstructed in the heyday of modernism – have regained currency since the mid-1980s, and are always understood in collective terms (collective as opposed to either individual or universal). A great deal of the art of the 1990s, and an even greater deal of the discourse in support of it, was about group identity and group representation. Sooner or later, though, this discourse is bound to face difficulties, not least the ghettoisation of group identities. I have not encountered a sincere advocate of multiculturalism who refuses to admit that all humans have something in common and that art, if it is any good, addresses that something beyond and across cultural particularities. What the sincere multiculturalist argues is that, although perhaps true, such blanket humanism is useless, and serves to cover up differences, contradictions and conflicts in the real world. Granted, again. But the difficulties do not evaporate just because some embarrassing words have been made taboo. It may be better to work out the difficulties and reclaim the embarrassing words. For example, better to reinterpret modernism, which has often been described as a crisis of *representation*, one of whose symptoms was the advent of non-represent-ative (non-figurative) art, as a crisis of representativity, affecting the legitimacy of artists to speak on behalf of all of us. In a nutshell, I believe multiculturalist discourse to be mistaken in making universalism the target of its critique, when it should be *representativity*.

The problem with representation lies not in its figurative nature but rather in the representativity the concept implies. Works of art are embodiments of aesthet-ic judgements that are evaluated by way of aesthetic judgements. Genuine works of art are the incarnate outcome of myriad aesthetic decisions resulting in a final decision that declares the *thing* the artist was working on a *work*, that is, finished, ready to be exhibited, and subjected to the judgement of others. Of all others; of an indeterminate other. If Kant was right, as I am convinced he was, this means that genuine works of art contain a universal address. Does this suffice to make the work itself 'universal', i.e. to ensure that the artist is speaking in anyone and everyone's name? Do artists legitimately speak on behalf of all of us in their work? The answer to this question hinges on the relationship between the universal *address* involuntarily or automatically contained in every pure aesthetic judge-ment and the universal *mandate* whereby artists allegedly speak on behalf of hu-manity. In other words, the relationship between the 'all of you addressees' of the work and the 'all of us humans' in whose name the artist can – or cannot – be said to have made it. Either mandate is the ground for address, or vice versa. Such is our alternative. In terms of the alternative between the standard reading of Kant and my slight shift of emphasis, this amounts to emphasising either the theo-retical necessity of endowing all human beings with the faculty of taste or the quasi-ethical obligation of endowing all human beings with the faculty of agree-ing. I am defending the second branch of the alternative: address is the ground for mandate – with the proviso that neither branch establishes a ground in the sense of 'if A, then B'. The grounding happens retroactively, in accordance with Kant's conception of a reflexive judgement: the whole *Critique of Judgement* is one long intellectual unfolding of what every aesthetic judgement does.

It is ironic, given they are arch-enemies, that both multiculturalism and formal-ism defend the first branch of the alternative. Multiculturalism sees no problem in making mandate the ground for address, provided the mandate is not universal; artists being spokesmen for a particular group is far less contentious than artists being spokesmen for humanity. But because the address contained in aesthetic judgement is inevitably universal, and because multiculturalism denies art's claim to universality, it is bound to focus its critique on aesthetics as such. If the 1990s were the decade of the return of the real – i.e. of representation – this was clearly prepared by the 1980s, which were the decade of the anti-aesthetic.[5] But you can't help aesthetic decisions being the stuff that genuine works of art, good or bad, are made of. It is no surprise that ghettoisation of group identities ensued, for multi-culturalism makes mandate and address congruent, restricting both to particular, non-universalizable groups. What we risk having is black art addressing the black community, gay art addressing the gay community, and so on. That said, there must be some valid reasons for the otherwise weak and problematic position of the multiculturalists and post-modernists of anti-aesthetic persuasion, or those movements would not have enjoyed the success that made them seem the best alternative to universalism in art and art politics. As I said, difficulties do not evaporate simply by making embarrassing words taboo. Recognising the valid reasons behind the mistakes of multiculturalism and the anti-aesthetic will lead to the most delicate shifts of emphasis, perhaps amendments, required to update Kant's third *Critique*. We will have to part company with Kant, at least momentarily. But where? The best place to start is the strange collusion between multiculturalism's and formalism's choice of the first branch of the alternative.

Formalism, too, makes mandate the ground for address, provided that mandate be universal this time. Whether we are talking about the aesthetic experience of art lovers or artists embodying aesthetic decisions in their work, it is their representativity vis-à-vis humanity as a whole, which, according to formalism, legitimates their claim to universal approval. What does the most prominent advocate of formalism have to say on this topic? In 'Seminar II', Clement Greenberg declares:

> In aesthetic experience you more or less distance yourself from [your]self. You become as 'objective' as you do when reasoning, which likewise requires distancing from the private self. And in both cases the degree of objectivity depends on the extent of the distancing. The greater – or 'purer' – the distancing, the stricter, which is to say the more accurate, your taste or your reasoning becomes. To become more objective in the sense just given means to become more impersonal. But the pejorative associations of 'impersonal' are excluded here. Here, in becoming more impersonal, you become more like other human beings – at least in principle – and therefore more of a representative human being, one who can more adequately represent the species.[6]

No doubt Greenberg's unabashed confidence in the objectivity of his taste, and thus his own representativity, betrays itself at its best here. We must definitely part with Greenberg and Kant here, but not before dissociating ourselves from the many readers of Greenberg who take him to be an orthodox Kantian, forgetting his infamous claim, in 'Can Taste Be Objective?': 'I realize that I take my life in my hands when I dare say that I've seen something better than Kant did.' For Chrissake, what did Greenberg think he saw better than Kant?

> Kant believed in the objectivity of taste as a principle or potential, and he postulated his be-
> lief on what he called a *sensus communis*, a sense or faculty that all human beings exercised
> similarly in aesthetic experience. What he failed to show was how this universal faculty could
> be invoked to settle disagreements of taste.[7]

When Greenberg speaks of settling disagreements of taste, he means deciding whether Ms A is right and Mr B is wrong, not that they are both right. This is a severe misreading of Kant, and one that has harmed the discipline of aesthetics enormously, because it was long taken for granted by readers of Greenberg only too happy to throw the baby out with the bath water, and spare themselves the difficulties of reading Kant for themselves. Kant never believed in the 'objectivity of taste', and *sensus communis* is not 'a faculty that all human beings exercise similarly in aesthetic experience'; it is merely the transcendental idea of such a faculty. An incurable empiricist, Greenberg not only refutes Kant on the basis of experience, but lends him an empiricist reading of his own transcendentalism, which is properly aberrant. But let that be. Greenberg was an art critic, not a philosopher, and I still admire the risks he took venturing onto philosophers' terrain, because I share some of his motivations. Aesthetics for aesthetics' sake interests me no more than it did Greenberg; what interests me is the impact aesthetic theories have on the art world, and the endeavour to arrive at the best possible theory – by which I mean the one most truthful to experience and most liberating for art practice. This is why I think the articulation of the transcendental and the empirical deserves the most careful attention. In this respect, Greenberg may have been closer to Kant than his preposterous claims in 'Can Taste Be Objective?' make it appear, and this forces us to fine-tune where, exactly, we need to part company with Kant. Erroneous as it is, Greenberg's 'distancing from the private self' nonetheless dovetails with the Kantian motif of disinterestedness, and his striving for objectivity understood as impersonality corresponds to Kant's maxim of a 'broadened way of thinking' from § 40: to 'override the private subjective conditions of [one's] judgement [...] and [to] reflect on [one's] own judgement from a *universal standpoint* (which [one] can determine only by transferring [one]self to the standpoint of others)'.[8] This is where we must part with Kant. Not because such an endeavour is scandalous in itself or simply beyond our reach; nor because it smacks of enlightened condescension and privilege, though that's obvious. No, the reason why we must part with Kant exactly here, regarding aesthetic judgement's universal claim interpreted as a claim to universal representativity, is that the issue of 'whether taste is an original and natural faculty or only the idea of an artificial one yet to be acquired', is here made to hinge on our actual capacity of putting ourselves in other people's shoes. With the maxim of a 'broadened way of thinking', Kant himself invests his hopes in the wrong articulation of the transcendental and the empirical. Perhaps I have been too hard on Greenberg, in accusing him of an empiricist reading of Kant's transcendentalism. For in the passage where Greenberg's reading comes closest to the Kantian text, Kant himself waxes dangerously empirical:

> We must take *sensus communis* to mean the idea of a sense shared by all of us, i.e. a power to judge that in reflecting takes a priori account of everyone else's apprehension, in order as it were to compare our own judgement with human reason in general and thus escape the illusion that arises from mistaking subjective and private conditions for objective ones [...]. Now we do this as follows: we compare our judgement not so much with the actual as rather with the merely possible judgements of others, and thus put ourselves in the position of everyone else, merely by abstracting from the limitations that attach to our own judging; and this in turn we accomplish by leaving out as much as possible whatever is matter, i.e. sensation, and by paying attention solely to the formal features of what we apprehend.[9]

If you are looking for a passage in Kant on which to base your rejection of Greenberg's formalism, this is it. Formalism is indeed the embarrassing legacy of the third *Critique*. How to salvage Kant from his own formalism without destroying the whole edifice is the question that must be answered before I can repeat that Kant got it right and that, in spite of the huge crisis of representativity brought about by modernity, artists do legitimately speak on behalf of all of us. To this I shall devote the fifth and last part of my paper.

The wisdom of everyday language

Formalism has been added to the list of embarrassing words such as universalism and humanism. Let's leave them behind for the time being and consult everyday language instead. In order to encompass the whole human species, everyday language has three expressions, all of which have interesting properties, not least that they are utterly Kantian in postulating the species' common humanity without defining it in any way. Those expressions are: *anyone and everyone, all of us*, and *you and me*. All three avoid intensional definitions of what makes all humans human (the big, embarrassing words) and replace them by deictics. Deictics are empty, purely formal words devoid of matter or sensation. They can be said, in Kantian terms, to constitute the transcendental schematism of all perceiving and speaking beings. If we follow Kant, in the *Critique of Pure Reason*, we learn that schematism gives humans an inborn articulation of the transcendental and the empirical. Deictics remain a priori, devoid of matter or sensation, only so long as they are not accompanied by a second, empirically embodied, deictic. If I say 'this' without pointing at something, you will not know what I'm talking about. With our attention focused on the pointing finger – that is, the second deictic – we can turn to the three expressions everyday language uses to replace the big, embarrassing words with their small, vernacular, democratic and light-hearted equivalents – to wit, replace humanity and universality with *anyone and everyone, all of us, or you and me* – and see whether they do not rescue the big words, formalism included, from the bad name they deserved as long as they depended on representativity.

Anyone and everyone and, better still, *anybody and everybody*, equates 'every' with 'any', bypassing representativity in favour of embodiment. Neither 'every' nor 'any' are deictics strictly speaking, but they are a priori in the same way deictics are. Both are poised on the threshold of the empirical world, in need of a second deictic to become embodied—whether it is the counting finger that numbers 'every', or the designating finger that incarnates 'any', thereby changing 'any' into 'this'. Using 'everybody' and 'anybody' interchangeably puts the burden of invoking what the sum total of 'bodies' supposedly shares on the act of singling out one 'body' at random. The absence of criteria for the selection short-circuits representativity, disqualifying it as the key to universality. The expressions anybody and everybody, and, better still, anyone and everyone, imply that singularity is the key to universality, and its true content. The interchangeability of 'any' and 'every' postulates that what makes humans human is, precisely, that they are not interchangeable. Humans have in common that they are unique. Everyday language is spontaneously humanistic here, and its humanism is of the Kantian, transcendental kind.

All of us is humanistic in another sense, equally Kantian if not more. It postulates that the human species is not an amorphous mass; instead, it is capable of assuming the first person plural. It forms an 'us'. What does this mean? 'First person' means that the deictic or pronoun 'we', like 'I', designates the speaker, and 'plural' means that the speaker is not alone. 'We' ranges from 'the two of us' to 'all of us'. Save in exceptional and disquieting cases, where a group speaks in a single voice, the speaker who says 'we' sets him- or herself up as spokesperson. By what right? Has s/he been appointed to speak for the others, and in their name? Is s/he a legitimate delegate of the group? – or the species, if the group extends to all? *All of us*, it seems, has smuggled in through the back door the representativity which *anyone and everyone* had chased through the front. Does assuming the first person plural inevitably mean presuming to be representative? Does everyday language vindicate Greenberg's reading of Kant? For an answer, we must turn to the third of our vernacular expressions, *you and me*.

You and me is the most remarkable of the expressions of which everyday language has availed itself in order to encompass the species in its shared humanity. *You and me* is commonly used to signify 'all of us', even when the 'you' is understood as singular. How come? The pronoun 'we' can be broken down in two ways: either into 'she and I' ('he and I', 'they and I') or 'you and I'. Linguists call the former exclusive and the latter inclusive, but this is misleading; in most cases both exclude as much as they include. In itself, the pronoun 'we' doesn't say whether it is exclusive or inclusive, any more than it says who its members are. Let us talk in examples, and enlist our friend Howard Caygill here – shall we agree on this, Howard? Did you notice? I just switched from the first to the second 'we' in the same sentence, and changed alliances by the same token. I spoke of 'our friend Howard', addressing you, the audience, including you in my putative friendship with Howard, thereby excluding you from the 'we' as if you were absent or not listening. Gosh, I just did it again. Good thing I swivelled my head. I meant 'we', the audience, and you, Howard. In addressing you I am thereby excluding them. I mean them, the audience, which is therefore no longer an audience – witnesses, at most. We'd better stop trying to explain deictics with the help of deictics—they move too quickly – or we'll find ourselves in conundrums worthy of *Alice in Wonderland*. Take a 'we' of two consisting of Howard and Thierry. It is exclusive when Thierry addresses the audience and inclusive when he addresses Howard, and violent in both cases. Assuming the first person plural means assuming its inherent violence. Assuming in the theoretical sense of presuming, and in the quasi-ethical sense of shouldering. We are all – and here I mean 'all of us humans' – capable of assuming the first person plural in the sense of presuming, simply because we are speaking beings. Assuming the 'we' in the sense of shouldering its non-violent ethical purport is another matter. One of the consequences of my shift of emphasis in the direction of Kant's scepticism is that it becomes less and less sure that *sensus communis* can be conceived as the faculty of agreeing. Another is that postulating that it nonetheless *ought* to be increasingly approaches ethical obligation. A third is that the question of 'whether taste is an original and natural faculty or only the idea of an artificial one yet to be acquired', though it will never be settled theoretically in the empirical world, is nevertheless made to hinge, in practice, on our actual ethical capacities. But these no longer boil down to a capacity for putting ourselves in other people's shoes. They are more like the moral courage it takes to put the a priori 'we' to the test of the second, empirical, deictic. What is certain is that violence and exclusion accompany the assumption of the first person plural.

Why, then, has everyday language availed itself of *you and me* to translate 'all of us', and to signify the potential unanimity, or peace, that 'all of us' seems to promise? Is there some logical reason justifying the optimistic naïveté of everyday language? Obviously *you and me* doesn't always signify 'all of us'. Just a minute ago it referred to Thierry and Howard. So why does it sometimes signify 'all of us', in contradiction to its inherent violence? The answer, once more, is that everyday language is spontaneously Kantian, in yet a third sense. It practices reflexive judgement. It doesn't deduce from *you and me* that the whole human species is thereby designated – that would be absurd. It reflects on the fact that if the whole human species were to be designated by means of the first person plural, it could only be by a 'we' that has the form of a *you and me*, not of a *they and me*. A 'we' that is broken down into 'they and me' cannot possibly refer to us all, because it always leaves out at least one individual: the addressee. The condition of universality is negative and purely formal. Everyday language is not saying that all it takes is one outcast for humanism not to be universal (as I said too hastily in *Voici*);[10] that would be a reprehensible formalism, because such ethics are useless in the real world. Universalism and humanism deserve our mistrust, when we suspect them of being the harbinger of ethnocentrism, sexism, colonialism or imperialism. What everyday language is saying is that for the inclusive 'we' to deserve its name, to be devoid of violence and innocent of exclusion, it *must* be universal, it *ought* to be universal (a *müssen* for theory and a *sollen* for practice). That's not much, and it's of little help in the real world – the world of human relations, the world of the economy, or the political world. But it might explain why we have art.

Since the universally inclusive 'we' consists of *you and I*, and since the 'I' is by necessity an individual, the consequence is that it must be the 'you' that is universal. When it signifies *all of us*, *you and me* contains a universal address. Just like aesthetic judgements. A refreshing way of putting this would be to say that everyday language is a spontaneous artist. Its use of *you and me* to mean *all of us* is one of its most poetic, beautiful and profound tropes. It suggests that, though the question of whether the faculty of agreeing exists as a fact will never be settled, language itself postulates that it exists. According to Kant, to postulate that the faculty of agreeing exists is what aesthetic judgement does. The universal address contained in every pure judgement of taste indicates that the judge speaks on behalf of a universal 'we', a *you and me*, that translates as *all of us*. My reasons for saying that address is the ground for mandate, rather than the other way around, are now coming together. They stem from the following paradox, which is the difficulty some have with the 'Kant after Duchamp' approach: on the one hand, when looking at a work of art, you know that a number of intentional decisions are embodied in the work, and you tend to attribute your feeling of dealing with art to them; on the other hand, when looking at a natural object, you know that no such decision is responsible for your feeling of dealing with beauty. How can I maintain that in both cases we are dealing with pure aesthetic judgements in the Kantian sense, and that we are entitled to replace 'this (rose) is beautiful' with 'this (thing) is art'? Kant also had to deal with this paradox, but in a form that was mediated by representation. He could not have conceived of a mere thing, such as a snow shovel or 120 bricks, claiming the name of art. In his day, 'this thing is art' had to mean something like 'this picture of a rose is beautiful'. Kant solved the paradox with a double reflexive loop, when he said that 'nature is beautiful if it also looks like art; and art can be called fine art only if we are conscious that it is art while yet it looks to us like nature.'[11] In simple words: beauty in nature arises when we look at nature as if it were God-made, and beauty in art arises when we look at artefacts as if nobody had made them. No matter what creationists and religious fundamentalists believe, it is no longer possible to look at nature as if it were God-made. The question is whether we can still look at man-made things as though nobody had made them. The answer is not: yes, we can; it is: yes, we must. A strange 'must' on the verge of 'ought', as if poised between *müssen* and *sollen*. A quasi-ethical obligation to endow all humans with the faculty of agreeing, that overshadows the theoretical necessity to endow all humans with the faculty of taste. The emphasis is now on 'quasi'. Aesthetics stops short – must stop, ought to stop short – just this side of ethics. We have art to preserve this strange *heautonomy* that nature no longer guarantees. We have art that no longer looks like nature, because nature no longer looks like art, and yet art – and here I'm talking about the best art according to my taste – that somehow still has to look as if nobody made it.

This is where the involuntariness of the aesthetic judgement sets in. Spontaneity, lackadaisical brush stroke, *sprezzatura* and *non finito* have long been appreciated as signs that the accomplished artist is not the one in whose work everything feels controlled and willed. But it is only with the birth of the avant-garde in the nineteenth century that artists began 'pushing' the aesthetics of the sketch, deliberately refusing to 'finish' their work, or fostering naïveté and clumsiness for their own sake. These and other measures signified that they were giving aesthetic decisions priority over the determining judgements that go into making art. As the taste of the public caught up, each generation of avant-garde artists had to push the involuntary dimension of their plastic decisions to the point where they were felt to be no decisions at all. The surrealist expression 'automatic writing' encapsulates this tendency and reminds me that I called the involuntariness of the aesthetic judgement its 'automatic' character. Whereas theoretical judgements such as 2+2=4 are automatic in the sense that they are dictated by the laws of nature and the struc-ture of the understanding, and ethical judgements are acts of free will that cannot be automatic without ceasing to be ethical, aesthetic judgements are both free and 'automatic' in the sense that they are involuntary, and involuntarily addressed to all. Kant expressed this with the somewhat clumsy notion of disinterestedness – a notion that never fails to raise scandal in the anti-aesthetic camp because it ap-pears to posit an idealised subject detached from all worldly matters such as – top of the list – sexual desire and political struggle. With this clumsy word Kant avoid-ed raising a far greater scandal, one that must have been on his mind given what he said in § 59 about beauty as symbol of morality: the fact that aesthetic judgements are irresponsible. They have no merit in claiming universal assent. Thus they have no merit in endowing all humans with the faculty of agreeing. Why call this en-dowment a quasi-ethical obligation, then, as is implied by my choice of the second branch of the alternative? Why say that address is the ground for mandate? Why say that *you and me* legitimates *all of us*, and not the other way around? Everyday language in its poetic and philosophical wisdom is once again our best guide. It not only uses *you and me* to signify 'all of us', it does so even when the 'you' is un-derstood to be singular. And here again, it proves its ability for exercising reflexive judgement. A universal *you and me* of two would be a contradiction in terms if everyday language did not thereby intimate that it is you, the individual addressee, that legitimates *me*, the individual speaker, in uttering the universal *you and me*. Whoever assumes the universal first person plural signals that s/he is *irresponsibly* speaking on behalf of all of us, and begs the addressee to endorse this irresponsi-bility in his or her own name.

Such utterances are responsible only in art. Such a *you and me* is legitimate only in art. Everywhere else – in economics, politics, culture and human relations at large – to behave responsibly is to take others into account, or to act only with their mandate. Claiming the universal *you and me* is usurpation and abuse of power: my freedom stops where yours begins. Not so in art. A genuine work of art utters the universal *you and me* legitimately. It *is* such a *you and me*, both its sign and its embodiment. How do I know? How do I, the work's addressee, know that the *you* in *you and me* is universal? How do I know that the work contains a universal ad-dress? I don't know this, but if I am sensitive to art, especially if I am receptive to all the signs of freedom, *non finito* or maladroitness that testify to the involuntariness of the artist's decisions, I feel their involuntary address to all, and judge by dint of that feeling. Is it pleasure? Is it the feeling of beauty? Not necessarily. All feel-ings are admissible, including embarrassment, anger and even disgust, which Kant deemed incompatible with judgements of taste. If I am sensitive to art, there is not one feeling that I can exclude from the gamut of feelings resulting in my feeling that the thing I am looking at is art – least of all those feelings that put my trust in *sensus communis* in jeopardy, the ones I summed up, in *Kant after Duchamp*, as the feeling of dissent, the sentiment of dissentiment. I must discard *sensus communis* understood as a universally shared ability for sharing feelings – unless it shares the bad feelings as well as the good ones. What, then, is the decisive feeling? How do I know if the thing I am looking at has succeeded in transferring to me the irresponsibility, or freedom, that only art affords? I have no other way of knowing whether a work of art addresses all of us than the feeling that it addresses me personally. To judge whether it does is thus my responsibility.

Epilogue

Ms A and Mr B are at the Tate Modern quarrelling over Carl Andre's *Equivalent VIII*. Kant witnesses the scene. Ms A nods in approval: 'Ah! this is art.' Mr B shouts back: 'You're out of your mind, this is trash.' Kant feels on Mr B's side this time. Being broad-minded, he does his best to put himself in Ms A's shoes, but nothing doing. As far as he is concerned, the thing on the floor is just a pile of bricks abandoned there by some construction workers. Kant humbly insists in his effort, swallows his embarrassment, notices that there is a label on the wall naming the author. He tries to put himself in the shoes of this Carl Andre whom Ms A is ready to call an artist. He cannot fail to ascribe the form of the ridiculous thing he's looking at to the decisions this Carl Andre has invested in the work – if it is a work. The thing is definitely man-made, but it's not beautiful, it does not represent anything, and the so-called artist has not even touched the material it's made from. Anybody could have done this, Kant thinks. It looks so casual, so forlorn, so goddamn unmade, as if it had fallen from the sky. In entering the Tate Kant was expecting pictures of roses, and he doesn't feel ready for 120 bricks claiming the name of art and intimating him to side with Ms A. Claiming? Intimating? What is this strange sentiment verging on obligation that Kant feels growing in himself, competing with his puzzlement, his embarrassment and his impending anger? What is this even stranger feeling of exhilaration he senses as he starts to reflect? Kant was about to leave the room with a shrug, but the bricks are beckoning.

RESPONSE TO THIERRY DE DUVE

Howard Caygill

Ｉt is a pleasure and a privilege to be able to respond to Thierry de Duve's question 'Do artists speak on behalf of all of us?' and to reflect on the puzzling character of complicity and divergence that I experienced on hearing him now, as well as on previous readings of his work. I find myself in complete agreement with Thierry's premises and conclusions, but arrive at the latter by a different route. Thierry's work has convinced, indeed taught me and others, that aesthetics is central to the understanding of contemporary art, and that the reading of Kant's *Critique of Judgement* is central to aesthetics. His claim that this text of 1790 must be read 'after Duchamp' is a genial and productive proposition which has revivified my and many others' readings of the *Critique*, as has his claim that Kant 'got it right' with respect to aesthetic experience and judgement. Departing from the same premises, we seem to arrive at the same conclusion that aesthetic legitimacy depends not on an artist's 'universal mandate' but on the 'artwork's universal address'. Yet following the path of Thierry's argument from premise to conclusion I find we diverge radically, but perhaps in complementary ways.

My divergence from Thierry's line of argument might be summed up in rephrasing his question 'Do artists speak on behalf of all of us?' as 'Must artworks speak on behalf of all of us?'. The change in emphasis indicates a reorganisation of the Kantian structure underlying Thierry's question, remaining within the framework of the *Critique of Judgement* but emphasising different aspects of it. These differences may be summed up in terms of the categorical nature of aesthetic judgement and the emphasis accorded to the ontology or the being of the work of art.

Kant's account of aesthetic judgement parallels his accounts of theoretical and practical judgement in the first two works of the critical trilogy, *The Critique of Pure Reason* and the *Critique of Practical Reason*. In all three critiques the power of judgement is distributed across the four interlocking fields of quantity, quality, relation and modality. The salient characteristics of these fields in the *Critique of Judgement* are the disinterested, the universal, the non end-directed and the necessary quality of the judgement of taste. Variants of 'Kantianism' may be identified by the privilege accorded to one or other of these fields or to the subgroups (Kant always identifies three) within them. The form of Thierry's question 'Do ...' corresponds to the hypothetical subgroup of modality, my rephrasing of it relocates it in the subgroup of necessity. This rather dry distinction nevertheless exposes some interesting implications: by asking 'do ...' Thierry is asking a question of fact—do artists actually speak on behalf of all of us?; by asking 'must ...' the terrain of questioning has shifted from fact to obligation. In Ms A and Mr B's quarrel over a rose, the argument moves from feeling to imputation, and nested within this is a necessity or an 'ought' sustained by the *sensus communis*. Beginning with the necessity of the 'ought'—you must find this rose beautiful—shifts the terrain of argument from feeling to a place located between the rose and the obligation it summons.

Another categorical decision also informs the direction of Thierry's argument, namely that of quantity: the 'all of us' in Thierry's question is a place-holder for 'universality'. In his deductions of theoretical, practical and aesthetic judgement Kant privileged the categorical fields of quantity and modality—judgements must ultimately be legitimated in terms of universality and necessity. Aesthetic judgements exemplify this privilege; they must be universally and necessarily valid, an outcome achieved by the *sensus communis* in the ways shown by Thierry. Yet there is room for emphasising one or the other of the two fields: either the question of universality or that of necessity, and the choice of emphasis entails a decision, and brings with it a number of argumentative opportunities, dangers and consequences. Thierry's emphasis on universality orients his reading of aesthetic judgement towards the response to works of art and the negotiation between individual feeling and universally valid experience. This is elegantly prosecuted in the three conclusions leading to the derivation of the *sensus communis*—'aesthetic judgements imply a universal address', they call for agreement 'by dint of feeling involuntarily addressed to all', and aesthetic judgement is ultimately detached from the object and is concerned with the agreement in feeling. We must necessarily agree in our aesthetic judgements because of the universality sustained by the *sensus communis*.

There is certainly a great deal of textual warrant in the *Critique* to support this reading of the dematerialisation of the object of pleasure – Thierry cites sections 22 and 38 – but it sits alongside other possible readings. One that would begin from necessity might follow a different argumentative route – the primacy of necessity over universality begins with the question of why certain 'objects' must provoke certain responses – i.e. universality follows from necessity. Thierry maintains a reference to necessity, to the ought, throughout his account of the *sensus communis*, implicitly calling upon it to support universality; yet how would it look if scrutinised in its own terms? It could neither be logical nor moral necessity, but one somehow provoked in the place between, where between certain subjects and certain objects are able to encounter each other in different ways.

The focus on the universality of a judgement of taste orients the account of aesthetic experience toward the *subject*, individual and collective, of aesthetic judgement, while a focus on necessity opens the possibility of an account oriented towards the object, that is, towards an ontology of art. In Thierry's talk, and in his other work, the patient analysis of universality indeed arrives at, and is perhaps even motivated by, an ontological rephrasing of aesthetic judgement, evident in the 'is' of 'this is art'. Here Thierry makes an important contribution to the ontology of art, first by shifting attention from the art as object to its status as place, and secondly by regarding such a place as one 'where hope in the ethical destiny of the human species was put to the test'. The first shift frees the ontology of art from the subject/object distinction, thus respecting Kant's strictures against art objects while also opening the possibility of an ontology of art as place. What this entails, although Thierry does not here explicitly state it, is that the place of art succeeds the *sensus communis*, that an ontology of art emerges out of the aporias of feeling and universality described in the tension between individual feeling and universal agreement.

By arriving at this position by means of the analysis of universality instead of necessity, the unfolding of its full implications remains vulnerable to being pulled back into an aesthetics of subjectivity. This seems to me to take place in Thierry's

analyses of deictics, which are ingenious and subtle, but perhaps reinstate a subjective aesthetics. Art as place, the ontology of art, sees art as putting to the test the
human possibility of living peaceably. Here, testimony is made by the place of art,
yet in the subsequent argument Thierry moves from art's challenge to us – the
moral demand to us, by art, you *must* live in peace – to the use of art as an occasion
for us to test our claims to community. Instead of the place of art calling us and
our very judgement into question – the work pointing implacably *at us* – we point
it out to others as a means of negotiating our community and our differences.
This subjective perspective provokes the problems raised in Thierry's discussion of
formalism and multiculturalism, and the legitimacy of artists, which may not arise
in the same way, if at all, were we to depart from an ontology of art in which art
necessarily challenges and tests *us*, even to the point of its own destruction.

In his closing lines Thierry imagines Kant on a visit to Tate Modern. Kant witnesses the modern incarnations of the rose-lovers Ms A and Mr B arguing over
whether *Equivalent VIII* is art, and begins to construct a *sensus communis* between
them, himself and Carl Andre. Yet what insists itself upon him are less the feelings
and judgements of his fellow spectators and even the artist, but the 'abandoned'
pile of bricks. The strange sentiment provoked by the challenge of the work
provokes affect and reflection, and draws Kant into the place of the object. At this
moment of conclusion I find myself in complete agreement with Thierry: the work
is what makes the challenge. Witnessing Thierry witnessing Kant witnessing Ms A
and Mr B witnessing... I am left with the thought that maybe we could have made
it to the work sooner by means of the category of necessity and an explicit and
declared ontology of the artwork. While the *sensus communis* of Ms A, Mr B and
Mr Andre may in the end have brought us to the place of the work, what emerges
as important is the challenge it poses, its ontological status as holding its place,
lingering to point at and question us, at least for now.

THE DE-STRUCTION OF ART

Howard Caygill

The following thoughts on the destruction of art emerge from a fascination with the relationship between philosophy and its others – art but also politics, science and medicine – and a preoccupation with the question of why and how things come to be, stay and pass away. Reflection upon the specific case of why and how art comes to be, stay and pass away quickly runs into the difficulty of distinguishing between the apparently secured conceptual contrasts of becoming, being and annihilation or, to shift from a metaphysical to an aesthetic register, creation, conservation and destruction. The recognition of the mutual implication of being, becoming and annihilation, subject to debate in metaphysics since Hegel's *Science of Logic* 1812, will be turned to the problem of understanding the meaning of the destruction of art.

I hope to show that the destruction of works of arts – their passing out of existence – is perhaps closer to their creation than has been fully appreciated by modern aesthetics. The latter continues to be guided by Schiller's obsession with creativity or the coming into existence of works of art, to the extent, in The *Aesthetic Education of Humanity* 1795, of seeing in the creative 'play-drive' the condition of the possibility of works of art. The focus on the creation of works of art is complemented by a view – expressed in the concept of 'iconoclasm' – that their destruction somehow befalls them from without, motivated by some combination of psychological, religious or political pathology. Instead of confirming the assumption that creation and destruction are discrete events that befall works of art, I will begin from the idea that works of art are finite, already and always undergoing destruction. The finitude of art may be disclosed by attention not only to the acts of their creation and destruction but above all to the care for works of art in the face of their finitude or inevitable destruction. While the initial steps of such an analysis are indebted to Heidegger's modes of analysis of care in *Being and Time*, the concept is not primarily understood as ethical. Rather, the ethical and aesthetic issues of care are translated into terms of energetics.

In this view a painting, for example, is a system of energy transfer – it absorbs and transmits energy to and from its environment – at certain frequencies of light as colour, at others, as heat. From this perspective, care for a painting involves maintaining for as far and as long as possible its equilibrium of energy transfer; if this deviates from equilibrium the painting's passage out of existence – its ongoing process of destruction – is accelerated. In the limit case, when a painting absorbs traumatic quantities of energy from its environment, as in the heat transfer of a fire, the intrinsic destruction of the work is drastically accelerated. Understood in these terms, the issue of care in the context of inevitable destruction introduces a new level of complexity to the issues of creativity, conservation and destruction of works of art.

One way to approach this complexity is to inquire into the right to existence of a work of art. This approach immediately shifts attention from the triumphant Schillerian chain of freedom, creative intention and objective expression to the vulnerability of the work, or the possibility of its imminent passing out of existence – its destruction. Such an inquiry asks after the character of the investments that keep works of art in existence, the values with which they are irradiated. Is the duty of care motivated by their aesthetic value, their market value or their political/religious value, or are there also ethical and ontological values at work? I hope to show that the context of care may involve any or all of these values, but that their operation is in many ways quite intangible. Where it becomes visible is in those cases where the destruction of a work of art is traumatically accelerated – when it passes out of existence at an unexpected rapidity. At such moments, the care that was sustaining the work in existence – otherwise taken-for-granted, intangible and invisible – comes into view.

The ethical reflection provoked by the destruction of art is an experience with which most us are familiar. It is usually associated with *iconoclasm* or the intentional destruction of works of art. In the logic of iconoclasm destruction is visited upon works of art from without, the context of care catastrophically ruptured. The most recent case of the spectacular iconoclastic destruction of art was the destruction of the second-century monumental sculptures known as the Bamiyan Buddhas by the Taliban government of Afghanistan in March 2001. This event served as a powerful example for what Bruno Latour and Peter Weibel called 'iconoclash' – and is one that recurs throughout their iconoclash project as the most recent moment of a long history of iconoclastic onslaughts against Mahayanna Buddhist artefacts. The destruction sharpened aesthetic and ethical perceptions of a global cultural heritage for which global civil society and its institutions had assumed a responsibility of care – the statues were reproduced, projected on the Pompidou Centre, and after their destruction reflected upon and thought about. The event disclosed a fundamental lack of consensus surrounding the grounds on which these statues might be said to have a right to exist. In 1999, following international cultural diplomacy, the Buddhas were placed 'under the protection' of the Taliban government, an assumption of responsibility which Mullah Omar not only subsequently rescinded but even atoned for with the sacrifice of 100 cows.

The destruction of the Buddhas, while bringing into visibility an implicit sense of global ethical responsibility for works of art – even among those who did not previously know of the existence of such statues – also highlights the limits of thinking of the destruction of art in terms of iconoclasm. The Taliban government did not consider themselves to be destroying works of art, but as purifying their land; in the words of Mullah Omar: 'How could we justify having left these impurities on Afghan soil?' The question, note, is not of justifying why the statues were destroyed, but the hypothetical case of why they should not be destroyed: what right had they to continue in existence? The statues were destroyed as Idols, since not destroying them would have signified an impious care for their existence.

The attempt by the representatives of UNESCO to save the statues by arguing that they were works of art and no longer of primarily religious significance spectacularly backfired. It was because they were not of religious significance, there no longer being a significant Buddhist community in Afghanistan, that they had to be destroyed. Mullah Omar, perhaps disingenuously, maintained that if they were of religious significance to a hypothetical Afghan Buddhist community, then their right to exist would be secured: 'If they were objects of the cult of an Afghan minority, we would have to respect their belief and its objects, but we do not have a single Buddhist in Afghanistan so why preserve their false idols? And if they have no religious character, why get so upset; it's just a question of breaking stones.'[1] In the face of iconoclastic logic modern aesthetics is literally disarmed. If the only recognised ground for care is religious, then arguments to aesthetic and perhaps even economic and political value are irrelevant. Iconoclasm is indifferent to art, it is aimed at attacking the beliefs of others, or underlining the belief of one's own community, or usually both. The destruction of *art* is collateral damage – art is destroyed for what it is taken to mean to others rather than for what it means for itself. Iconoclasm uses the continued existence of a work of art as a means to attack the context of care that sustains it in existence.

It is widely assumed that iconoclasm is paradigmatic of the destruction of art – Latour and Weibel's extraordinary *Iconoclash* project is a comprehensive statement of its paradoxes – yet it seems a special and very particular case. In the first of three contributions to the *Iconoclash* catalogue dedicated to the destruction of the Bamiyan Buddhas, Pierre Centlivres points towards a complex notion of destruction. The Buddhas had already been defaced, allegedly the work of Aurangzeb in the seventeenth century. Centlivres cites the archaeological argument of Zemaryalai

Tarzi that the Buddhas were not the objects of iconoclastic violence but had been created already defaced – that the faces depended on the ceremonial care of a Buddhist community that would adorn them with painted wooden masks. Their destruction was thus already inscribed at their creation. From this point of view the statue invokes at its origin a call for care, for a liturgy or work of care to complete it and to keep it in existence. The work of art is the possibility of its destruction, it is emblematic of a future breakdown of care. In this case, UNESCO was unable to assume the duty of care passed on by the extinct Buddhist community, exposing the statues to the karma that presided over their birth.

The inscription of destruction at the moment of creation seems to point to a richer and more complex conception of the destruction of art than that performed in iconoclasm. The iconoclastic attacks on works of art such as the *Rokeby Venus*, Michelangelo's *Pietà* and the Barnett Newman actions of the 1980s in Berlin and Amsterdam deny the work's right to exist, but in the name of the values that it allegedly embodied – patriarchy, catholicism, international modernism.[2] The destruction of art has broader implications, and reveals more aesthetic and ethical complexity, than the attack on values that informs the actions of art assailants such as Mullah Omar and Josef Kleer.

Some of these implications become evident in the motiveless destruction of works of art, as in the destruction of contemporary British art in the Momart warehouse fire in London in May 2004. The destruction of contemporary art in this fire brought to light a number of interesting issues, such as the ethical reluctance of the Senior Fire Officer Gary Fredericks 'to put firefighters' lives at risk for art' and Tracy Emin's circulated text message: 'I was OK now I'm hurt. But no one died and ideas continue. The war in Iraq is wrong x.' But the fire also disclosed other issues regarding the relationship between care and art.

One of the works destroyed in the fire was Helen Chadwick's *Unnatural Selection: Opal* 1996 (iris print, perspex 100 x 80 x 8). While not a victim of any iconoclastic logic, the destruction of Opal provokes reflection on the relationship between creativity, care and destruction. 'Unnatural selection' reworks Darwin's term 'natural selection' (where survival of the fittest entails destruction of the unfit) and emerged from Chadwick's residency at the Assisted Conception Unit at King's College Hospital, London. It controversially used embryo images, in particular those which were unnaturally selected. The image of the foetus has been at the centre of recent quasi-iconoclastic struggles in which Chadwick's was clearly an intervention.[3] But what is striking about the destruction of this work is the contrast between the lack of motivation – it was not destroyed for the sake of anything – and Chadwick's effort to give existence through art to these foetuses by encasing them in a durable material like perspex. The attempt to redeem and give life to the foetus through art was itself vulnerable to destruction – its attempt to sustain those images in existence by means of the care of art did not itself succeed. The logic of this destruction seems more difficult to think about and to raise more questions than that of iconoclasm. It exceeds any iconoclastic logic, and points beyond the idea that the destruction of art is necessarily a motivated, exceptional event. Perhaps it is the norm – more work has been and will be destroyed than has been conserved – indeed the work is always on the verge of destruction, has to be kept in existence, perhaps, even especially, at the moment of its creation.

Early in the last century George Lukács posed a Kantian question that for him was at the core of aesthetic reflection: 'We have works of art: how are they possible?' The implicit answer is usually along the lines of 'because they have been created'. However, we might try a different approach to answering the conditions of art's possibility – namely 'we have works of art because they have not been allowed to succumb to destruction'. This raises the further questions of the vulnerability of a work of art and the character and limits of the aesthetic and ethical care that sustains it in existence. But before doing so I would like to show how far this line of questioning is from the dominant Schillerian line of aesthetic reflection. I'll do so by quickly pointing to some elements of complexity in Kant's formidably subtle and ambivalent *Critique of Judgement*.

One thing that is troubling about Kant's enigmatic text is that it does not assume that the work of art has any ethical or aesthetic right to existence. An aesthetic judgement for Kant is not only possible without the existence of works of art, but indeed requires their non-existence. It is, bluntly, an account of aesthetic judgement founded on the destruction of art, one justified, aesthetically and ethically, in the name of freedom. Kant formally declared four conditions for a valid aesthetic judgement of taste: that it be disinterested, that it hold for everybody, that its object be complete in itself, and that it necessarily pleases. These conditions – the moments of the quality, quantity, relation and modality of a judgement of taste – are insistently subjective, prescinding from any assumption concerning the existence of works of art: quantity and modality by definition, quality and relation more indirectly, more perversely. Kant begins with the all-important 'quality' of an aesthetic judgement, claiming that the delight in the beautiful object cannot be interested in its existence. For to be concerned or to care about the existence of a work of art is to have an 'interest' in it, one which for Kant is ineluctably bound up with the faculty of desire. The claim for the disinterested character of the aesthetic judgement is not simply an act of theoretical *epoché* or a logical act of abstraction from the existence of works of art; it is rather more. In §2 of the *Critique of Judgement*, Kant gives an example of disinterestedness. He imagines being shown a beautiful palace – and then insists that his lack of interest in its existence exceeds even that of the judge who 'does not care for things that are merely made to be gaped at', or that of the incongruous Iroquois in Paris who preferred restaurants to palaces, or even that of Rousseau who saw in the existence of such an object the wasted sweat of the people. None of these care for the continued existence of the palace, but Kant's position is even stronger; he explores his disinterest by indulging a fantasy that combines Robinson Crusoe with the Arabian Nights: he says that were he to find himself on an island and could bring the palace into existence with a single wish he would not do so if he had a comfortable hut. So little does he care about the existence of the beautiful object that he would not bring it into existence even if it were gratuitous to do so.

Anyone making a judgement of taste must have no care for the existence of the object of judgement. The reason for this 'complete indifference' to existence is given toward the end of the section on quality: 'An object of inclination, and one which a law of reason imposes on our desire, leaves us no freedom to turn anything into an object of pleasure.' The existence of a work of art places us under an obligation to it, and this responsibility limits our freedom. The freedom to make anything into an object of pleasure – even a urinal – means that *nothing* can make any claim on us to be such an object. This primacy of freedom constitutes limitless creativity – freedom consists in assigning its pleasure where it will – yet to grant the right to exist to an object beyond the moment in which it is chosen for pleasure is to compromise the ethical value of freedom. What this translates into is an insistent and perpetual destruction: at the same moment as freedom brings objects of pleasure into existence it must cancel that existence, or find itself obliged to care for it. This is an extreme statement of what would later be known as creative destruction and destruction art – that free creativity must be spontaneous and not bound even or above all by its own creations.

Perhaps this is one of the reasons why Kant has notoriously little to say about works of art in the *Critique of Judgement* – for if the interval between creation and destruction is distended then the work not only exists, but lays claim to existence. Freedom in this case is succeeded as ultimate aesthetic and ethical value by the value of care for the existence of the work. Kant's results as ever are splendidly ambivalent. For with the same movement by which freedom, spontaneity and creativity replace the work with the ever repeated moment of creation, the issue of time becomes crucial and the problem of the existence of the work is that it must be poised between creation and destruction. One reading – Schiller's – is that freedom and spontaneity are always creating new works and nothing has a right to exist; the other is that works are always poised between creation and destruction, always posing the question of their right to exist and demanding care. We might rephrase Lukacs's question – We have works of art: how are they possible? – as 'Works of art are made to be destroyed: why do some continue to exist?' One approach to an answer is to focus on the notion of poise – the work of art poised or lingering between creation and destruction – which requires viewing it as primarily an event rather than an object.

There are a number of beginnings to think about this moment of poise: Plato's late dialogue *Parmenides* develops the rather inconspicuous and subsequently overlooked notion of *exaiphnes*, the unpredictable moment or instant between coming into and passing out of being, describing it as of 'an uncanny sudden nature'. Walter Benjamin developed a similar notion – *Ursprung/Origin* – explicitly with respect to the work of art, as an 'eddy in the stream of becoming'. Such focus on the event of art displaces many of the emphases of Schillerian aesthetics – works of art exist not only because they have been created but also because they have *not yet* been allowed to pass out of existence. The question of what is a work of art usually answered in terms of something created becomes the question of the when of the work of art, and, collaterally, why it has not yet been allowed to go away. In approaching a work of art in this way we can ask the aesthetic question of how it is preserved in existence and the ethical question of why care is taken to do so. The beginnings of such reflection on art are to be found less in aesthetics and art history than in museology and the theory of restoration. A thoughtful example not much heeded by philosophical aesthetics is Cesare Brandi's *Teoria del restauro* 1977, which distinguishes between the various phenomenological temporalities of the work of art – creation, emergence, its arrival to the present and its future – according to each moment its own specific responsibility.

Rather than dwell on this example, I would like to move toward an ending by way of some intriguing 'works of art' that do not make a lot of sense in Schillerian terms. The first is a ghost of a work that has long fascinated me, Picasso's *The Guitar Player: Construction* 1913, traces of which I first saw in the 'Picasso and Photography' show and that was allegedly destroyed by its creator.[4] The 'work' appears over five photographic prints, four of which apparently stem from a single or two slightly displaced negatives. The four closely present manipulations of a studio scene, the first apparently documenting a large work in progress cropped vertically to the right, the other three more severely cropped and worked on through the additions of line and the blanking out of areas of the image.[5] The fifth, or perhaps the first image – the position with respect to the others is, as we shall see, debateable – features a self-portrait of Picasso sitting in front of the work in progress. The 'work' did not survive, at least not as an object independent of its photographic traces.

Dominating the studio space of the four prints is a work in progress, *Construction with Guitar Player*, dated to Picasso's studio in 242 Boulevard Raspail where he moved in 1912 and stayed until the summer of 1913. In the first (11.8 x 8.7) print the large canvas occupies a large part of the image, but is surrounded by other objects.[6] Of all the prints it most approximates to a documentary record of the destroyed work, except that it deletes almost a quarter of the canvas to the right. Moving from the upper left, the first object to be inventoried is a part of a poster with the prominent letters SSO and a partial A, advertising Picasso's retrospective exhibition in Munich during Spring 1913.[7] Immediately below the poster are two works by Picasso, the papier collé still life *Au Bon Marché* and a sketch of the bottle of Anis del Mono. Below are a number of canvases, in the foreground three small and medium reversed rectangles, the one or perhaps two oval and one large rectangular canvas prepared with a sketch. In the centre foreground is a small round table with the paraphernalia of a still-life model: bottle, pipe, cup, newspaper and a white shape which appears to be the cutout of the hand that appears superimposed on the tuning key of the guitar in the self-portrait. In three of the prints the first finger of the cutout seems to be bent up, in the fourth it is flat. Behind the table is the greater part of a large canvas that makes up the 'guitar player'.

The studio scene, beside its collection of work from Picasso's recent past, also situates itself in a number of his creative series. It is one of a number of studio scenes, as is the related self-portrait print part of a series of studio self-portrait photographs, of which the self-portrait of the artist as a boxer of 1914–15 is perhaps the best known. The work in progress comprises a series of vertical planes sketched in charcoal in the upper section and intersected by an oblique plane with geometrical lines. A guitar is suspended at an angle to the surface of the canvas by a diagonal cord attached to the top of the canvas and another to its right-hand side. Two hands cut out of newspaper play the guitar, one forming a chord, the other slapping the instrument below the frets. Below the guitar is a sketch of an exploded guitar, with the sounding box protruding in the shape of a cone that ends with a number of sketched letters. To the right of the guitar is the shape of an upturned bottle, which on closer inspection emerges as the fret (with hand) and a tuning peg of a guitar. Above and to the left is part of an assemblage attached to the canvas that is more fully revealed in the other prints forming this series.

The first print offers a comprehensive precis of Picasso's work to date, a retrospective so to speak. Thematically it rehearses the themes of the guitarist that Picasso began painting in 1908, as well as the guitar itself, a repeated motif culminating in the New York Museum of Modern Art's papier collé 'Guitar' of 1913 and sculpture of the guitar – a spatial negative so to speak of the volumes of the instrument – of 1912–13. The collage *Au Bon Marché* and the dappled bottle on the wall in the photograph look back to the work of 1912 and forward to that of 1914–15, while the guitar player itself combines the linear investigations of analytical cubism with papier collé and collage. The painting assumes sculptural values, with all the elements gathered together in the space of the photograph.

In the following three prints the picture plane has shifted up and towards the left, including, in the 7.8 x 5.8 print, a full view of the affixed assemblage only partially revealed in the first print. However, the print has been marked with a series of lines that seem both to map and project a series of possible spatial transformations. Most prominent are two diagonal arcs, one with its centre in the guitar, the other in the vertical line following the left side of the assemblage. A diagonal intersecting the longer arc and another descending from an intersection with it form a parallelogram within which a vertical intersects a deltoid form, descending to rotations of the curve of the guitar centred upon the right hand of the guitarist. The lines offer a diagram for the spatial transformation of the shapes making up the motif. The diagram can be understood either as an analysis of the organisation of the existing work, or its projection toward a new work: in either case the photograph of the guitar player is substantially obliterated. The other two prints take this process further, using the selective under-exposure of the negative as a means to cut into the space of the image. In the 11.4 x 8.8 print a large part of the image has been erased leaving a fret-like form moving up through areas of shade from the table, through the guitar to the wall. Similar but more drastic surgery has been conducted on the print in the 11 x 9 version where a large jagged area has been deleted from the right, and a square and a rectangle from the left and a large rectangle from the centre. Amid these manipulations of the image it becomes increasingly unclear where the work is to be located, whether outside the photograph as documented object, in each of the prints, or in the ensemble of all manipulations understood as a series. Given that the 'original' work is destroyed, all that remains are the photographic traces, but their progressive deletion of the original work points to the emergence of something new from its remains.

Finally we may turn to the ambiguous self-portrait – 'Self-Portrait in front of *Construction with Guitar Player*, Paris, Studio Boulevard de Raspail, Summer 1913' (16.6 x 10, Picasso Archive, Musée Picasso, Paris). The date and place of the photograph have been difficult to fix. Baldassari reports that in 1950 Christian Zervos dated it to 1912, Jaime Sabartes in 1954 relocated it to the studio in Rue Schloelcher in 1914, while for Edward Fry in 1988 it reappears in the studio at Boulevard Raspail in 1913. Baldassari opts for locating the other photographs at Ceret (March–June) 1913, and the self-portrait after 20 June when Picasso returned to Paris.[8] What is at stake in the decision regarding the time and the place of the photograph is the character of the self-portrait – whether it portrays the creator at the beginning of the work or the destroyer pausing while removing it from existence.

The issue provokes even the admirably sober curator Anna Baldassari to speculate. She dates the photograph *after* the destruction of the work, seeing it as an 'epilogue' to the experiment in construction, and describes it as 'portraying Picasso in front of *Construction with Guitar Player* when the work was dismantled or destroyed... His hands seem to hold an invisible guitar, as if, by means of a photographic substitution, the artist has taken the place of his ephemeral creature of string and paper.'[9] The act of destruction is redeemed by the substitution of the body of the artist – miming a guitar player for the destroyed work. Yet it is by no means clear whether the artist can be definitively located at the moment of creation or destruction. The denuded state of the canvas can equally mark a time before creation as after destruction. Baldassari's evidence is a questionable mark left by the glue of the right arm – that could easily be a mark for the application of the glue and the arm. More persuasive is the hand on the fret – in the earlier, replete photographs the paper hand was still on the table. In the case for destruction it would have been applied late to the work in progress and also removed at the very end, after the self-portrait. Even with evidence for the contrary – Picasso is not dressed for the Parisian summer – the image is wholly equivocal (perhaps ambivalent) – undecidable between whether this is the artist before the moment of creation or after the moment of destruction of the work of art, benign creator or art assassin. It is a moment of poise – with a number of strange features such as the crease of the edge of the canvas at the lower right continuing to form a triangle with the crease of Picasso's sleeve – that is somehow emblematic of the ambiguity that informs the relationship between creation, care and destruction in these photographs and in the artistic personal and working practices of Picasso.

The ambivalent condition of the work of art in Picasso's photographs, destroyed or conserved and transformed through photography and the manipulation of photographs, becomes an organising principle of the early work of Robert Rauschenberg, which collapses the distinction between artwork and photograph. These works also elegantly stage many of the dilemmas of care that we have explored and return them firmly to the context of energetics. *The White Paintings* 1951 inhabit the uncanny space between painting and photography occupied by Picasso in 1913, and operate by staging the energy transfer that constitutes a work – retransmitting energy inputs from the environment as images of the viewers. This unusually delicate energy system is extremely vulnerable and undergoes rapid destruction; as a result it requires enormous care, with the artist stipulating periodic repainting of the surface. At the other extreme of the energy-transfer spectrum, the near-contemporary *Black Paintings* absorb energy from the environment, reflecting much of it in heat and thus too undergoing destruction. The ontological inseparability of creation, conservation and destruction that is staged in these works and underlies perhaps all works of art is given an iconoclastic staging in Rauschenberg's *Erased De Kooning* drawing, which superimposes the acts of creation and destruction, transposing their ontological status to the level of artistic intentionality.

But I would like to conclude with some reflections on the complexities that attend the destruction of art in the context of conservation. The paradoxical complicity of creation and destruction evident in the cases of Picasso and Rauschenberg also attends the particular case of the care for art represented by 'conservation'. On a recent visit to Ghent I was struck by the care lavished on the Van Eyck brothers' *Altarpiece of the Lamb* in the church of St Bavo. Removed from its chapel to a closed environment, presumably for the purposes of conservation, the work might seem to exemplify the paradoxes of conservation and destruction. The casing of the Altarpiece in 'protection work' might also be understood as 'destruction work'. The front and rear of the painting are subjected to a barrage of lights amounting to a colossal bombardment of energy, one which is resumed daily and probably without the gradual change in energy levels represented by the gradual exposure to natural light in the original location. With the additional energy sources of light bulbs in the room and the attendant's reading light, the ban on using flash cameras seems hypocritical. The unprecedented levels of energy that the painting now has to absorb has the benefit of provoking extreme visibility at the level of visual frequencies but may also be provoking chemical change, a process exacerbated by the black frame designed to enhance visibility but at the expense of raising heat levels.

While it can be assumed that the energy parameters surrounding the painting are being carefully monitored, it seems undeniable that such conditions must be distorting the delicate equilibrium represented by the continued existence of this object. Conservation in this case may unwittingly be contributing to changing the equilibrium of the work and hastening its destruction. But before calling upon UNESCO to intervene it is important to reflect once more on the structure of care within which the Altarpiece finds itself. The painting has to be made available to a mass audience, a value which has to be balanced against the absolute value of conservation. At an extreme, these might require that the work be removed from the public gaze or returned to its original location, rigorously controlling its condition and severely limiting access. Even a brief reflection on the implications of such a move reveals once more the complex set of investments, implications and consequences that attend the care for a work of art in the face of its inevitable but deferred destruction.

RESPONSE TO HOWARD CAYGILL

Thierry de Duve

T hanks, Howard, for your thought-provoking reflections on the destruction of
art. The question you raise—why and how art comes to be, stay and pass away—is
broad; much broader when cast in such organic metaphors than when confined to
the art-institutional register. There is a vitalist thread running through your paper,
the way I read it. Why do we have art? Works of art are mortal, and therefore alive,
exactly the way people are, and this is why we care—we *ought* to care—for art. You
may find this reading too romantic and not sober enough to keep with the tone
of your text. Your way of keeping romantic and vitalist metaphors under check, it
seems to me, was to focus on case studies implying aggression against art and the
violent negation of *sensus communis*, the better to probe the positive articulation
of aesthetics with ethics. Negative instances are the best test, no doubt.

The thoughts your talk prompted in me cannot possibly do justice to the
meandering line of argument that had you weave seemingly unrelated concerns
into such a dense fabric. I say 'seemingly unrelated' because I must confess that
at first I resisted your idea of coupling the destruction *of* art with destruction *in*
art. I couldn't see what the Talibans' decision to destroy the Bamiyan Buddhas
had in common with Rauschenberg's decision to erase a de Kooning drawing and
make it a work of his. But reading further, I realised how much you saw the *Erased
de Kooning* work in continuity with the *White Paintings*. And those, as you rightly
insist, require enormous care, with the artist stipulating periodic repainting of the
surface. I agree. I don't see much difference between de Kooning offering the
brash young Rauschenberg one of his drawings, knowing that he would destroy it,
and Rauschenberg handing over the responsibility of repainting the *White Paintings*
to Brice Marden, knowing that this, too, would destroy the original work. The point
is that Rauschenberg did not entrust his *White Paintings* to just anybody. Brice
Marden is a colleague of whom Rauschenberg knows that he cares for painting.
Of course the same holds true for de Kooning in relation to Rauschenberg; he

wouldn't have let him destroy his work otherwise. The long and *careful* paragraphs you devote to Picasso's *care* in letting us know how much he *cared* for a work he ultimately destroyed testifies to the fact that, beyond destruction, the real object of your philosophical concern is the care for art. Your move from Lukacs' Kantian question, 'We have works of art: how are they possible?' to a more sceptical and anxiety-ridden one, 'Works of art are made to be destroyed: why do some continue to exist?', is a radical move. Though I think it is excessive to claim that art is made to be destroyed, I definitely share your view that the right to existence of works of art is not self-evident. Adorno said as much in the very first sentence of his *Aesthetic Theory*.

With Picasso and Rauschenberg in mind, the connection you make with the Bamiyan Buddhas is logically understandable: they had been created already defaced, you argue, and were handed over to the ceremonial care of a Buddhist community that would adorn them with painted masks. However, I don't think I can follow you in your conclusion that their destruction was already inscribed at their creation. My reasons have to do with a distinction I think we ought to make between works of art produced, shown and, as the case may be, destroyed *as* art, and works of art produced, shown and destroyed *in the name* of art. I have no doubt that the sculptors who carved the Bamiyan Buddhas were aware of being artists and that they looked at their own production as being art. But they were not acting in the name of art. They were acting in the name of their religious faith, and so did the Taliban when they destroyed the statues. You made a strong point when you underlined that UNESCO's plea to the Taliban, arguing that the Buddhas were works of art cleansed of their religious significance, spectacularly backfired. Art emancipated from religious significance is the gist of the Western, modern idea of the autonomy of art. As we know, this idea is the regulative idea (in the Kantian sense) that presided over the birth of museums in the eighteenth century. Works of the past that had survived destruction then began to be collected and preserved in the name of art, although most of them had been made and hitherto cared for in the name of religion. It is only when artists began to work with an eye on the museum as sole destination for their work that works of art could be created and/or destroyed both *as* art and *in the name* of art. Picasso and Rauschenberg were working within the Western, modern paradigm, whereas the sculptors of the Bamiyan Buddhas and the Talibans were not.

Works of art are objects, and even with the best conservation techniques, objects ultimately succumb to the law of entropy. Though not made to be destroyed, works of art are made in full awareness that they will not last forever. Again, reading you, I resisted at first the amalgam you seem to make between art wilfully and art accidentally destroyed. And here again I yielded when I realised that the real object of your concern was the care for art – and beyond the care for art, the care for people. They sometimes run hand in hand (or so the humanist view on art has it), and sometimes counter to each other. There is a beautiful though painful allegory in the story of the fire officer refusing to put the life of his men at risk in order to save lives that had been symbolically rescued by a work of art. Helen Chadwick's encased embryo images displaying her care for unborn children had to be balanced against the officer's care for his men, when the Momart warehouse where Chadwick's work was stored burned down. This made me think that from the vantage point of museum curators and conservators, there is little difference indeed between acts of vandalism and natural catastrophes. Museum people have to deal with the consequences, not with the motives or absence of motives of the destruction, except that they must factor in the cause of a destruction into their protective measures in order to prevent its repetition. The iconoclastic attack not on one but on two Barnett Newman paintings at the Stedelijk Museum in Amsterdam is a tragic but interesting case, in this respect. The same man who had slashed *Who's Afraid of Red, Yellow and Blue III* with a Stanley knife in 1986 came back eleven years later to inflict the same damage onto *Cathedra*. Both paintings have the same broad horizontal format and are among Newman's greatest masterpieces. The slashes on both are virtually identical, running horizontally across the whole length of the paintings, and are literally the signature of the perpetrator, as in a parody of a grandiose abstract expressionist gesture. The vandal, it turned out, was a failed artist with a pathological hatred for the high modernism those paintings exemplify. He destroyed art in the name of art, though sustained by an aesthetic ideology diametrically opposed to the one informing the art he destroyed. The story, alas, doesn't stop there. Restoration of *Who's Afraid* was confided to an American restorer who had been recommended by the painter's widow, and who ruined the painting a second time, of course with the best intentions, that is, in the name of faithfulness to Newman's art. He repainted the large expanse of red that constitutes the quasi-totality of the canvas's surface, allegedly with a roller, matching Newman's colour as well as he could but neglecting that it was the visual result of the painter's multilayered technique. Whereas Newman's red made full use of the transparency of oil paint and let the yellow underneath shine through, the restorer's red is a dull and flat vermilion verging on orange. When *Cathedra* was in turn vandalised by the same man who destroyed *Who's Afraid*, the museum decided to do an in-house restoration and conducted the job with infinitely more care. Though the seams are faintly visible, at least the colour is right. The epilogue of this sad story raises the same questions you asked yourself after visiting Van Eyck's *Altarpiece of the Lamb* in Ghent. There is no law in the Netherlands adequately protecting works of art from vandals, and the man who destroyed a Newman painting twice is free. Even if it were technically possible, museums are not allowed to blacklist this particular person, let alone other potential vandals. After the restoration of *Cathedra*, the Stedelijk Museum officials found themselves facing a cruel dilemma, pitting ethics against aesthetics. As representatives of a public institution, their duty is to make their treasures available to the widest audience, in viewing conditions that respect the spirit of the work. Thus, restricting access to Newman's paintings or framing them behind glass was out of the question. An awkward corral was built to keep the spectators at bay, with glass partitions rising to shoulder level and letting the gaze reach the paintings unhindered, but from a distance. Here, two different notions of care for art are conflicting. I, for one, who care for Newman's paintings, will never again be able to indulge in one of my favourite viewing behaviours in front of *Who's Afraid*. I used to walk swiftly parallel to the painting with my nose almost on its surface so as to let the energy of the red overwhelm me and the yellow stripe at the right end of the canvas catch me by surprise. This I am no longer allowed to do and, given that Newman wanted his paintings to be looked at from nearby, I feel that an essential dimension of their aesthetic experience is now lost. But I do care enough for *Who's Afraid* to put up with its awkward new viewing conditions. Even though I tend to see them as an aesthetic betrayal, I have to admit that care for the physical maintenance of the painting has priority. You are right in speculating that the contradictions between the aesthetic and the ethical notions of care are bound to be more and more irresolvable, should the modern ethic of art as cultural service to the community continue to prevail. As you say, modern aesthetics is literally disarmed in the face of iconoclastic logic. If, as you suggest, the said logic is not reducible to vandalism but testifies to the 'ontological inseparability of creation, conservation and destruction' of works of art, then another aesthetics is urgently needed. I suspect that this is the broad horizon you set your eyes on with your paper.

CLONING TERROR: THE WAR OF IMAGES 2001–04

W J T Mitchell

I   Biopictures

In 1992 I coined a phrase, 'the pictorial turn', that has become something of a cliché, sometimes even an interesting concept, in the criticism of culture, society and politics. My idea (hardly an original one) was that the image had become a conspicuous problem, both in popular culture (where 'image is everything' was the mantra of the day), and in the study of the arts, the media, cultural theory and philosophy, where a turn from language to the image seemed to be occurring. Richard Rorty's 'linguistic turn', in other words, was being succeeded by another shift, this time to pictures, images, iconic signs in all the media. The idea was given other elaborations – the 'iconic turn' of Gottfried Boehme, and the 'visual turn' of a newly invented proto-discipline called 'visual culture' or 'visual studies'.[1]

I want to describe another version of the pictorial turn, a turn toward what we might call the 'biopicture', or the 'biodigital picture', the icon 'animated' – that is, given motion, expression, by digital animation or DNA, which treats the image as an organism, the organism as an image. The biopictorial turn can be best summarised with a still image from Stephen Spielberg's *Jurassic Park* showing a Velociraptor with the letters of the DNA code projected on its skin. (fig. 1: Digital

fig. 1 Digital Raptor: film still from *Jurassic Park*
dir. Stephen Spielberg (1993)

Raptor) In the film narrative, the Raptor has just broken into the computer control room of the dinosaur park, and has accidentally turned on the film projector loaded with the park's 'orientation film'. The letters of the DNA code that governs the cloning of the park's dinosaurs are being projected onto its skin. The still captures in a single image the entire premise of this film: that dinosaurs have been cloned from extinct DNA, and creatures that previously existed only in pictorial or sculptural re-creations have now been literally resurrected from, not just death, but species extinction. These are not merely 'ghostly' reanimations of the dinosaur as image, in other words, but all too real, embodied, and fleshly. But of course at the same time we know that this is only a film, and these images are merely shadows. The revealing of the code of life here also suggests a strictly cinematic technology, the code of digital animation which was pioneered in *Jurassic Park* and displaced the older analog animation technology of robotics and animatronics. This is the first explicit avatar of what I want to call the 'biodigital picture'.

The biopicture, then, is the fusion of the older 'spectral' life of images (the uncanny, the ghostly) with a new form of *technical* life, epitomised by the contemporary phenomenon of cloning. What we are seeing in the 'digital raptor' of *Jurassic Park* is a 'cloning of terror', literally, the artificial duplication of a life-form, the *dinosaur*, whose name ('terrible lizard') is synonymous with terror.[2]

II   Cloning Terror

If the biopicture or animated icon is the technical foundation of the contemporary version of the pictorial turn, its political, moral and aesthetic foundations are located in the twin phenomena of cloning and terrorism. We are in the midst of a double revolution, one involving the mutation of political violence into international terrorism (and the 'war on terror'), the other based in technical innovations in the biological sciences. The convergence of these two revolutions is what I call 'cloning terror', by which I mean 1) the paradoxical process by which the war on terror has the effect of producing more terror, 'cloning' more terrorists in the very act of trying to destroy them, and 2) the horror or terror of cloning itself, which presents a spectacle of unleashed forces of biological reproduction and simulation that activates some of our most archaic phobias about image-making. Cloning and terror converge, in other words, at the level of images understood as life-forms–the biopicture. The figure of the clone as digital raptor perfectly captures this logic, showing the monstrous new life-form at the moment when it is invading the control room of Jurassic Park, threatening to devour the controllers who created it in the first place. The linchpin between terrorism and cloning is the image in collective fantasy and memory, endowed with an unprecedented virulence by the new technologies of capture, storage and transmission provided by the digital revolution.

The terrorist and the clone, then, are the mutually constitutive figures of the pictorial turn in our time. (figs. 2 and 3: Masked Palestinian Fighters; Helmeted Stormtroopers from Star Wars: Attack of the Clones) That is why the terrorist is often portrayed as a clone, a headless or at least faceless automaton, masked and anonymous, a mindless, pathological and suicidal life-form comparable to a virus, a cancer, or a sleeper cell that 'incubates' inside the body of its host, turning the body's defences against itself in what Jacques Derrida has diagnosed as a socio-political form of autoimmune disorder.[3] The clone, in turn, embodies a host of ethical, religious, and aesthetic horrors: the reduction of human beings to mere instrumentalities or commodities (what Giorgio Agamben calls 'bare life'); the impious effort to 'play God' with technology; the spectre of reproduction without sexual difference which leads quickly to fantasies of unleashed homosexual reproduction; the figure of the macho gay male (popularly known as a 'clone') who subverts the reassuring stereotype of the sissy;[4] the spectre of abortion raised by the technique of cloning, which involves the destruction of what some regard as an embryonic organism in order to create a new life-form; the spectre of the

fig. 2 Masked Palestinian fighters
from Betar-Tagar, UK, The Zionist Movement

fig. 3 Cloned Stormtroopers
from *Star Wars: Attack of the Clones*
dir. George Lucas (2002)

'monstrous double' or 'evil twin' who perfectly simulates the 'donor' or 'parent' organism, and threatens to replace it with a new race of aliens, mutants or replicants. The real horror of the hooded suicide bombers, then, is not that there is some monstrous face concealed under the mask, but that when the mask is taken off, the face might be that of a perfectly ordinary person who could mingle among us, turning us against ourselves. The figure of Dolly the Cloned Sheep is not frightening because she is a wolf in sheep's clothing, but because she is a *sheep* in sheep's clothing, impossible to distinguish from the 'real thing' by visual, or even genetic examination. The clone represents an even deeper threat than easily profiled aliens or 'racial others' who 'all look alike', as the racist stereotype would have it. The clones do not necessarily look like each other (thus, no profiling stereotypes are available), but they may very well look exactly like *us*, and thus be indistinguishable and unclassifiable. Like terror, cloning takes the logic of the image as figure of resemblance, similitude and copying to the limit of virulence, toxicity and insidious invisibility.

Perhaps the most vivid fantasy of terrorist as clone (and vice versa) is a report in the online tabloid *Weekly World News* that the 'mad mullahs of Iran and Syria' are cloning 'toddler terrorists' from 'the DNA of ruthless SS men who once formed Adolf Hitler's elite bodyguard'.[5] CIA 'sources' (unidentified) are quoted to emphasise that 'the most insidious part of the scheme is that these killers won't look like Arabs, and no traditional form of racial profiling will work to screen them.' This 'invincible army of "superior" German warriors' will be trained to speak English with an American accent. A 'respected Israeli historian and intelligence expert', Aviv Shimson, supplies the connections between Nazi Germany and Middle Eastern terrorists, reminding us that one of the most 'notorious allies' of the Nazis was Haj Amin el-Husseini, the Grand Mufti of Jerusalem. Islamic fascism's anti-semitic and anti-American alliance with Nazi Germany was only waiting for the technical breakthroughs of human cloning to produce its invisible Aryan army.

Bizarre as these associations of cloning and terrorism may seem, they would not have any efficacy if they did not engage some level of historical reality and collective fantasy in the American populace. The fact is that the onset of the current epoch of terrorism in 2001 was launched in the context of a national debate in the US about cloning and stem cell research. The off-lead in the *New York Times* on 9/11 was, in fact, a story about the National Academy of Sciences report that came out in support of cloning to produce new lines of stem cells. Nor was this some kind of anomaly or coincidence. The lead story in American newspapers throughout the summer of 2001 had been the cloning debate, and the 9 August decision of President Bush to prohibit the development of new stem cell lines. The cloning issue was 'buried', as it were, by the onset of the terrorist attacks, but it seemed to hover over the ruins of the World Trade Centre, as if the grey dust that hung in the air for weeks after their destruction contained traces of the DNA of the victims.

Since 9/11, an intense new epoch in the pictorial turn has opened up, a 'war on terror' triggered by and waged against images. To call this a war of or on images is in no way to deny its reality or to minimise the real physical suffering it entails. It is, rather, to take a realistic view of terrorism as a form of psychological warfare, specifically a use of images, and especially images of destruction, to traumatise the collective nervous system via mass media and turn the imagination against itself. It is also to take a realistic view of the 'war on terror' as quite literally a war against an *emotion* (like 'pity' or 'love' or 'hate'). It is thus a war on a projected spectre or phantasm, a war against an elusive, invisible, unlocatable enemy, a war that continually misses its target, striking out blindly with conventional means and waging massive destruction on innocent people in the process. The aim of terrorism is, in fact, precisely to provoke this overreaction, to lure the 'immune system' of the social body (its military and police powers) into responses that will have the effect of increasing the power of the terrorists, in effect 'cloning terror' in the process of trying to destroy it.[6]

If terrorism is primarily a war of images, however, we must ask what images are and what they are becoming in our time, when the biodigital picture has emerged at the technical frontier of image production and circulation. This necessarily involves a moment of aestheticisation of the images loosed upon the world since 9/11, a consideration of their formal, sensuous, affective properties within the epoch they have come to define. The moment has evidently passed when the image repertoire of the war on terror (the whole sequence, from the attacks of 11 September through the Abu Ghraib photos) can have an immediate political impact. In fact, for many months leading up to the November 2004 Presidential election, it was widely believed that these images were revealing the naked, awful truth about the futility and horror of the War on Terror, and that they would have enough power to bring down the Bush administration. Now that their immediate political urgency is behind us, the moment has arrived for a more considered analysis of what these images mean, even as the historical epoch they marked fades in memory.

2001–4 was an epoch marked and defined by unforgettable and traumatic pictures, from the destruction of the World Trade Centre to the photographs of torture taken in Abu Ghraib prison. I want to trace a pattern in these images which expresses the logic of the biopicture. I have in mind, first, the obvious fact of a new, virulent life afforded to images with the invention of the internet and digital photography, the way images 'clone' themselves, and circulate with incredible rapidity, sometimes reversing their meaning and coming back to haunt their producers. I also have in mind the figure of the terrorist as clone in the sense of 'double', twin or mirror image of his opponent; the spectacle of terror as iconoclasm, the destruction and mutilation of images (especially the image of the human body) as itself an artificially 'produced' image, or 'photo-op'; the recurrence of the headless, faceless, and hooded figure, or what Jean Baudrillard has called the 'acephalic clone', a mindless repository of 'spare parts' or an automaton without will or agency; the reduction of the human form to 'bare life', and the (usually futile) attempt to censor, prohibit and contain these reductive images. I will conclude, finally, with a meditation on the Abu Ghraib photographs, which I believe define a certain kind of end to this epoch, though its consequences are still unfolding for us as I write.

III   The War of Images

Twin Towers

> 'As though architecture … was now merely a product of cloning.'   Jean Baudrillard

The destruction of the World Trade Centre in New York has provided the most memorable image of the twenty-first century so far, destined to join the iconic mushroom cloud as the principal emblem of war and terror in our time, leaving behind it a space known as 'Ground Zero', a label that links it (quite inaccurately) to a nuclear bomb. The 'twin-ness' of the towers and their destruction has frequently been noted: the initial doubling of the image of destruction by the two moments of impact and the two moments of collapse, followed then by the indefinite doubling and redoubling of every detail, every conceivable angle of perspective on the disaster. The towers themselves were, of course, understood as iconic forms in their identical twin-ness and their mutual facelessness. Jean Baudrillard compared them to bearers of digital information, the 'punch card and the statistical graph', 'as though architecture, like the system, was now merely a product of cloning, and of a changeless genetic code'.[7] The World Trade Centre was already a global symbol, a 'world picture' in its own right as well as an epitome of the 'biodigital' moment of the pictorial turn. Its destruction had been foretold since the moment of its building, staged repeatedly in disaster films, and even attempted in the early nineties.

The destruction of the twin towers was a classic act of iconoclasm (the destruction of the 'idol of the other') as the creation of a counter-icon, one that has become, in its way, much more powerful as an idol than the secular icon it displaced. The site was immediately declared 'hallowed ground', the victims apotheosised as heroes and martyrs. This is a process similar to the elevation of the Final Solution from a hideous extermination program into a 'Holocaust', a sacred sacrifice, tech-

fig. 4 Kevin Clarke and Mikey Flowers
From Dust to DNA (2002)
Photo Collage
Permission of the artists

nically, a 'burnt offering'. The monumentalisation of the holy place has proceeded with similar grandiosity, most notably in Daniel Liebeskind's proposed 'Freedom Tower' which, exactly 1776 feet high, and with features such as the 'Park of Heroes', the 'Garden of the World' and 'Memory's Eternal Foundations', will surpass even his Jewish Museum in Berlin as a coercively allegorical contribution to the trauma industry.[8]

A more open and evocative memorial was provided by the Kevin Clarke/Mikey Flowers photo collage of the ruins overlaid by the dust-filled scrim inscribed with the DNA code. (fig. 4: Clark/Flowers: From Dust to DNA)[9] Flowers, an Emergency Medical Technician, took the pictures of the smoldering ruins in the days immediately following 11September, and Clarke (an artist who also lives in lower Manhattan) overlaid the image with the letters of the DNA code (a practice he had been using for a number of years to create what I would call 'deep portraits' or 'biopictures' of human subjects). This image evokes the longing for traces and relics of the victims that was so vividly evident in innumerable informal memorials that attached themselves to the site, and throughout lower Manhattan. But it recodes this longing as a desire for literal biological reanimation, just the reverse of the funerary liturgy, 'ashes to ashes, dust to dust'. The logic of *From Dust to DNA*, by contrast, leads on to 'from DNA to cloned resurrection'. Or if not resurrection, at least identification of the particular victim whose dust has been reclaimed. The Clarke/Flowers image is also perhaps a reminder of the biodigital picture that was already inscribed in the twin towers, their monumental flaunting of doubleness, twin-ness and architectural cloning, and hints at the ironic coincidence of cloning and terror in the summer of 2001. While the men of al Qaeda were making their final plans, while Richard Clarke, the head of US counter-terrorism, was vainly trying to get the attention of the White House to warn them of the impending threat, the Bush administration was preoccupied with stopping the dangerous acceleration of biomedical research in cloning.

Uncle Osama: The Uncanny Double

> 'We have met the enemy and he is us.'   Walt Kelly, Pogo

'Only when modeled, shaped, or even cloned from those interacting with them can terrorists become terrorists,' notes sociologist Vincenzo Ruggiero.[10] The mimetic symmetry between the sovereign and the terrorist is vividly displayed by the TomPaine.com anti-war cartoon of 'Uncle Osama', a graphic clone of Uncle Sam. (fig. 5: Uncle Osama) Uncle Osama hails American recruits with the message: 'I WANT YOU to invade Iraq.' Why? As a recruitment device for al Qaeda. The image illustrates perfectly the assessment of counter-terrorism expert Richard

I WANT YOU
TO INVADE IRAQ

Go ahead. Send me a new generation of recruits. Your bombs will fuel their hatred of America and their desire for revenge. Americans won't be safe anywhere. Please, attack Iraq. Distract yourself from fighting Al Qaeda. Divide the international community. Go ahead. Destabilize the region. Maybe Pakistan will fall — we want its nuclear weapons. Give Saddam a reason to strike first. He might draw Israel into a fight. Perfect! So please — invade Iraq. Make my day.

TomPaine.common sense

Osama says: 'I Want You to Invade Iraq.'
TomPaine.com *features reasons why we shouldn't.*

© 2002 The Florence Fund, PO Box 53303, Washington, DC 20009

NYTimes 9/25/02

Clarke: 'The ingredients al Qaeda dreamed of for propagating its movement were a Christian government attacking a weaker Muslim region, allowing the new terrorist group to rally jihadists from many countries to come to the aid of the religious brethren.'[11] The war in Iraq was a double blessing to bin Laden, and a double mistake by the US. It turned attention away from him and toward Saddam Hussein, who was easily rendered as a symbolic substitute. And it served as a recruiting device for jihadists. The problem is that the irony of this image was evidently lost on many viewers. Its mimicry of the prevailing fantasy was a bit too literal. After all, when George W Bush took his 'Mission Accomplished' bow on the deck of an aircraft carrier, he explicitly linked the war in Iraq to 11 September himself. Uncle Osama could have morphed into Bush himself at that moment, urging young men to sacrifice their lives on both sides, calling for the Iraqi resistance to 'bring it on'.[12]

Hoodwinking Saddam
Wars of images are clone wars. They require a mirroring of the faceless enemy and his acts. Even better is the *headless* enemy, what Jean Baudrillard calls the 'acephalic clone':

> On the other side of the Atlantic Ocean, headless frogs and mice are being cloned in private laboratories, in preparation for the cloning of headless human bodies that will serve as reservoirs for organ donation. Why bodies without heads? As the head is considered the site of consciousness, it is thought that bodies with heads would pose ethical and psychological problems.[13]

If one cannot remove the head, however, hooding it is almost as good as a way of eliminating the 'ethical and psychological problems' presented by the sight of a human face. The so-called 'interrogation hoods' made famous by the images propagated at Abu Ghraib prison have served this double purpose: the hoods serve as torture instruments, rendering the victim helplessly blind and vulnerable to smothering and unpredictable blows, while protecting the torturers own anonymity, and from the possibility of human identification or empathy. The hoods have the effect of stifling the cries of pain, and render the victim faceless and anonymous.

No surprise, then, that the preferred photo op of the American army on entering Baghdad was the hooding of Saddam Hussein's statue with an American flag. (fig. 6: Hooding of Saddam Hussein's Statue) In a moment of temporary sanity, however, it was apparently realised that this image would not suggest liberation from tyranny to most Iraqis or the rest of the world, but would look like a trium-

**fig. 6 Hooding of Saddam Statue with American flag
by Cpl. Edward Chin, April 9, 2003**
AP Photo/Laurent Tebours

phal emblem of American imperial occupation. The hood was quickly removed (but not before it was photographed and circulated throughout the world). The more traditional iconoclastic tactic was then deployed, and Saddam's statue was pulled down. If the aim was to produce a mimesis of the destruction of the World Trade Centre, laying low the phallic verticality of the enemy's monumental erection, it was something of a botched job. Saddam's statue turned out to be difficult to pull down, and it leaned over at a semi-tumescent angle before the engineers were able to complete the job.[14]

Saddam's Dental Examination

The hooding of the head, and especially of the 'head of state', is an ideal strategy for humiliating the enemy in a war of images. But an even more inventive treatment of the 'head' was afforded by the actual capture of Saddam Hussein in December

fig. 7
Saddam's Dental Examination on T-Shirt
Photo by Janice Misurell Mitchell

2003. (fig. 7: Saddam's Dental Examination) The once-powerful tyrant had to be paraded for the cameras in a scene of abjection and humiliation, but not one that would suggest cruelty or torture. Some inspired genius in the Pentagon's media liaison team must have come up with the idea for what became the iconic photo op of Saddam's capture: his dental examination. This image is, in a very precise sense, an inversion of the hooding of the head in that it penetrates the head, goes inside it to illuminate its dark interiors. A video loop of the dental examination, with a tiny flashlight being inserted into Saddam's mouth, lighting up his cheeks from within, was run repeatedly in the hours and days after his capture. The sheer repetition of this image rivalled the repetition of the images of destruction of the Twin Towers, rendering it the single most memorable image of the whole capture episode. Other images, like the removal of lice from Saddam's hair, or shots of the dark interior of the 'spider hole' where he had been hiding, were simply not formally compelling enough to sustain interest. But the dental examination had the virtue of adding several symbolic components to the primary effect of humiliating the 'head of state' in the most literal possible manner. First, it defused any hint of cruelty by staging Saddam's captors as looking after his health, perhaps determining whether he had developed any cavities or abcesses during his underground existence, or preventing him from committing suicide with a cyanide capsule embedded in one of his teeth. Second, it suggested that the US military had finally achieved the elusive objective of total victory, since now it had penetrated 'inside the head' of the head of state. Any remaining secrets would now come to light, and it did not take long, in fact, for the image to be reproduced with a new caption: 'looking for weapons of mass destruction.' Third, the real purpose of the dental examination may well have been to extract a DNA sample from Saddam's mouth, to determine with certainty that the man in US custody was not one of Saddam's many notorious doubles. Of course, if the captured Saddam was a clone, then even a DNA test would be unable to differentiate the original from a copy.

Cloning Bodies

'The human body is the best picture of the human soul.'

Ludwig Wittgenstein, *Philosophical Investigations*[15]

'We don't do body counts.'

General Tommy Franks

Until Spring 2004, the war of images was mainly running in favour of the United States. Inconvenient images of Iraqi civilian casualties had been successfully censored. The American army had made it clear that the Powell doctrine of 'no body counts' (either of 'enemies' or 'innocent bystanders') would be continued. The

only bodies counted, the only bodies that *counted*, were those of American troop
Then, in May 2004, images of bodies began to proliferate in the mass media, an
a new kind of photo op emerges: atrocity photographs and videos of the beheac
ing of American hostages; the dismemberment of American contractors and th
display of their mutilated bodies on a bridge outside the city of Fallujah; the flag
draped coffins of American soldiers; and the scandalous torture photograph
from Abu Ghraib prison. The first two groups of images were photo ops delibe
ately staged by the enemy, the Iraqi resistance. The second two were produced t
Americans themselves. Let's start with the 'enemy images'.

Horrible as they are, the images of decapitation betray a kind of symmetr
with the hooding of Saddam's statue and the dental examination. The justice
an eye for an eye escalates to a head for a head, and a symbolic decapitation
trumped by the staging of the real thing. Although these images were immed
ately declared 'barbaric' and 'savage', decapitation was a standard (and litera
form of 'capital' punishment in European nations up to and including the Fren
Revolution, which invented the guillotine as a 'humane' form of quick and ea
execution, and it is still the legal form of capital punishment in Saudi Arabia toda
The 'clinical' treatment of Saddam's head was answered, in other words, by the 'j
dicial' treatment of American hostages, whose beheadings were accompanied t
the trappings of a legal execution, complete with the reading aloud of the charge
and the circulation of the images on the internet to the global media.

The Fallujah photographs carried the staging of horror to a new extreme. On
March 2004, the bodies of four American contractors ambushed and killed outsi
Fallujah were set on fire, mutilated horribly in a kind of echo of the European pra
tice of 'drawing and quartering', and then the remains of two of them were strur
up as trophies for display from a bridge over the Euphrates river. The behaviour
the crowd of Iraqis before the camera made it clear that the photographs were n
merely the spontaneous recordings of a passing journalist, but staged photo o
meant to outrage the eyes of the enemy.[16] Like the bystanders and participants
American lynching photographs from the early twentieth century, the assemble
crowd expressed unabashed delight in the spectacle they were creating for the can
era, and held up signs declaring Fallujah to be a graveyard for Americans. In co
trast to the decapitations, there is no attempt to stage these photo ops as records
judicial proceedings. They portray the rough, anarchic 'frontier' justice carried o
by an angry (and exultant) mob, a spontaneous act of violence meant to expre
the collective will of the city of Fallujah to be 'the graveyard of the Americans'. O
sensed from the moment that these photographs appeared that this message wou
be taken literally by the Americans, that the city of Fallujah was doomed, and th
collective punishment would be carried out sooner or later. The siege and destru

tion of Fallujah, a city of 300,000 people, was duly executed by American forces right after the American Presidential election in the Fall of 2004.

A corpse is the primeval form of what I have been calling a biopicture. It is 'only an image'–a still, dead, motionless image - of what was once a living form. And yet it is still alive, taboo, uncanny. The mutilation of a corpse is, from a rational perspective, a futile exercise. The person, the subjective consciousness, who was or once inhabited the corpse cannot feel the wounds. And in fact, the wounds are not meant to inflict pain on the actual victim. They are meant to be transmitted in images designed to terrorise the enemy.[17] They are not images *of* trauma, but images designed to traumatise the viewer, especially those who identify with the victim. When propagated by digital reproduction and global circulation they produce a kind of effect quite different from modern(ist) 'shock', which had its therapeutic, defamiliarising aspect. There is nothing like 'shock therapy' in the realm of trauma.[18] These images are designed to overwhelm the viewer's defences, and that is why many of the news services that carried them on 1 April 2004 elected to *blur* them, rendering their contents almost unreadable.[19]

The mutilation of a corpse is thus the mutilation of an image, an act of iconoclasm that is reproduced as an image in another medium–in verbal reports and rumours, in the memory of an impression, in photographs that can be propagated indefinitely. But this is a form of iconoclasm that goes well beyond the prohibition on images shared by Islamic, Jewish and Christian versions of the second commandment. If the human body is created 'in the image of God', and is the sacred handiwork of God, then its mutilation–even as a corpse–is an act of desecration. One of the leading clerics of Fallujah accordingly declared that the mutilation of the contractors' bodies was a 'desecration', and a violation of Islamic law.[20] From a Christian point of view, the mutilations were a double outrage, triggering not only the tribalistic reaction to the treatment of a 'member' of the social body, but also constituting a theological outrage, a crime against God–or the *imago dei*–himself ('desecration' in the fullest sense). The mutilations added force, in other words, to the sense that the US is engaged in a Christian 'crusade' in the Middle East, not just an effort to bring secular democracy to the region. The images were perfectly designed to stoke the passions of a holy war.

Modern warfare is often portrayed as a derealised spectacle, a mere simulacrum on the order of a video game. And indeed, that is the way the American media and its political minders would like to portray it: a war of faceless enemies marching in anonymous ranks to be vaporised by superior weapons from a safe distance. But television also has the capacity, as Edward R. Murrow pointed out long ago, to present the 'little picture', up close and personal. And it can reduce our distance from events, even as it seems to distance us. Marshall McLuhan's vision of a 'global village' has come to pass, not as the idyllic utopia that is often (wrongly) attributed to him, but as the terrifying *immediacy* of viscerally intimate violence portrayed in real time. Archaic forms of tribal violence designed to elicit the tribalistic reactions of the American public can make the global village a very dangerous place, especially when the full force of American military power is mobilised in reaction to a local provocation. And thanks to the invention of digital media, these spectacles, the violent dismemberments of the biopicture, can be cloned indefinitely and circulated globally. They are the poisonous 'gift that keeps on giving', taking on a perverse life of their own in the world's nervous system.

Clonophobia

'The revulsion prompted by cloning points to its problems – the very asexuality of this kind of reproduction; the prospect that cloned human beings will, by constitution, be physically or socially inferior to others; conversely, the possibility that the genetic manipulation of cloning science will bring about a superspecies, an absolutizing of the divide between haves and have-nots; the use of cloned persons, or cloned embryos, as means toward ends belonging to others.'

James Carroll, 'Cloning, Terror, and Our Humanity', *Boston Globe*, 7 January 2003

Perhaps it becomes clearer now why so many scenes of sexual humiliation have come out in the scandal of Abu Ghraib prison. Suspected Arab terrorists must be subjected to this form of dehumanisation because, according to racial profilers like Raphael Patai who provide guidance to US military treatment of Iraqis, 'the' Arab male is extremely insecure about his masculinity.[21] But it turns out the *American* male is too, and what better way to secure one's masculine superiority than forcing another male to submit to domination by women, or to be thrown into piles of anonymous, headless, 'homosexual' bodies?

The famous photograph of the pile of naked, hooded, male bodies served as a screen-saver on one of the computers in the military intelligence office in Abu Ghraib prison. No ordinary 'cover up' of these images seemed possible in May 2004 when they were first released to the public. They could not be completely censored the way the images of flag-draped coffins were. Instead, the neutralising tactic was, as Mark Danner has pointed out, to focus attention directly on the images themselves, 'the garish signboards of the scandal and not the scandal itself'.[22] This focus on symptoms rather than causes facilitated the 'deviant behavior' and 'few bad apples' defence, which scapegoated those seven soldiers who were stupid enough to stage themselves as jubilant torturers within the pictures. All right-thinking people (led by President Bush himself) could declare themselves 'disgusted' at the images and deplore the conduct depicted there. When questions about the causes and the systemic basis for the images were raised, the pornography industry made a convenient scapegoat. The actual architects of the global detention and torture system that these photographs represent were kept invisible and unnameable, except at those moments when they–Geoffrey Miller, Donald Rumsfeld, Albert Gonzalez and others who designed, approved, and justified the flagrant violations of international law and common human decency–emerged to express their horror at the 'deviant' conduct they had made possible and even inevitable.

In Spring 2004 these photographs were greeted by many Americans as the 'smoking gun' that would finally reveal the moral bankruptcy of Bush's 'war on terror', and produce a scandal that would force the resignation of the most incompetent Secretary of Defense in US history. But the images rapidly faded out in the course of the 'news cycle' of the American mass media. They were no longer news within a month, disappearing down the memory hole along with Richard Clarke's revelations about the incompetence of the Bush administration's counter-terrorism policy. The Democratic Party chose not to make them an issue during the election campaign. The system that produced them–the Bush White House, the Pentagon and the shadowy world of 'intelligence'–now seems immune to investigation and exposure. Hundreds of the photographs with reportedly even worse images of rape and child abuse remain classified, and the internet is awash with fraudulent, staged photos that undermine the credibility of even the most firmly legitimated photographs.

So why bring them back now? What is to be seen? Now we can concentrate on the images as symptoms of a systemic problem that goes well beyond the Bush administration, to the 'system beyond the system', the culture that could be exploited by vague bureaucratic euphemisms about 'unlawful combatants',' 'high-value detainees', 'sleep adjustment' and 'enhanced interrogation tactics' to produce these specific images. Now we can see their relation to standard practices in American prisons, to the history of lynching photography (especially in their status as photographic trophies to be circulated, complete with the exultant faces of the torturers), and to the homophobia that is so deeply entrenched in straight American male culture.[23] Now we are in a position to diagnose the systemic problem as a *clonophobia* that provides the general logic of these images. The steps in clonophobia are as follows: 1) project an image of yourself, a narcissistic self-portrait; 2) reverse the valence of that image so that it becomes the 'evil twin' of yourself, the repository of your darkest desires and fears; 3) project that image as a mask, veil or hood to conceal the humanity of another person; 4) subject the person on whom that image has been projected to the most degrading humiliations you can devise.

Why is this clonophobic procedure necessary? Because the 'bad guys' (as they are routinely labelled in American military lingo) do not wear uniforms (except, perhaps, the racial uniforms of brown skin and Arab names): they look like civilians, like the friendly Iraqis the 'war on terror' was supposed to liberate. They do not identify themselves as combatants like our 'honest soldiers' do. They do not obey any rules. And we have no rules for telling the innocent from the guilty, the good guys from the bad guys (85–90 per cent of the detainees in Abu Ghraib prison were innocent, rounded up in random nighttime sweeps; they had little or no intelligence value, and were a product of 'cordon and capture' techniques that treated non-combatants as illegal combatants).[24] That is why the perverse logic of clonophobia has to begin, not with a simple stereotype of 'the other' as a clearly marked alien, but with the *self* as a figure of even deeper anxiety. The racial version of clonophobia is the distinctly American ritual of blackface impersonation, in which the mask is applied to the *self*, not the other, and one temporarily 'assumes the position' of negritude in order to enter a carnival atmosphere of unleashed role reversal. It doesn't seem accidental that the sexual humiliations of the Iraqis were accompanied by a fair amount of sexual experimentation (also documented photographically) by the American MPs themselves. The right-wing radio personality Rush Limbaugh was not completely off-base, then, when he noted that the sexual humiliations of the Iraqi men at Abu Ghraib were something like an 'American fraternity initiation', perhaps even the sort of thing portrayed in the film *Animal House* as the quasi-Nazi initiation rituals of the 'good' fraternity; perhaps even something like George W Bush himself had to endure in his initiation to Skull & Bones at Yale. This is why we must not overlook the obvious signs of obscene enjoyment in the faces of the torturers, the clear signals that they were 'just having fun' with their Iraqi captives. It was, in a certain rather precise sense, all part of the initiation into the brotherhood of American democracy.

Cloning Jesus

'The God of Islam is an idol.'   William Boykin

Or perhaps we should say, initiation into American *Christian* democracy, because the US is, after all, one of the most religious countries in the world, and the war on terror is a holy war, a crusade against evil. In unguarded moments, this view is expressed with remarkable clarity, as it was by Bush's appointee to the position of Undersecretary of Defense for Intelligence, Lt General William Boykin. General Boykin's speeches to Christian audiences have included declarations that 'the God of Islam is an idol', and that the war on terror is a war against 'Satan'. Bush himself, of course, declared the war on terror by characterising it as a 'crusade', an incau-

fig. 8 Hooded Man
US Department of Defense

tious remark that he later avoided (though the language of 'evil' has continued).

The most vivid example of the monstrous double is the image that has now become iconic of the entire Abu Ghraib scandal, and perhaps of the whole 'war on terror'. That is the famous 'Hooded Man' with a black cloak standing on a box of C-rations with electrical wires connected to his hands and genitals. (fig. 8: Hooded Man) It has been obvious since the first appearance of this image that there was something special about it, something that differentiated it from the degrading, pornographic spectacles of enforced nakedness and humiliation that character-ised the other Abu Ghraib photographs. The image is, to begin with, formally simple and memorable, quite unlike the chaotic, almost unreadable piles of naked bodies with their air-brushed genitalia. It achieves an instant recognisability that is easily reproduced in other media. There is also a curious air of dignity about the image, a suggestion of poise and balance under severe stress, that invites the viewer to empathise and identify with the figure despite (or is it because of?) its hooded anonymity. If one tries to project oneself into the experience of the figure, one must imagine being blinded and stifled by the hood, and then terrified with the warning that, if one falls off the precarious pedestal, one will be electrocuted. A few carefully administered electric shocks to sensitive areas of the body would make this seem far from an idle threat. When one combines this empathic exercise with the stillness, symmetry and balance of the image, one notes an immediate paradox, and that is the transformation of an image of humiliation, terror and abjection (as imagined from inside) into a figure of poise (as seen from outside). A fleeting moment of balance has been frozen by the still photograph into an image of endless equilibrium.

The Hooded Man has clearly been transformed into a 'Christ-figure'. It seems very unlikely that this was anyone's intention, though some of the other torture images (a naked, excrement-smeared Iraqi compelled to stand in a cruciform pos-ture with his legs crossed) make one wonder. If the pornographic images seem to record a homophobic ritual of 'fraternity initiation', this one registers an even more profound transformation of the (suspected) terrorist, the tool of Satan, into the avatar of the Christian 'son of god' himself. The figure of the (supposed) Islamic martyr, a warrior prepared to sacrifice himself in holy jihad, is converted into the Christian martyr, the patient 'suffering servant' who endures terrible pain and humiliation without protest, as an expiation for the sins of mankind.[25]

Look at this image through the eyes of an iconologist, and you will see some-thing even more specific, and that is the particular stages of the passion narrative that are echoed by the Man with the Hood. This is clearly not a crucifixion: the arms are at the wrong angle. It is, rather, a synthesis of three distinct moments

fig. 9 Fra Angelico
Man of Sorrows
Bayerische Staatsgemaldesammlungen, Alte Pinakothek, Munich

from the iconography of the passion of Christ: the first is the mocking of Christ (which usually shows him blindfolded); second, the Ecce Homo ('behold the man') when Jesus is presented to the crowd as a mock 'king', wearing the Crown of Thorns, sometimes standing on a pedestal; and third, the 'Man of Sorrows', a non-narrative image that shows Jesus taken down from the cross, his body washed, and often displayed (as in Fra Angelico) with his arms out at 4 and 8 o'clock. (fig. 9: Fra Angelico, Lamentation. Alte Pinakotek, Munich) It also evokes certain treatments of the resurrected Christ, arms extended in a gesture of welcome and blessing.

Although the Abu Ghraib image is generally reproduced as a singular, isolated iconic form, it implies an address to and relation to others that is a central feature of the tortured and dying *imago dei* in Christian iconography. We know that the torturers are not far away, and we know from the pornographic images that they were having a good time, giving the 'thumbs-up' sign to the camera as they gloated over their victims. But this, too, is a central feature of the photographs, which, like canonical scenes of the passion of Christ, incorporate the torturers as an essential part of their iconography. Did Lynndie Englund know that a frequent motif in scenes of the mocking of Christ is the leading of him on a leash? Certainly not. These tableaux are not to be taken as expressions of the intentions of the torturers, but symptoms of the 'system behind the system' that brought them into the world.

It seems only fitting that, in May 2004, just at the moment that American Christians were wallowing in Mel Gibson's sadistic portrayal of torture in *The Passion of Christ*, an image should surface in the mass media that synthesises the phases of the passion into a single memorable icon as a kind of summary of everything accomplished by the American crusade in Iraq. On the one hand, the image is a kind of ideological X-ray, exposing that mission as a Christian crusade that aims to 'convert' the Muslims into Christian martyrs. On the other hand, it provides (like the Uncle Osama poster) a kind of mirror reversal of its intended purpose. Instead of eliciting useful intelligence about the Iraqi resistance, it had the effect of intensifying that resistance, serving as a recruiting poster for jihadists throughout the world, and destroying the last, threadbare alibi for the American occupation of Iraq. By this point in that war, all the pretexts for pre-emptive war – the weapons of mass destruction, the notion of Iraq as a haven for terrorists, the linkage of Saddam Hussein with 9/11 – had been shown to be utter illusions, if not outright fabrications. The only casus belli remaining was the moral crusade of 'liberating Iraq' from tyranny and bringing democracy there, a pretext that was rather effectively undermined by the Abu Ghraib photos, especially this one.

If ever an image has been 'cloned' in the circuits of the mass media, this one was, both in the sense of indefinite duplication, and in the further sense of taking

fig.10 Hooded Man and Statue of Liberty (grafitti)
AP Photo/Karim Kadim

fig. 11 Guy Colwell
***The Abuse* (2003)**
Permission of the artist

on 'a life of its own' that eludes and even reverses the intentions of its producers. The Man with the Hood appeared throughout the world, on television, over the internet, in protest posters, and in murals, graffiti and works of art from Baghdad to Berkeley. It became so ubiquitous and recognisable that it could insinuate itself subtly into commercial advertisements for the I-pod in New York subways, where it merged almost subliminally the figures of 'wired' dancers wearing I-pod headphones, and the Man on the Box with his wired genitals. Within Iraq, it took on a quite specific role in its renaming as, and 'twinning' with, the Statue of Liberty. An Iraqi mural artist, Sallah Edine Sallat, captured this double cloning in a wall painting that pairs the Hooded Man with a Hooded Statue of Liberty. (fig. 10: Sallat, Baghdad Mural: Hooded Man & Statue of Liberty) The difference between the two figures is as simple as black and white–the black robe and hood of the Iraqi, and the white robe and hood (with eyeholes) of the Statue of Liberty, portrayed as a knight of the Ku Klux Klan. The Statue of Liberty's arm is raised, not to hold up the torch beckoning immigrants to America, but to flip the electric switch connected to the wires on the genitals of the Iraqi prisoner. This image undoubtedly took on a bit of extra irony, given the conspicuous inability of the US occupation forces to restore electric power and other vital services to the Iraqi infrastructure.

The cloning of the Man with the Hood was made even more emphatic by San Francisco artist Guy Colwell, who portrayed the figure as *triplets* in a tableau reminiscent of the surrealist artist Paul Delvaux. (fig. 11: Guy Colwell, The Abuse) Three hooded men with wires on their hands and genitals stand on pedestals, stripped naked from the neck down (perhaps to emphasise their connectedness to the pornographic scenes from Abu Ghraib) while American MPs brandish nightsticks and chemical lights, the now-familiar instruments of sodomy, and a blindfolded Statue of Liberty is led into the room, perhaps to 'witness punishment'. The San Francisco gallery that dared to show this image was attacked by vandals and had to shut down, perhaps a forecasting of the American reception of these images.[26] Although images, especially photographs of this sort, are extremely powerful in exposing people to the truth, they are not all-powerful, and they can be neutralised by clever strategies of containment, censorship and outright denial. Even the straightforward realism of the video of Rodney King's beating by Los Angeles police, for instance, was finally overcome by a defence team that cleverly treated the video to a slow-motion, frame by frame analysis that deconstructed its plain evidentiary character. It's as if the longer and more intensely one contemplates these kinds of images, the more opaque they become. As Mark Danner puts it:

> The images themselves… having helped open the door to broader questions of how the Bush administration has treated prisoners in the War on Terror, are now helping as well to

fig.12 Hans Haacke, *Stargazer* 2004

block that door; for the images, by virtue of their inherent grotesque power, strongly encourage the view that 'acts of brutality and purposeless sadism', which clearly did occur, lay at the heart of Abu Ghraib.[27]

Danner's own investigation into the 'hidden story' behind the images (which the official investigations are doing their best to keep hidden) has tried to keep the door open. And the work of Seymour Hersh, and the initial interpretations of them by Susan Sontag and others, have made it clear that a great deal more lies behind the door. Certainly, in a world where the notion of human rights and international justice had any force of law, the United States' actions in Iraq would be condemned as those of a rogue state placing itself above the law. The flagrant disregard for international law that was expressed by the highest officials of the Bush administration (including the President) would, in a just world, be grounds for criminal proceedings. But we do not live in a just world, and international law has no way of enforcing itself. So the question remains: what is to be done with and about these images once their 'hidden story' has been revealed, and their political efficacy has (at least for the moment) been exhausted?

The answer, I think, lies in that 'inherent grotesque power' that Danner observes in the images. Although this power can have the effect of blocking a concentration on the narrative and documentary meaning of the photographs, it can at the same time open up new dimensions of meaning in them–what I have called the 'system behind the system' that made them possible–and that made something very like these images inevitable. What I am suggesting, in other words, is that there is something more to be learned from these pictures than the story of what happened at Abu Ghraib, and who is to blame for it. These images were, after all, paid for with the tax dollars of American citizens. We own them, and must own up to what they tell us about who we are, and what we are becoming in the age of the biodigital picture.

Let Hans Haacke have the final word in his stunning image, *The Stargazer*, (fig. 12) which shows a man in an orange jump suit with a star-spangled blue hood over his head. This image summarises perfectly the whole complex of biopictures we have been exploring, from the 'acephalic clone' to the hooded terrorist or torturer to the hooded terror suspect transformed into a torture victim. The hood as an instrument to produce the faceless anonymity and blindness of the torture victim has been synthesized with the emblem of American sovereignty, summarising the American 'war on terror' as the self-destructive process it has been.[28] The curious mirroring of the torturer and the victim is eloquently expressed by a subtle ambiguity about the location of agency in the figure. On the one hand, the star-spangled hood stages this figure (like the hooded Man on the Box, or the statue of Saddam Hussein) as the passive, suffering trophy of American power. On the other hand, the man's white skin and relaxed arms (no 'stress positions' here) and the title of 'Stargazer' hint that this man has pulled the hood over his head all by himself. Stargazing Americans have indeed hoodwinked themselves with a peculiar combination of ignorance and idealism, blindness and innocence, a refusal to understand the consequences of their invasion and occupation of Iraq, coupled with the utopian rhetoric of freedom and democratisation that has been employed throughout this war. So Haacke's image may also be suggesting that the wearer of this hood is capable of removing it and seeing things as they are. Whether the American people are ready to look without blinking at this and the other images of the war on terror, to face what they have done to Iraq, to themselves and to the world order, is quite another question.

RESPONSE TO WJT MITCHELL

Griselda Pollock

Musing on the role of certain iconic images of recent atrocity, destruction and torture that form a visual history of the United States of America's troubled entry into the twenty-first century, Tom Mitchell offers us a new chapter in his study of the 'pictorial turn'. The new dimension hinges around the *bio-digital image* that, in various ways, conjugates the always fragile and mutable human(istic) body, now leaking into the post-human body as code (DNA), with the rapidly expanded and widely accessible digitalised forms of image-creation and dissemination – a choice of words on my part that also tries to hold the logical and the physiological together with the often deeply sexual unconscious of verbal rhetoric.

My major concern lies with the use of the journalistic proposition 'cloning terror' as a means of analysis of highly charged and politically complex historical events that themselves replay but also revise the historical legacies that determine them. While the inevitability of rhetoric often serves to illuminate the novelty of a situation, it can also confuse and even distort.

Terrorism is not a war of images even though the image-world is clearly one of its propaganda arenas. Terrorist bombings are real violence causing indescribable mutilations and suffering. They leave scattered and dismembered body parts that are never imaged. In place of the ghastly horror of what even do-it-yourself explosives do to the body, we are offered iconic images of the aftermath through mangled cars, burned-out buses, collapsed buildings. I am interested to ask: what can we bear to see – as well as never see? In 1945 there was no alternative but to show in graphic detail photographs of the atrocity because words so palpably failed before the unimaginable. In the case of the Twin Towers, however, we had to watch the so-called real footage over and over precisely because we were so well prepared. Through video games and disaster movies we were so used to its computer-generated simulation in films such as *Independence Day*, which staged a world threatened by an alien amoral other bent on destruction. Furthermore, that process of aestheticisation by showing the images of cause and effect – crash and collapse – involves some evasion. The collapse of the Twin Towers after the assault seems to have in part been due to the architectural design faults that failed to contain the fires in the higher floors and thus melted the entire metal infrastructure within an unexpectedly brief period of time.

The repeated viewing of the attack on and collapse of the Twin Towers was not, I would suggest, a cloning of the image, but a sign of a traumatically induced repetition-compulsion through which symbolic mastering of the traumatising loss might slowly be assumed in the manner Freud postulated with the famous story of his grandson's game of fort-da. In difference from Mitchell, therefore, I would stress the subject's encounter and transformation via that encounter with the image rather than the image's proliferation as if it were some kind of organism: cloned. I would rather introduce the psychoanalytical concept of doubling.

In 'the Uncanny' 1919 Freud tracks the psychological foundations of the sensation of uncanny anxiety through the concept of the double first explored by Otto Rank. The double originates in an infantile attempt to overcome a dread of extinction. Sublimated and transformed culturally, this motivation generates the projection of an immortal soul or the belief in a resurrected self such as the Egyptians elaborated in their culture of the afterlife complete with replication of the living self encasing the embalmed dead body. Formed optimistically in infantile fantasy, the double, however, turns uncanny in its later return; it becomes the harbinger of the death it was incited to forfend. Doubling with its inherent inversion and displacement, moreover, links back with repetition, introducing, however, the disturbing shift of the mirror that reverses the image. Although what we see in the doubling of the mirror-image appears identical, it is not. Positionally, it is the opposite and thus entirely different in its orientation, presenting the viewer with an 'other' self made radically strange, no longer secure in its imagined self-knowledge and localised delimitation. As the argument progresses, Freud allows into view the deeper source of the uncanny as the radical alterity that inhabits the subject: not only its own unconscious but the non-human dimension beyond the unconscious registered in the death drive symptomatised by the compulsion to repeat. In one of his strangest texts, *Beyond the Pleasure Principle* 1921, Freud proposes the most radical of psychic theoricisations – the death drive – by means of reminding us that the strangest of all phenomena with which the psyche struggles is the coming of life itself, the electro-chemical shock that jolts inanimate matter into life at the level of the initial cell. Why I invoke Freud is precisely not to set psychic against biological but to draw back into view the difference between his difficult acknowledgement of the dialectical transformation of physiological life into psychic representation through which alone we know it, fantasise, or register its pulse as radical, unthinkable but active alterity.

The biologisation of the terrorist as virus or contamination, however, as a kind of disease creeping unseen through society as an amoral force of violence that does not value human life, its own or the other's, per se falls dangerously into the racialising rhetoric that I presume the American liberal left wishes to denounce with these kinds of analysis. This again makes unclear the difference between a rhetoric used to register the nature of anxiety in face of a new enemy (what of sleeper cells of Cold War espionage days?) and the nature of fascist thinking that is defined precisely by the suspension of the shared humanity of the other because that other is represented in reduced, biologised terms. Hence the matching visions of resurrected raptors and T-Rexes and replicating terrorists. Once hooded for anonymity in the perpetration of crime, the new suicidal enemy makes his or her own videos to secure their claim to posthumous martyrdom and renown.

To clone is to use the DNA of one living organism to replicate an identical copy that is not 'fertlised', hence mediated, by difference which is, as evolution teaches, the basis of creativity and transformation. Cloning is, I suggest, an inadequate metaphor for the proliferation of the socio-historical factors that might increase the number of jihadists prepared to fight against the Allies in Iraq or elsewhere. The political is not only midwifed by longer plaits of history, but the complex product of 'many determinations and relations' (Marx) which need to be distinguished from, although they often impinge upon, the ethical and the aesthetic. I find the transposition of cloning, however metaphorically, to a scene of political and historical events such as the insurgency in Iraq or the dissemination of images of Allied prison abuse both misleading and conceptually confusing. What fosters recruitment or preparedness to die is not cloning or even twinning but a political situation completely screened by the use of such terms. Furthermore, the reviewing of the West through the mirror-image of the terrorist cannot be used to confuse the fundamental, political differences between flawed democracies, however politically misguided we feel their administrations to be, and various forms of fascist behaviour, however just their sense of oppression might be. Cloning is not reproduction, but active connivance to produce the identical: thus it is ahistorical. Its use erases much of the political complexity that alone allows us to grasp the aftermath of a totalitarian sectarian state torn between competing models of its political future.

Cloning seems also to come into play in Mitchell's text as a means of reconfiguring the iconological recurrence of a visual trope. What makes an image iconic such as that of the hooded man so central to Tom Mitchell's argument? This has been a central puzzle for art historians who try to think what makes art *historical?* What allows art to have a history at all since the aesthetic might be claimed as transcending historical particularity. How do particular semiotic systems transfer beyond the semantic community in which they were produced? Formalism allowed us to bypass the semiotic question that iconological analysis takes as its central problem. The mnemonic function of gestures and figurations that are called upon by image-makers when they need to charge an image with an emotional freight (the echo of the pathos of the crucified in the photo of the man on the box) was named by Aby Warburg *pathos formel*, placing the affective rather than the cognitive as the means of historical transport precisely because he argued that the image operates symbolically rather than purely semiotically in the *interval* between the conscious and unconscious, between the historically contingent and the structurally recurrent which twentieth-century theory named 'the symbolic'.

In introducing both Freud's theory of the uncanniness of the double and Warburg's theory of 'the iconology of the interval' that hinges emotion and thought, time and system, I wanted to allow psychic ambivalence rather than biological replication into play.

The most horrific image of the attempt to reconstruct an individual from some remnant of their DNA code occurred in *Alien Resurrection* where Ripley (Sigourney Weaver) reappears only to be revealed as a mutant behind whose apparently flawless reproduction in human form lie two horrors. Ripley is a mutant combining her own and the Alien's DNA, enhancing her powers but splitting her loyalties dangerously. The second is the discovery of all the horrific—and acutely suffering—failed versions of this grotesque experiment to regenerate her who beg to be released into death. This scene confronts Ripley with multiple doubles across whom is disseminated any remnant of coherent selfhood. The *Alien* movies internalise and yet narratively problematise what I would identify as a legacy of 'the concentrationary universe': what Cayrol and Resnais also named in their warning of recurrent fascism at the conclusion their collaboration *Night and Fog* 1955 as 'the concentrationary disease'. Significantly depoliticised, the Company with its robotic technocrats and scientific officers, created to look or pass as humans and who, usefully lacking the sentimental susceptibility to human compassion and species identification, are exclusively loyal to the commercial profit motif of their creators and managers, insinuates into popular culture a fascist vision that reveals how the latter lines the underside of unmitigated capitalism. Fascism suspends the right to life of fellow-humans whose humanity is annihilated by decree of power. Our only resistance to its invasive corruption of ethics and permeation of aesthetics in both untrammelled capitalism accumulation as well as fundamentalist terrorisms of all kinds is a political understanding based on deep historical knowledge sensitised by awareness of 'the psychic life of power'.

DYING
SEEING
FEELING

TRANSFORMING THE ETHICAL SPACE OF FEMINIST AESTHETICS

Griselda Pollock

Thinking memory and art together involves articulating art with trauma and its foreclosure.[1]

Wit(h)nessing the traumatic Thing-Event cannot give a proper witnessing concerning the event, but it attests to its uniqueness and validity, creating a space for it in the world by aesthetic means that becomes of ethical value.[2]

I   Photography and Trauma Culture: the Orphic Gaze

Working on the process of moving from trauma to cultural memory, I am concerned with the problem of looking back, of that space between memory and history. I am worrying away at the historian's problem of reviewing the image archive which serves at once as *evidence* of an event (the document) and of its institution as history (the archive): a condition that requires a retrospective witness to an event otherwise lost in the passage of time. Thus we encounter the ethical as the gaze of retrospect.[3]

Barthes argued that truly traumatic photographs are rare: 'for in photography the trauma is wholly dependent on the certainty that the scene "really" happened: *the photographer had to be there* (the mythical definition of denotation).'[4] The photograph is a witness of an event we otherwise retrieve from a historical, hence rhetorical, distance that 'sublimates and pacifies' the traumatic which is itself 'a blockage of meaning'. Photography and trauma are already involved in an internal contradiction. Since its invention, we have relied on photography to function as a privileged verification of events we might otherwise never know. In the twentieth century, photography was called upon to verify what we could not even imagine and hence not believe.[5] Yet in being so directly contiguous with the event, the photograph risks becoming as ahistorical as trauma itself. Its shock value is directly in inverse proportion to its knowledge value. Denotation cannot survive connotation. Barthes places the trauma registered by the existence of the photograph, rather than its content, on the side of indexical denotation.

This overlooks the condition of photography: the gaze of both the photographer and his/her substitute, the viewer. The (f)act of someone seeing, registered by the photographic apparatus as indexical proof of that look in time, defines, to some significant extent that may or may not be mobilised, the effect of the image on its viewer, on the someone who looks at the photograph – the existence, but not the rhetoric or form, of which is witness to an event or a moment in time. That moment is for us inconceivable since meaning is a product of paradigmatic accumulation reviewed from elsewhere and later. Barthes argues, furthermore, that supplementing this denotational, evidential level tied at once to actual time and to the no-time of the extreme situation that overwhelms as traumatic, the photograph of a catastrophic event is, however, depleted at the connotational level. He says it is the photograph about which there is nothing to say.

I assume that this means that the intensity and immensity of what it has witnessed overwhelms whatever else we might be tempted to say about its manner of representation because the traumatic substance demands an ethical rather than either an aesthetic or a cognitive reaction to what we now, too, witness, via its perpetual mediation: its ahistorical present. If the photograph were to generate a discourse beyond its indexicality, would that not be necessarily other to its structure as event and encounter with another's catastrophe that is the death of meaning and the positions from which to make sense of it? If included in discourse, the photograph would then evidence, for instance, a history of photography and its tropes, a history of events and their narratives, questions of form or quality and so forth. On the other hand, such traumatic photographs, once *repeated* for their documentary, knowledge-value in books on wars or history, become the talismans of something quite other: namely, cultural memory, furnishing a visual access to a past in the museum or history book that raises the spectre of memory by means of the representations' indexically uncanny, but now iconic, relation to lost events. Such memory production may be traumatising. But, as paradigmatically corralled icons of cultural memory, it is hard to recover the traumatic quality of each image precisely in the terms of an unrepeatable indexicality.

A particular photograph appears regularly in museums dedicated to the memorialisation of the Holocaust. I first encountered it in a large anthology of pho-

fig. 1
Photograph of Nazi soldier shooting mother clinging
to child, variously located at Czechoslovakia or Ukraine
from The Pictorial History of the Holocaust

tographs of the Holocaust, the album titled *The Pictorial History of the Holocaust.*[6] (fig. 1) Then I found it again – recognising in that repetition a new significance attached to its selection – at the Holocaust Memorial display in the Spertus Museum in Chicago which I visited in 1997. In both cases it was untitled, unlocated, unspecified except as a German soldier shooting a woman in an unknown location. Only in 2004 did I discover another reproduction that tied it to a specific history. In *The Pictorial History of the Third Reich*, the image was reproduced as a double-page spread with the following caption: 'When Heydrich the hangman was killed by the Czechs, every man, woman and child in Lidice was killed; the village was then burned to the ground.'[7] (fig. 2a) Here I discovered that the first version was cropped, excluding a huddled group to the right of the mother and child. Then, in 2005, the catalogue to the newly reopened and designed museum at Yad Vashem, *To Bear Witness*, illustrated this same, extended image, captioning it as evidence of an *Aktion in Ivangorod, Ukraine, 1942.* (fig. 2b)

fig. 2a
from The Pictorial History of the Third Reich

It is one of the curious facts about the history of representation and the Holocaust that for decades, the normal scholarly identification of photographs for location, photographer and what they actually witness was missing. Sybil Milton was one of the first to begin the task and in the later 1990s a new generation of scholars began to work on Holocaust photography in all its varied aspects.[8] For many decades, the sheer horror seemed to overwhelm the normal categorising imperative so that unlocated and unidentified images floated freely across the varied museum, book and media sites, as icons of the event, becoming generic rather than historically identified in terms of what was being witnessed, and above all by whom and why.

In the three crops of the actual photograph (fig. 3) the reproduction quality of the book radically modifies the photograph we see. In addition, cropping and contrast alter the preferred position of viewing because of the amount of ground that is allowed between viewer/photographer and the event, the amount of visible

fig. 2b
Aktion in Ivangorod, Ukraine, 1942

detail that will stimulate or frustrate vision. In the Yad Vashem catalogue the image is reproduced panoramically across a double-page spread. Its quality, however, suggests that it has been grabbed from within a film. The extended landscape format and reduced foreground bring us, the viewers, closer to an action that in fact becomes derealised by the degree of blur created by (what seems to be) its relation to the filmic process. The viewer is placed in greater proximity to the action/ Aktion and the dominant contrast is between ground and figures who are blocked in bold, dark silhouette. In *The Pictorial History of the Holocaust*, with its portrait format, starker contrasts eliminate the background and bleach the foreground so that the two figures, the killing man and the dying woman, arrest our attention in a dramatic duet of gender and death. In the much cheaper and dubious *Pictorial History of the Third Reich* a general graininess of poor-quality reproduction evens out the strange expanse of grassy field in which we have soldier and mother with child on one page and then the huddled mass of three or four figures on the right,

fig. 3
Anonymous Aktion in Ivanagorod, Ukraine 1942
Collection Jerzy Tomaszewski

the fold of the binding dividing the two arenas.

The contested captioning serves to reveal the non-unitary character of all the events subsumed under the belated and confusing term 'the Holocaust'. Does the image mark an event in Czechoslovakia or the Ukraine in 1941 or 1942? Between the necessity of knowing, so that the image can function evidentially, and the fact of it existing, which functions traumatically, what should be our ethical position in relation to viewing any such image as the proof of someone's death and suffering? The existence of this photograph is not like those created by the liberating forces for the purposes of proving to an unbelieving world the atrocity they were seeing for themselves. Who took this photograph and why? How did it survive? Why would a perpetrator document this scene?[9]

The ubiquity of this photograph as a kind of mnemonic for the mass atrocities of the Holocaust forces us to ask: Why was this photograph chosen, and why so often? Is it traumatic or is it iconic and hence a fetishising displacement of what its existence indexes? Is it, in its reduced form of soldier and mother and child, somehow more bearable to look upon because its stark simplicity reiterates some deeper, mythic troping of gender and death: normalising the aggression of masculine violence, and the suffering of woman as the perpetually dying?[10] Is it repeatable because mythically the mother is not only the giver of life but also the dreaded portal of mortality? Undated, unlocated except as a singular moment of the military executions of civilian populations that took place in the Soviet Union after the German troops invaded in the summer of 1941, the photograph is, however, both more and less than representative of the chaotic photographic memory archive of this experimental method of killing, preceding the enactment of the industrialised Final Solution.

A single soldier is being photographed at the precise moment at which a bullet from his aimed rifle has lifted the body of a clothed woman holding her child into the air. Death is happening before the eyes of the camera positioned at right angles to the event it registers; the click of its shutter must have coincided almost precisely with the pulling of the trigger, a doubling that renders the photograph itself a deadly witness as well as a witness to dying. The photograph is starkly divided into two sections, neither of which locate the scene nor provide identification for the photographic point of view. The curvature of the lighter ground that forms the foreground and lower half of the photograph might be the edge of a pit, the edge of an abyss into which this momentarily raised and suspended body still hovering between living and being dead will, in a moment that will never come, fall lifeless – and what we ask of the child? Is this an experiment in killing two with one bullet, is this the reason for the solitariness, and for the proximity? Is this the last survivor of a mass execution, all of whom now lie in the pit beyond, the gaping hole in the centre of the photograph in this no-land of destruction? Is this a political execution of a resistance fighter additionally tortured by being made to take her child with her to her death?

In the historically created difficulty of knowing the conditions and context of this image, two things serve my purposes here. One is formal, the other psychoanalytical; yet neither is truly separable. The almost classical formal decision of the photographer to 'shoot' this moment as a composition does not *at all* catch the chaos of what we otherwise know of the historical process of mass *Einstazgruppen* killings whose excess and unprecedented yet organised violence has no prototype in the archive of cultural memory.[11] Other photographs of this process are more drenched in the terrible pathos of the methodical violence of forcing people out of their homes and towns, making them dig trenches, stripping them of their clothes in chilly weather conditions and as an act of traumatising dehumanisation, before forcing them to line up and move in procession towards a summary execution that they can hear being inflicted on those ahead of them in this queue.[12] Such images, which I will not show here since they risk inflicting by exposure some of that pain upon those trapped under the documenting perpetrators' gaze, have no formal shape, and it is often hard to discern the meaning of the image since what it shows has no precedence in the annals of art and visual culture which might shape the photographic unconscious in choosing such and such an angle, moment or scene.

In this photograph (fig. 1), however, a predetermined aesthetic derived from a genealogy that runs from Jacques Louis David (*Oath of the Horatii* 1784) and Francisco Goya (*Third of May, 1808* 1814) to Edouard Manet (*Execution of Maximilian* 1867) finds in this scene a powerful formal opposition between the militarised, deadly certainty of the killing man seeking to inflict death as he looks down his phallic prosthesis and, on the other hand, the almost fused conflation of the woman and child, clasped together in a final embrace of failed maternal protection. This becomes, therefore, the siting of the feminine, annihilated but also deflecting the full horror of this seen event by the normalisation of a feminine troping of protective vulnerability and dying.[13]

Thus, in the two cases that crop the image, (fig. 1 and 2) the excision of the other group and the dramatic confrontation between soldier and mother appears overdetermined as a formal structuring from the other scene, the phallocentric unconscious, by means of which the confrontation with criminal atrocity becomes an image that we can bear to look upon even while it is shown to us as evidence of what should traumatise us.

Who are we now as we look again and again at such a photograph? With what gaze – created by the action of making of a photograph in such circumstances – are we potentially aligned, whatever our own conscious political, historical or social resistance to its interpellation, by the internal absenting of the frame from which the photograph was taken? If the photograph's existence is indexical of such a moment, its own aestheticising formal construction effaces its location and the political absence of an ethics involved in this doubled 'shooting'. The photograph formally evacuates the signs of its own productive hence ideological location, its purpose; it does not tell us who was there to stand by with camera instead of a gun to mark the triumph? the duty? the beauty? the trauma? or the crime? of this moment whose meanings are so terrifyingly politically unstable and yet, in gendered terms, so certain. Does/can the photograph pass its image of this event onto us as trauma or are 'we', its imagined viewer, saved/protected/positioned by the gap that yawns between the execution and the place of viewing mediated by the space of composition? Might we be positioned with what, only in retrospect and from a non-fascist and feminist subject position, we can name a genocidal gaze that

Orphically kills again as it looks back?[14]

No one can engage in this debate about looking (back) on atrocity through photography without reference to the work of Susan Sontag, who resumed her discussions of photography and trauma in her book about photography and the pain of others in 2003.[15] Let me remind you first of another iconic photograph, from the liberator archive, posed and taken by American war photographer Margaret Bourke-White after the liberation of Buchenwald for *Life* Magazine dated 7 May 1945. (fig. 4) It stands apart from the many that form the horrific archive for all its figures are survivors, blessedly clothed and still, just, alive. What interests me is the encoding of a gaze.

Bourke-White has composed her image across the horizontal axis with no relief of background as a potentially limitless frieze of faces who stare out at the viewer from another world. Yet those spectres who look at us, the spectators, are divided from us by a fence that cuts horizontally across their prisoners' vertically striped garb as a barely visible barrier. What these men have seen and what they will never cease to carry as images burned into hunger and pain-dulled minds, our sight of them from this side of that frontier cannot imagine. The photograph makes them the metonyms of their own unimaginable trauma that is not shown but is encrypted in their deadened gaze. Beyond the limits of all representation, before all that they experienced there, representation of their suffering fails. Yet the structure of the photograph indexes something significant: a gap and their suspension as survivors between two worlds, two deaths: the death their humanity suffered in that place and the relief of a death their bodies will later deliver—or that they will, like Primo Levi, Paul Célan, Jean Amery and so many others, actively seek by their own hands. Yet, for us, not to look back, not to consider again and again this horizon of our present that is cut into history at that razored wire, is to obliterate all that these men look for, mediated into history by the photographer's presence, in meeting whoever is there, on the other side of the wire, any time the image is viewed. The photograph installs an ethical appeal to us as the missing *human* other, the necessary witness that, in this 'event without a witness', as Dori Laub defined the event, can partially restore a shared human bond.[16]

Hardly equivalent in horror and abjection to the myriad images that were rushed down the wires to the world's newspaper readers, Bourke-White's photograph from Buchenwald once shared with those I choose not to show the power of a terrible novelty. As Susan Sontag, the cultural critic who mused so instructively on photography long before it had attracted much serious theorisation, wrote of a moment in her life in July 1945:

One's first encounter with the photographic inventory of ultimate horror is a kind of revela-

fig. 4
Margaret Bourke-White
Photograph of the liberation of Buchenwald, May 1945
Courtesy Margaret Bourke-White / Time & Life Pictures / Getty Images

tion, the prototypically modern revelation; a negative epiphany. For me, it was the photographs of Bergen-Belsen and Dachau which I came across by chance in a bookstore in Santa Monica in July 1945. Nothing I have ever seen – in photographs or in real life – ever cut me as sharply, deeply instantaneously. Indeed it seems plausible to me to divide my life into two parts, before I saw those photographs (I was twelve) and after, though it was many years before I understood fully what they were about.[17]

Susan Sontag bears witness to a sight that forever changed her life. But she asks:

What good was served by seeing them? They were only photographs – of an event I had scarcely heard of and could do nothing to affect, of suffering I could hardly imagine and could do nothing to relieve. When I looked at those photographs something broke. Some limit had been reached, and not only that of horror; I felt irrevocably grieved, wounded but part of my feelings started to tighten; something went dead; something is still crying.[18]

Typical as a defence against the threat of the traumatic image, a certain withdrawal or an overaffectivity floods the viewing subject. Individuals as well as cultures defend themselves against these terrible wounds and what was once the overpowering impact of a real transmitted by the photograph becomes derealised by the very existence of the image under its repeated exposure.

To suffer is one thing; another thing is living with the photographed images of suffering, which does not necessarily strengthen conscience and the ability to be compassionate. It can also corrupt them. Once one has seen such images, one has started down the road of seeing more and more. Images transfix and images anaesthetise. An event becomes more real than it would have been if one had never seen a photograph. But after repeated exposure to images it also becomes less real.[19]

Susan Sontag seems to suggest images *happen* to us: marking us by an exposure to a sight. That is, there is a subject who is affected by the encounter with *an image* of the pain of the other. Images may wound *us*, can transfix *us*, Medusa-like in the confrontation with an indexical witness to horror that breaches the outer ramparts of our discrete subjectivities to lodge the pain of others in our memories. Of a terrible event, photographs can also be traumatising, drawing from the Greek root of this word the idea of both the cut or a wound, but mostly the wound that pierces the defences of the psyche. Yet Susan Sontag suggests that even the most shocking of images of atrocity towards the fellow human cannot retain its initial power. This shock of the first time may happen for individuals as they too come across this archive, marking the date of the encounter as the passage from innocence to an unbearable knowledge that she felt as a decisive breach. But as a culture, the repeated image cannot hold this terrible rupture before us any more. The Orphic gaze kills the power of the traumatic encounter by virtue of our inevitable defences resuscitated by repetition – and hence anticipation.[20] The image becomes known as the image of ...

Although no repetition dulls the recollection of that moment of first encounter that seemed to mark a burning line in time: before and after the knowledge the image traumatically projected into her being, Susan Sontag must admit that repetition does *inure* us. The photograph of Holocaust atrocity and suffering – and these are differently adjusted possibilities of what we are shown – guarantees the evidence of first-hand witnesses that defies the deniers. Now of course, in the age of digital fabrication, that last tenuous and indexical link has been severed and all reality is in *potentia* virtualised. So we swing back from the initial function of the indexical photographic archive as proof, witness in the first person, the image alone able to register in its poverty something of the horror the rhetoric of language could not encompass without returning it to known tropes, to think about other modes of encounter via an image archive that becomes a transport to and from the suspended historical moment of this and other traumas mediated to us by both public and familial photographic traces.

II

    At the end of a sun-filled day, disaster ... at the beginning catastrophe

Let me introduce another image of the pain of others, one that includes a doubled position of viewing which qualifies this question of who we are when we look at images and what images do to frame and condition our subject positions as viewers, onlookers or readers. In an unsigned and undated canvas Breughel pictured the scene from Ovid's *Metamorphoses* that gives this large landscape its textual anchorage: *The Fall of Icarus.* (fig. 5)

Icarus was the son of Daedalus the legendary artist and creator. Flying too near the sun, Icarus's waxen wings melted and he plunged helpless to his watery death. Destroyed between the necessary but also deadly elements, light and water, Icarus allegorises ambition, hubris and tragedy. Faithfully reproducing the poet's moral message about the quotidian indifference of the earthbound working men – the ploughman, the shepherd and the fisherman, ruled by the cyclical rhythms of seasonal labour – to the heroic disaster that happens within their working spaces but not their confined life-worlds of labour and reproduction of life, Breughel's painting endlessly incites writing and response. If I now pluck it out from its place in the visual choreography of art history in the Musée Royale des Beaux Arts in Brussels and from its many citational sites in modern literature – Auden's poem of that title comes to mind – and from my own memory of direct encounter with a fellow art historian who has also written a feminist text upon it, in order here, to frame it as an image of the pain of others, I call upon it to answer some questions about how paintings function between art and ethics and the problem of trauma and inurement. To follow that through I want momentarily to remind the reader of a photograph that set me thinking about this genealogy with a difference,

In September 2003 *The Observer* featured Associated Press photographer Richard Drew's series of photographs that he started taking at 9.41am on the morning of 11 September 2001. I think I am looking at digitally enhanced close-ups of a still sequence that has the effect of appearing as frame-by-frame break-up of film. These images were not shown at the time. They came to light later. They were published in *The Observer* on 7 September 2003 (the second anniversary edition) under the title 'The Falling Man'. They were framed by a discussion of the taboo on showing these photographs, themselves existing as Richard Drew's compulsive photographic witness to an unfolding event. The hesitation about publica-

fig. 5
Breughel. *The Fall of Icarus*
Courtesy Musees Royaux des Beaux Arts, Brussels

tion concerned sensitivity to the unknown identity of the individual thus shown on his way to his horrible death as one tiny moment of a vast catastrophe. As in so many instances of this event, the frame immediately shifts from the political documentation of an event witnessed by the news photographer to that of portraiture, individuation and familiarisation of a person with mourning relatives in which this image becomes a memento of a singular death and a family's grief.

Crumpled newsprint gives the reproduction its own locality, reminding us of the material conditions of the circulation of images. In the zoomed-in close-up that artificially takes human sight closer to what was from the normal viewing distances a tiny almost unrecognisable spot of movement, a man is eternally suspended against a massive Bridget Riley whose variegated stripes perhaps residually mark the volumetrics of the skyscraper. Here they have become instead a formal index of the verticality that both confirms the fall and holds it forever above the earth where an already happening dying will be unimaginably horribly affirmed. Is Drew's gaze as deadly as the photographer in the Ukraine or can the image in its own semiotic structuration of elements and focalisation *difference* the Orphic viewer of this man's dying?

Icarus, the heedlessly overambitious son of a creator-artist, plunges to his allegorical death that Breughel registers with complete evacuation of dignity. All we see are naked legs of the inverted man as his head and torso disappear beneath the water. Yet closer inspection reveals an upturned face just visible beneath the waves. (fig. 6)

A moment of intersubjective connectivity is instituted only when examination of the painting's surfaces reveals this almost obscured invocation of the subjectivity of Icarus in his final and eternal appeal to someone else than the indifferent bystanding workers. It is a painting of a face that invokes an ethical other to confirm the singular nature of this event as human tragedy. Icarus, as it were, looks back from beyond his dying to call out, visually, for an Other to witness it and affirm its tragic status.

This incident is miniaturised by scale. The viewer must work hard to see its strange dislocation of face and ungainly body while everywhere within the painting there are other focalising elements to catch our attention and narratively signify inattention or preoccupation and thus conflict between the daily movements of human life-making and the extraordinary ambition of human attempts to defy its materiality and earthbound destiny. These are not the shocked bystanders shouting–'Oh my! He's fallen!' as they are recorded screaming, 'Oh my God! They're jumping!' in New York on September 11. Nor are they witnesses within the paintings that serve semiotically to mark looking and seeing as the cognitive activity (see for instance how this works in Caravaggio's *Betrayal of Christ* 1602) and the theological aesthetics of display or showing and seeing. By contrast, the formal element of the tightly framed photographs by Richard Drew inscribes into the structure of the photograph a singular viewing of a singular event. He has paid attention. He was called to witness in a form that becomes a document both of the event and of the witnessing. Where does that leave us?

Breughel's extraordinarily arresting painting sucks the viewer into itself, the diffusion of the colour that logically stems from the setting sun creates a cone of brightness into which the viewer's look is drawn, forging the space for an experience of subjectivity that is independent of the depicted characters who are not surrogates. The painting creates a distance as well as summoning us into its fictive space around which we travel interrogatively, putting its elements into semiotic play, finding meaning in the dissonance of its combination of a death and on-going daily life. This death occurring in the presence of the indifferent cohabitants of this shared world is not, I think, traumatic but rather it is made dramati-

fig. 6
Breughel. *The Fall of Icarus (detail)*
Courtesy Musees Royaux des Beaux Arts, Brussels

cally significant and thus capable of enjoining the pathos of intersubjectivity that renders the event tragic. The painting is a set of propositions about hubris and the pathos of heroism that is the foundation of tragedy. The only way the pathos of the heedless youth whose overweening ambition and disobedience has led him to his premature death can be pictorially signified is through the creation of a space of ordered time and regular labour: the world carrying on its business. Yet his face beneath the waves inscribes a gaze into the painting that invites identification as against the focused otherness of the peasants at work. The aesthetic – the distillation of a practice to the point of its satisfying realisation of this complex series of ethical, ideological, intellectual propositions by means of a created space – is at once an ethic establishing the terms of relations to others that are the grounds of painting's production of its subjects, not as witnesses, documentators, but as visual thinkers. However enthralled I feel to this painting whose discovery of what painting could be made the art historian in me gasp (and ask how long it would take for another painter to realise what Breughel had done here and build upon it?), it operates in a historical, social and subjective space of pathos and tragedy, not trauma or horror. For the subject, Icarus, can be made to look back, to connect with the gaze outside his time and space.

III   Transcryptum, Metramorphosis and a Feminine Ethico-Aesthetic

I am guided throughout these researches by the work of a contemporary artist, Bracha Ettinger, for whom the relations between looking back (the surviving photographic image) and the deaths of others (a history both imprinted on family memory and in the world after Auschwitz) form the central problematic of a haunted subjectivity identified as 'the second generation'. The concept of 'transposition' was proposed by psychoanalyst Judith Kestenberg when she worked with children who knew what their survivor parents could not remember. 'Transposition describes the uncanny experience where the past reality of the parent intrudes into the present psychological reality of the child.' Although such seepage from parent to child is part of normal, non-verbal cultural transmission, the transposition of massive trauma: the blockage of meaning and the deflection of the subjectivity's present/presence is 'transgenerational transmission run amok' for it 'turns the ordinary dimensions of time and space inside out.'[21]

The parents' past usurps the current life of the child who may become aware that s/he must process what s/he did not experience on behalf of another unable to even know what has been transmitted to him/her. The traumatised parent passes on not merely the unremembered pain but also the depressive consequence of impossible mourning for the lost others the parent still holds in her own psyche as loved objects. As the parents' inner life is turned back, to the past, and to the field of unmournable deaths, the child, unconsciously seeking connections with the living but, in André Green's theory of the effect of parental depression, 'dead mother', travels in time and space with the adult and is infused in her own psyche with those she never knew, never forgot yet remembers.

It is on this paradoxical ground that it becomes possible to pose a non-fascist, feminist ethico-aesthetical intervention that takes us beyond the two scenarios I have sketched above, both of which placate, pacify and sublimate the pain of others. The question is how to process that pain by means of the encounter generated at the threshold between past and present, self and other than can be, specifically, generated in that sphere we can still call the aesthetic so long as that term is understood as profoundly remade 'after Auschwitz'. Can the encounter be transformative not only on an individual level, as in extreme cases of psychologically transmitted trauma, but culturally, where the relay between image and knowledge exposes us to transhistorical transmission?

I want thus to conclude with the interrelations between ethics and aesthetics that Ettinger explores in her working practice between photographic document become psychological archive and the potentiality of painting as a transferential encounter through which the blockage of meaning that is the immemorability of trauma can be processed without its usual risks of Orphic voyeurism, inured familiarity or sublime pathos.

Ettinger works in a space she theorises as a *transcryptum*. This neologism adds what she has introduced into psychoanalytical aesthetics as a *matrixial* register of trans-subjectivity, subjectivity-as-encounter and originary severality[22] to the concept of the crypt derived from psychoanalysts Torok and Abraham where the crypt is a mental space that results from 'a traumatic loss without memory'.[23] Secret and unknowable, the crypt is a result of a 'brutal change in the maternal imago' caused by a trauma in the mother. 'Thus the subject (in this case, a child) can libidinally invest the traces of someone else's trauma (in this case, the mother's) within its psychic apparatus.' In other words, the psyche has the capacity to hold the phantom of an Other in its own crypt. It is in art-working that 'we are called upon to think of the enigma of trans-subjective memory and joint affectivity.' 'The idea of producing traces of memory of/in/for/with the other invites a further elaboration of the uncanny aesthetic effect.'[24]

Not thinkable within strict Freudian or Lacanian models, Ettinger argues for a means by which a belated subject, coming after, can, nonetheless, open a passage by means of which the kind of spectatorship proposed by both Sontag and Drew is bypassed in favour of transformation. Here art that is oriented to the processing of the traumatic remnants of human catastrophes is considered, through this psychoanalytical perspective, as a specific apparatus soliciting and providing occasions for moments of trans-subjectivity that can traverse or suspend linear-time-space and work through the traumatic event that itself as trauma remains unforgotten and unremembered outside of time and place. Bracha Ettinger has written:

> 'The place of art is for me a transport-station of trauma: a transport-station that, more than a place, is rather a space that allows for certain occasions of occurrence and of encounter, which become the realisation of what I call *borderlinking and borderspace in a matrixial trans-subjective space* by way of experiencing with an object or with a process of creation. The transport is expected at the station, and it is possible, but the transport-station does not promise that passage of the remnants of trauma will actually take place in it; it only supplies the space for this occasion. The passage is expected but uncertain; the transport does not happen in each encounter and for every gazing subject.[25]

As created borderspace, art is neither pure content nor image nor mere expression. It creates an *occasion* for subjectivity to be affected along strings or cords that run through an 'object or a process of creation', the *poiesis* itself. This depends on the subjectivities, histories and sensibilities potentially brought into tune with each other – but there is no guarantee or prediction. This is neither in the realm of pure denotation nor of connotation but specifically brings into view both the ethical, the relation or openness to the other, and the aesthetic, as an instance of a non-cognitive transferential possibility of changing the inner world of an other.

What is, furthermore, critical here is that this proposition emerges at the unexpected conjunction of a painting practice and a feminist psychoanalytical discourse through which what occurs in *poiesis* can be articulated, otherwise, to elaborate its theoretical implications, but from which the ethico-aesthetic specificity of art must necessarily fade away as it becomes a theory of subjectivity and aesthetics.

The painting practice of Bracha Ettinger returns repeatedly to certain 'documents', photographs from the archive of the Shoah that are both personal, from a family album, and impersonal from the vast uncatalogued mass with which I started. One photograph that has been her companion over fifteen years is as emblematic as that shown at the beginning. It appears in Resnais' *Night and Fog* 1955 and many Holocaust Memorial museum displays. It too stems from the *Einstatzgruppen* murders in the territories of the Soviet Union around 1941–2. Not an isolated woman and the single deadly soldier performing a neo-classical gender duet, this second image calls upon another kind of classical *pathosformel*: the frieze or procession that we might recall from the Parthenon. The women here are processing towards their own unprecedented and undeserved deaths. Three figures in this desperate line form a trio to which Ettinger repeatedly returns in her paintings: the traumatic inversion of a famous Western threesome: *The Three Graces* realised in oil paint at that precious moment of figurability we call the Italian Renaissance by its epitomising painter, Raphael. His painting method, visible in the background of his tiny painting of idealised female nudity and rhythmic repetition, offers itself as the very source for Ettinger's own delicate and refined oil painting technique even to its limited and haunting colour range.

With Adorno's strictures in mind about the civilisation that produced the Shoah, we can set Raphael's perfect iconisation of that culture against the photographic index of mass murder: the trio of a woman turning her unseen face towards the catastrophe, a woman turning her desperate face in appeal to whomever meets her gaze beyond the field of this terror, and a woman clasping to her in tenderness insufficient to protect it, her naked child. These three form what I name the 'Graces of Catastrophe'.[26]

The indexicality of the photographic image is sustained by Ettinger in a reprographic technology that suspends its photographic status to allow it to become a temporal screen. The photograph is passed through a photocopier but that process is interrupted where a scatter of photocopic dust begins to reconfigure the rough masses that form a never-fixed trace of the image as a past held between appearing and fading. Suspended in black ash, the re-apparition is suspended between past and present on a paper that becomes a threshold for a returning gaze of the painter/viewer that is constantly dispersed across the surface by the membrane of painted colour that builds up sometimes in specific area, sometimes across the whole image so that seeing can not rest and find a focused image. A different kind of gazing-encounter is disseminated at the threshold of encounter–holding firmly to the modernist concept of the surface and indelibility of the support while blasting that formalism apart with the intensity of affect generated from the two sides of the historical meeting re-created through what Ettinger names *artworking*–reminding us of Freud's *Traumarbeit* and *Trauerarbeit*. Enfleshed, as it were, by the materiality of the paint that builds its veils and opacities, leaving its encounter traced in pulsing touches or smeared screens of colour, a tactile seeing serves also as a tender protection of the bodies that might otherwise be exposed again to the Orphic gaze (that kills again).

This painting practice enables a different kind of scopic encounter with the trauma of the other that is called *matrixial*. This meeting may engender a different moment or stratum of subjectivity in the viewer who, in being affected by what s/he did not herself witness or experience, processes some of its traumatic freight by receiving it not as an image (that can shock or traumatise) but as connectivity.

The materiality of painting's combination of mark, flow, rhythm, definition and opacity are what the artist names *metramorphosis*. Enacted upon an undoing of photography's *fixing* of an image by light and chemicals, Ettinger's work reveals the ever-present property of metramorphosis for the affective recharging of a dispersed visuality that she names the matrixial gaze. This differs from the Oedipal gaze of mastery, clearly defining self versus other in an almost unavoidable hierarchy of narcissistic self-consolidation as well as being distinct from what, after 1963, Lacan theorised as the gaze as *objet 'a'* namely, the trace in the scopic field of the severance in which the phallic subject is formed, leaving both a longing and a dread encoded in the visual.

Neither the single image that can compose a world such as we saw in Breughel nor the fragmented frame by frame of the photographic or cinematic image of Drew, Ettinger's serial paintings (Brian Massumi notes that they always come in series[27]) are hung in variable combinations that spread the viewer's gaze across each moment to a field that can never be one. The gaze does not halt to see or fix or know or recognise; nor does the image assault the unprotected viewer. It neither loses the subject in sublime excess nor offers the solace of complete optical mastery. The matrixial gaze at the metramorphosis of painting becomes the potential occasion for the passage not merely of affect but of the remnants of trauma from the site of a historical other captured facing the horror of death and being held before us through the indexicality of the photographic image under the perpetrators' doubled and deadly aim.

For Ettinger, painting after painting and after history has offered a possible moment of encounter with the traumatic event that is indexed by the photograph that could only exist because what it shows happened and someone was there to see it. As a perpetrator image and as a reproduced icon, the photograph as image cannot repeatedly perform that encounter-event; rather, it inures us by becoming a figuration of the Holocaust. Yet the conditions of that viewing and photographing, the perpetrator image or the genocidal gaze that solicits the Orphic second killing each time we look, cannot be allowed to rest as the only avenue back to the moment of the suffering of others. Thus a painting practice intervenes to mobilise the specificity of its long historical gestation as an instrument of human reflection and affective thought. By means of a strategic art historical intervention at the interface of the image archive, the technologies of reproduction and the space- and gaze-making properties of coloured earth mixed with oil that solicit subjective transactions at its surface, a proposition is made about the relations between event and encounter. This suggests that such a mode of trans-subjective encounter is a hitherto unacknowledged condition of subjectivity that binds the ethical and the aesthetic in this historical legacy. It can be mobilised to move us beyond trauma as either oblivion or desensitising familiarisation. Ettinger writes:

> Beauty that I find in contemporary art-works that interest me, whose source is the trauma to which it also returns and appeals, is not beauty as private or as that upon which a consensus of taste can be reached, but as a kind of encounter that perhaps we are trying to avoid much more than aspiring to arrive at, because the beautiful, as Rilke says, is but the beginning of the horrible in which–in this dawning–we can hardly stand. We can hardly stand at the threshold of that horrible, at that threshold which may be but, as Lacan puts it in his Seventh Seminar, the limit, the frontier of death–or should we say self-death?–in life, where life glimpses death as if from its inside. Could such a limit be experienced, via art-working, as a threshold and a passage to the Other? And if so, is it only the death-frontier that is traversed here? Is death the only domain of the beyond?[28]

Beauty–neither Kantian nor personal in taste–and not only as Lacan would have us think about a missed encounter with Death/the Real, can be otherwise. It can arise not as an aestheticisation of the suffering of others, but as the result of an affecting and transforming encounter that opens up a transport-station, a passage to a beyond that is not death, but a future in which trauma is carried, processed, remembered.

We cannot abandon the others at the mouth of hell. Yet ethically how can our looking back not condemn anyone caught in such images of atrocity to the repeated death structured into the photographic index of time and space? There is an intimacy between the aesthetic process, the relations of the making and positioning of a viewing subject–the creation of a kind of gazing that is the passageway of ethical encounter with an unknown otherness and with the unknowness of trauma–and the theoretical elaboration of this practice as metramorphosis and the matrixial gaze.

> Transcryptum is the art object or art event or art procedure, which incarnates transcription of trauma and cross-inscriptions of its traces, in which case the artwork's working through of the amnesia of the world into memory is a trans-cryptomnesia: the lifting of the world's hidden memory from its outside with-in-side. The transcryptum supplies the occasion for sharing and affectively-emotively recognising the uncognised Thing or Event. Art as transcryptum gives body to a memory of the Real consisting in memory traces of oblivion of the Other and of the world It generates symbols for what would otherwise remain as the unremembered trauma of the world, but which can be perceived when and if the threshold of our own fragility is lowered. Our post-traumatic era becomes, by virtue of this art, trans-traumatic. The forgotten trauma becomes transitive; its traces wander and are shared affectively.[29]

The ethical concerns the relations to the Other. A secondary responsibility lies to the image of the other at the moment of extreme vulnerability: death. The question of what the image may do to us–like Sontag's negative epiphany–can be extended to ask what the image may do for both us and the other across time and space. Can there be an encounter through aesthetic means that changes the terms of the ethical encounter to enjoin a co-subjectivity that is at once differenced and joint so that, in being affected, something of the other is processed by the viewer–not as a repeating trauma, but as a working through, as Freud conceived both transferential analysis and the work of mourning?

The image of the unknown falling man may already have transgressed and caused offence. Yet few raised that question in relation to images of the Shoah which also show named individuals. Bracha Ettinger cannot suspend such knowing. 'It could be *my* aunt', 'it could be *me*' is what she says, not 'look *they* are dying'. The encounter is impossible to avoid–the leakage of trauma cannot be contained by time. So Ettinger works to raise the impossibility of not sharing trauma to the level of theoretical recognition through the analysis of the effects occurring in and produced through her painting–aesthetic–practice. We are no longer witnesses like the photographer in the first image from the Ukraine or Richard Drew to the deaths of others. Ettinger posits the possibility of *wit(h)nessing* by means of a reconceptualisation of the ethical dimensions of a matrixial aesthetics.

The images that I have discussed concern death. The dead fall into the realm of the abject against which we have defences against contamination. Here I am suggesting that, in an ethical move of co- and trans-subjectivity, the sharing of the humanity of others or the dehumanising pain of others can be invoked in us by the creation of a threshold, a border-space that never collapses, never closes. (fig. 7).

fig. 7
Bracha Ettinger
View of studio
Courtesy of the artist

RESPONSE TO GRISELDA POLLOCK

Ethics, Aesthetics, and Trauma Photographs

W J T Mitchell

'Who are you, who will look at these photographs,

and by what right, and what will you do about it?'

James Agee, *Let Us Now Praise Famous Men*

Griselda Pollock makes a powerful case for an ethical reading of trauma photographs, one that rejects the 'Orphic Gaze' that aligns itself with the voyeuristic and sadistic impulse that produced the photograph in the first place, and seeks out a 'matrixial gaze' that veils the image, protecting it from unworthy eyes, and opens a space of potential connection to a beholder. This space, which may be designated as the site of art, or of a post-Auschwitz aesthetic, or of an ethics of photography, provides the possibility of an encounter with the traumatic event in a form that allows it to be remembered and worked through in a proper mourning. Some artists and artworks (the example here is Bracha Ettinger) provide such a space by producing a remediation of iconic Holocaust images that veils them with painterly effects—the 'allegorical ash' laid down by the interrupted photocopy, the 'veil or membrane of painted colour'.(p.232)

With uncompromising seriousness, Pollock faces the terrible paradox of trauma photography: that the photographic representations of atrocity, horror, and evil simultaneously demand an ethically responsible viewing, at the same time that this viewing is subject, as Susan Sontag noted, to corruption through repetition and familiarity. The trauma photograph has two radically opposite effects:'images transfix and images anaesthetize.' Marshall McLuhan once noted that insofar as media are 'extensions' of the human senses and organs, they simultaneously serve as 'prostheses' and as 'amputations', lengthening the reach of sight and hearing, touch and feeling at the same time they produce a 'numbness'. This is why Sontag is so emphatic that the view of such photographs is a secondary trauma in itself, not just because it provides a transparent witnessing of the suffering of someone else, but because it at the same time undermines that witnessing, rendering it inauthentic and impossible. This secondary trauma is not just the shock of witnessing another's pain, but the tertiary shock of shame at one's inability to intervene. The shock of what one sees is redoubled by the realisation that one (merely) sees, as a passive, remote, ineffectual witness.

'Can I feel another's pain?' was the question Wittgenstein asked, and if I understand him properly the answer is yes and no: yes, I can feel something, a sympathy or empathy or (in the case of the sadistic voyeur) a kind of perverse delight; but no, I cannot feel it from inside, from the point of view of the sufferer. Photography's mythic status as indexical trace of the Real, transparent window on the past to an ungrammatical 'this was', coupled with its inexorable tendency to pictorialise, anesthetise, and formally aestheticise thus reproduces the ethical dilemma of unmediated, immediate witnessing. Only the passage of time provides an excuse, a relief from the shameful accusation: you saw this, and you did nothing? The excuse: I came upon the scene too late to do anything. Or, I had, and have no power to intervene. It happened a long time ago. The photograph simultaneously accuses and provides an alibi.

I find Pollock's reflections on traumatic photographs and photographs of trauma very suggestive for working through the archive of photographs from Abu Ghraib prison. But rather than simply apply her insights to these images, I want to pose a set of questions based on some of the technical, aesthetic and ethical-political differences between them and the Holocaust photos.

1   What difference would it make if the Holocaust photographs (like those of Abu Ghraib prison) had been digitally produced? What would happen to their 'indexical link' to the Real?

Pollock notes that 'now, of course, in the age of digital fabrication, that last tenuous and indexical link has been severed and all reality is in *potentia* virtualised.' I wonder if this is true, and if it matters at all to the claims of an indexical connection to the real whether a photograph is digital. Certainly the digital does make a difference, but I suspect it has to do mainly with the repetition and circulation of images, not with their truth claims. If the Holocaust photos had been made today, their global circulation would have occurred much more rapidly. The arduous reception history of the Holocaust images, and their protracted status as enigmatic signifiers would have been radically truncated. The iconic figure of the Abu Ghraib scandal, the

Hooded Man on the Box, has now in less than two years acquired a proper name and appeared on the front page of the *New York Times*.[1] The rapid appropriation of this icon by anti-war groups would have been highly improbable in the pre-digital age.
2
What difference does the temporal lag encoded in these images make? The Holocaust photographs are of events now more than half a century removed from the present. The Abu Ghraib photos are of an event (and, more ominously, of a system) that is radically contemporary.

What is our responsibility to images of the Holocaust today? Certainly the moment for their judicial efficacy has passed. The trials of the perpetrators are ancient history, and the only residue of them is the occasional entanglement of a Holocaust-denier with laws criminalising this form of speech. Certainly we owe the images a certain respect and tact, and Ettinger's artistic practice is an effort to both protect them from what she calls the 'Orphic gaze' that 'kills again' and to transform them into into a 'transport-station … to a future in which trauma is carried, processed, remembered'. But it is not clear to me how this is accomplished by veiling the images in reproductive displacements, or overlays of paint. I suppose my preference is instinctively for a more direct address to the images, and that Ettinger's practice strikes me as perilously close to the aestheticisation of trauma she wants to avoid. The images, I want to say, have already been veiled repeatedly by time and forgetfulness; what they need now is something more naked and direct – though what that would be I am at a loss to say.

The contrast with artistic renderings of the Abu Ghraib photos is clear. Many of them are quite directly polemical and satirical, possessed of a political and even judicial urgency that comes with their contemporaneity. This doesn't, of course, make them better works of art. On the contrary, it exposes them more directly to the risk of kitsch and mere topicality. In both cases, then, the relation between aesthetics and the ethical/political is highly problematic, but in exactly the reverse proportion. For the Holocaust photos, the ethical and political issues strike me as mainly settled, and the aesthetic looms as the deeply disturbing area. For the Abu Ghraib images, aesthetics has to take a distant second place to the urgency of interpreting the images, and deploying them as instruments in a current struggle. But this doesn't rule out a longer-term reception in which we will have to come to terms with the aesthetic conditions, and the iconographic archives, that give them their meaning and effect. It is for this reason that Pollock's reflections on the iconographic precedents of the photographs that have emerged as emblematic in the Holocaust archive strike me as so useful. The images of atrocity, once loosed upon the world, are not merely scandalous bits of evidence, or occasions for secondary traumatisations, but for iconological analysis and a devotional aesthetics that refuses to reduce them to their merely narrative informational value, or what Barthes called their *studium*.

3   Is the choice between an Orphic and a Matrixial Gaze really a choice at all? Can one choose how to feel about these images, or is the question more one of what to do, what to say, about them?

I ask this question in all seriousness because I do not know the answer to it. I'm not even sure that Pollock is proposing the Orphic/Matrixial alternative as a choice in an ethical or political sense. It does seem to function as an aesthetic choice (one that is riddled with ethical and political considerations) for Ettinger's practice and for Pollock's appreciation of her work. My sense of the impact of the Abu Ghraib photos has been that they impose on an American viewer a sense of responsibility and complicity. These images were paid for by our tax dollars. We own them and must own up to what they say about the moral status of the nation that produced them. This is true even if we opposed the Iraq War, and express horror at the behaviour of our government. As Thomas Mann noted, his exile in the US during the Second World War did not excuse him from a conviction of responsibility and shame for what had been done in the name of the German nation. So I do not feel that I have a choice about what or how to feel about either of these image-archives, and this includes large doses of self-defensive disavowal and evasion. Oh, no!, I want to say. Not more trauma photographs! Enough, already! So the conversion of these images into 'transport-stations' to some possible future is an absolute imperative, but not only a future in which 'trauma is carried, processed, and remembered', but one in which the systemic causes of that trauma are recognised and deconstructed, and in which justice – always incomplete and imperfect – is done.

Notes

Introduction
pages 6–36

1   W J T Mitchell, *What do Pictures Want? the Lives and Loves of Images*, Chicago 2005, p.10.

2   Clement Greenberg, 'Necessity of Formalism', *New Literary History*, Vol. 3, No. 1 (fall 1971), reprinted in Robert C. Morgan, *Clement Greenberg: Late Writings*, Minneapolis 2003, pp. 45–6.

3   For an influential account of the post-modern as a moment within the modern, see Jean-François Lyotard, 'Answering the Question: What is Postmodernism?', the appendix to *The Post-modern Condition: A Report on Knowledge*, Minneapolis 1984.

4   Hal Foster (ed.), *The Anti-Aesthetic: Essays on Post-modern Culture*, Bay Press 1983, p.xv.

5   An early representative of the return of beauty in art criticism is Dave Hickey's polemical *The Invisible Dragon: Four Essays on Beauty*, Art Issues 1993. *Regarding Beauty*, the show curated for the Hirshhorn Museum and Sculpture Garden by Neal Benezra and Olga M. Viso in 1999, is representative of how exhibitions have addressed the topic.

6   Peter Schjedahl, 'Beauty is Back', *New York Times Magazine*, 29 September 1996, p.16.

7   Elaine Scarry, *On Beauty and Being Just*, Princeton 1999, p.57. Though probably the most widely read and influential expression of this position at the time these essays were composed, advocates of beauty have recently gained a more persuasive, philosophically fortified and eloquent champion in Alexander Nehamas's *Only the Promise of Happiness: The Place of Beauty in a World of Art*, Princeton 2007. This is an expanded version of Nehamas's Tanner Lecture on Human Value, of the same title, delivered at Yale on 9-10 April, 2001.

8   See Arthur Danto, *The Abuse of Beauty: Aesthetics and the Concept of Art*, Open Court 2003. For more on this see, Diarmuid Costello, 'On Late Style: Arthur Danto's *The Abuse of Beauty*' in *British Journal of Aesthetics*, vol.44, no.4, October 2004.

9   See Nehamas's Tanner Lecture for an overview. For Nehamas's commentary on a debate between Arthur Danto and Diarmuid Costello about the value of 'beauty' as a critical term in debates about art, see James Elkins (ed.), *Art History Versus Aesthetics*, Oxford 2006, pp.145–55.

10 Nicolas Bourriaud, *Relational Aesthetics*, Les presses du réel, 2002. For an overview, see Claire Bishop's entry 'Nicolas Bourriaud' in Diarmuid Costello and Jonathan Vickery (eds.) *Art: Key Contemporary Thinkers*, Berg 2007.

11 See, for example, Claire Bishop *Participation*, London 2006, and Kate Fowle and Ted Purves *Endless Terms of Engagement: Art and Social Practice*, New York forthcoming 2009.

12 See, for example, Claire Bishop, 'Antagonism and Relational Aesthetics', *October*, Fall 2004.

13 *Artforum* 36, no.9, May 1997. See also *Documenta X: The Book*, Ostfildern-Ruit 1997.

14 See, for example, the four 'Platforms' Okwui Enwezor's curatorial team developed in advance of Documenta XI (itself named as Platform 5 in the sequence), which defined the global political frame in which the exhibition sought to situate itself: *Democracy Unrealized*, (Platform 1); *Experiments with Truth: Transitional Justice and The Processes of Truth and Reconciliation* (Platform 2); *Créolité and Creolization* (Platform 3); *Under Siege: Four African Cities, Freetown, Johannesburg, Kinshasa, Lagos* (Platform 4), all four published by Ostfildern-Ruit 2002-3. For information about the symposia behind these publications see: http://www.documenta12.de/archiv/d11/data/english/index.html

15 For a conception of the aesthetic dimension of works of art as rhetorical along these lines see Arthur C. Danto, *The Abuse of Beauty*, op cit., chapter IV.

16 See for example: *Beyond Ethics and Aesthetics/Voorbij ethiek en esthetiek*, eds. Ine Gevers and Jeanne van Heeswijk, Nijmegen 1997; *Aesthetics and Ethics: Essays at the Intersection*, ed. Jerrold Levinson, Cambridge 1998; *Beauty Matters*, ed. Peg Zeglin Brand, Bloomington

and Indianapolis 2000; *Between Ethics and Aesthetics: Crossing the Boundaries*, eds. Dorota Glowacka and Stephen Boos, New York 2002; *The New Aestheticism*, ed. John Joughin and Simon Malpas, Manchester 2003. For a more empirical take on the ethical issues around contemporary visual art, see 'Ethics and the Visual Arts', eds. Elaine King and Gail Levin, New York 2007.

17 W.J.T. Mitchell, *What do Pictures Want? The Lives and Loves of Images*, Chicago 2005, pp.8 and 26.

18 One should not exaggerate the extent to which 11 September 2001 and its consequences mark a break with what went before. In some ways, they have just made it possible for long-standing, deep-rooted ideologies and systems of power to operate more openly.

19 J.M. Bernstein, *Against Voluptuous Bodies: Late Modernism and the Meaning of Painting*, Stanford 2006.

20 Ibid., p. 6.

21 Ibid., p.7.

22 Judith Butler, *Precarious Life: The Powers of Mourning and Violence*, Verso 2004; and *Giving an Account of Oneself*, New York 2005.

23 See chapter 3, in *Precarious Life: The Powers of Mourning and Violence*.

24 For an overview of the issues here, see Diarmuid Costello, 'Retrieving Kant's Aesthetics for Art Theory after Modernism: Some Remarks on Arthur C. Danto and Thierry de Duve', in T. O'Connor, F. Halsall and J. Jansen (eds), *Re-Discovering Aesthetics*, Stanford 2008.

25 For a substantial treatment of this topic see *Iconoclash*, ed. Bruno Latour and Peter Weibel, Cambridge 2002.

In Praise of Pure Violence
pages 37–55

1 Elaine Scarry, *On Beauty and Being Just*, Princeton 1999, pp.24–5.

2 Ibid., p.68.

3 Ibid., p.90; emphasis mine.

4 In Sigmund Freud, *Character and Culture*, edited by Philip Rieff, New York 1963. 'Reflections upon War and Death' was translated by E. Colburn Mayne; all quotes are from pp.122–4. For an interesting commentary on this essay, see Samuel Weber, 'Wartime', in Hent de Vries and Samuel Weber (eds), *Violence, Identity, and Self-Determination*, Stanford 1997, pp.80–105.

5 In *Character and Culture*, translated by James Strachey, p.149. The following quote is from p.150. I want to thank Paola Marrati for pointing out to me the relevance of this essay for my argument.

6 Apart from verb tense, I am of course quoting the opening sentence of T.W. Adorno's section 'After Auschwitz', in *Negative Dialectics*, translated by E.B. Ashton, London 1973, p.361.

7 Barnett Newman, 'The Sublime is Now', in Charles Harrison and Paul Wood (eds), *Art in Theory: 1900–1990*, Oxford 1992, p.573.

8 Henceforth all references in the text to FB refer to Gilles Deleuze, *Francis Bacon: The Logic of Sensation*, translated by Daniel W. Smith, London and New York 2003.

9 One might add to this list of devices Bacon's use of private or anonymous spaces (bathrooms, hotel rooms), the employment of arrows, the borrowings from Muybridge's action photographs and from K.C. Clark's book *Positioning in Radiography* (1929).

10 This way of construing Deleuze's argument makes it utterly proximate to Merleau-Ponty; indeed, there is little doubt that he means his Bacon book to be the successor to Merleau-Ponty's 'Cézanne's Doubt', in his *Sense and Non-Sense*, translated by Hubert L. Dreyfus and Patricia A. Dreyfus, Evanston 1964, ch.1, just as his philosophy as a whole is the successor to Merleau-Ponty's phenomenology.

11 Evidence for this reading of the body without organs as one which *intensifies* the comprehension of the body as a *living* thing emerges directly in Deleuze's analysis of Bacon, where making the representational image into the Figure is achieved through the dislocation or displacement of the head and the face (since the primacy of head/face just is the production of an hierarchically structured organism). Once the head/face dominance is disrupted, then Baconian figure can come to constitute 'a zone of indiscernibility or undecidability between man and animal' (FB, 21), and hence, by extension, the thought that the living flesh is already inhabited by the dead meat it will become. Roughly, Deleuze's complaint about the notion of organism is that it involves a logic that excludes the very 'life' thematised – because living is not a logic but a movement, a pathos, a sensation.

12 Henri Matisse, 'Notes of a Painter', in Jack Flam (ed.), *Matisse on Art*, revised edn, Berkeley 1995, p.42. Further references in the body of the text to this volume are to 'Flam.'

13 Although it is worth mentioning that John Elderfield, *Henri Matisse: A Retrospective*, New York 1992 is still feeling enjoined to make that argument in 1992, which is just two years after Yve-Alain Bois provided his forceful deconstructive reading of Matisse in 'Matisse and "Arché-Drawing"', in his *Painting as Model*, Cambridge 1990, pp.3–63. This is as good place as any to acknowledge the depth and pervasiveness of my debt to Bois, Elderfield, and Lawrence Gowing's *Matisse*, London 1979 for my understanding of Matisse. My effort here is not to contest their great efforts of art historical analysis, but to marshal their insights for a philosophical elaboration of the meaning of modernist painting. Other writings that I have found useful are: Alfred Barr, *Matisse: His Art and His Public*, New York 1951; Louis Aragon, *Henri Matisse: A Novel*, translated by Jean Stewart, New York 1972, 2 volumes; Pierre Schneider, translated by Michael Taylor and Bridget Stevens Romer, New York 1984; Yve-Alain Bois, *Matisse and Picasso*, Paris 1998; and, for an account of the much-disputed early Nice period, Dominique

Fourcade, 'An Uninterrupted Story', in Jack Cowart and Dominque Fourcade, *Henri Matisse: The Early Years in Nice 1916–1930*, New York 1986.

14 My thanks to Daniel Bernstein for bringing this to my attention.

15 Gowing, *Matisse*, p.181. Gowing continues: 'Even the diagonal march of space across the floor and up into the pictures is linked with a pattern of coinciding edges, connecting tables to chair and flowers to picture, *so that both are seen as natural properties of the picture's flatness and redness*.' Emphasis mine.

16 *Henri Matisse*, p.53.

17 *Moroccan Café* c.1913; *Woman at the Fountain* c.1917; through to the eerie *The Silence Living in Houses* 1947 and *Plum Blossoms, Green Background* 1948.

18 In 'Modernism and Tradition', Matisse says almost exactly this: 'A great modern attainment is to have found the secret of expression by color, to which has been added... expression by design: contour lines and their direction" (Flam, 121). I think it is because Matisse had neither a single practice of drawing, but a series of interconnected strategies, nor had a single term expressing his practice that it has been easy to overlook the equal centrality of his transformation of drawing (above and beyond drawing in colour). I am hoping that the notion of the arabesque can pick up the semantic slack in this area.

19 After completing this, I recalled hearing and reading a paper in 1999 by T.J. Clark, 'Modernism and Dialectics: Matisse's *Woman with the Hat*'. Focusing on just that one remarkable painting of Matisse's from 1905, Clark's paper leads to the very same conclusion as this one: the two-sidedness of Matisse's art, its work as a salvaging of the depth of things in the pure artifice of painting, of recovering human depth in flatness, and the utter proximity in Matisse of sensuousness, enlivenment and death. Clark's ideas have obviously worked on me.

Beyond Seduction and Morality
pages 63–81

1   All page references in the text are to *Walter Benjamin: Selected Writings*, ed. Marcus Bullock and Michael W. Jennings, vol.I, 1913–26, Harvard 1996.

2   Yves-Alain Bois, *Painting as Model*, Cambridge 1990, p.179.

3   For a further discussion, see 'Critique, Coercion, and Sacred Life in Benjamin's "Critique of Violence"', in *Political Theologies: Public Religions in a Post-Secular World*, New York 2006, pp.201-19.

4   Benjamin distinguishes between the 'the soul of the living' which, he claims, ought to be protected against violence, and 'mere life', which is not enough of a basis to justify non-violence.

Response to Judith Butler
pages 82–88

1.   'Music, Language, and Composition', in Theodor W. Adorno, *Essays on Music*, Richard Leppart (ed.), Susan H. Gillespie (trans.), Berkeley 2002, p.116.

2.   Theodor W. Adorno, 'The Relation of Philosophy and Music', in *Essays on Music*, p.141. For a full elaboration of this logic, see J.M. Bernstein, *Adorno: Disenchantment and Ethics*, New York 2001, pp.275–87.

3.   G.W.F. Hegel, 'The Spirit of Christianity and its Fate', translated by T.M. Knox, in G.W.F. Hegel, *Early Theological Writings*, Philadelphia 1975, p.227.

Art and Alienation
pages 89–109

1   Karol Berger, *A Theory of Art*, New York 2000.

2   This trichotomy still holds sway today. See Jurgen Habermas, 'Philosophy as Stand-in and Interpreter', in *After Philosophy* ed. James Bohman and Thomas McCarthy, Cambridge 1987.

3   See Iredell Jenkins, 'Art for Art's Sake', in *Dictionary of the History of Ideas*, ed. Philip P. Wiener, New York 1973, vol.I, pp.108–11.

4   Paul Oskar Kristeller, 'The Modern System of the Arts', in *Art and Philosophy*, ed. W.E. Kennick, New York 1979.

5   See M.H. Abrams, 'Art as Such: The Sociology of Modern Aesthetics', and 'From Addison to Kant: Modern Aesthetics and the Exemplary Art', in *Doing Things with Texts: Essays in Criticism and Critical Theory*, New York 1989. See also: Jane Forsey, 'The Disenfranchisement of Philosophical Aesthetics', *Journal of the History of Ideas*, vol.64, no.4 (October 2003), pp.581–97.

6   Miles Rind, 'The Concept of Disinterestedness in Eighteenth Century British Aesthetics', *Journal of the History of Philosophy*, vol.4, no.1 (2002), p.85.

7   John Wilcox, 'The beginnings of L'art pour l'art', *The Journal of Aesthetics and Art Criticism*, 11 (1953), p.363.

8   Larry Shiner, *The Invention of Art*, Chicago 2001.

9   Ibid.

10 M.H. Abrams, 'Kant and the Theology of Art', *Notre Dame English Journal* 13 (1981), pp.75–106.

11 Crispin Sartwell, 'Art for Art's Sake', in *The Encyclopedia of Aesthetics*, ed. Michael Kelly, Oxford 1998, vol.I. The isolation of art in our civilisation is also noted by John Dewey in his *Art as Experience*, New York 1934, p.337.

12 Jane Golden, Robin Rice and Monica Yant Kinney, *Philadelphia Murals and the stories they tell*, Philadelphia 2002.

13 See Noel Carroll, 'Art and Recollection', *Journal of Aesthetic Education*, vol.39, no.2 (Summer 2005), pp. 1–12.

14 In order to substantiate this claim, take note of perhaps

the most impressive recent defence of the autonomy of literature from the claims of truth, namely *Truth, Fiction, and Literature* by Peter Lamarque and Stein Haugom Olsen (Oxford: Oxford University Press 1994). Though it may not be immediately apparent, the position that this book defends is formalist. For the way in which its authors maintain literary artworks deploy concepts that apply to the world is not in order to propound truths, moral or otherwise, but to organise or colligate the disparate episodes, characters, descriptions and so forth of the text under overarching conceptions–like destiny. That is, artists and critics use such concepts in order to unify the text (or, at least large parts of the text) where *unity* is a formal feature of a work of literature. According to Lamarque and Olsen, the practice of literature is such that writers employ concepts not to advance truths, but to structure their fictions. This is alleged to be a premise of the institution of literature. But above, I will argue that with respect to some genres, literary and otherwise, it is part of the practice of the art-making under consideration to do more than present unified formal designs.

15 E.H. Gombrich, *The Story of Art*, New Jersey 1995, p.4. Also quoted by Jane Forsey, 'The Disenfranchisement of Philosophical Aesthetics', p.596.

16 For example, Tom Wolfe's recent novel *I Am Charlotte Simmons* has been roundly criticised for its presentation of prefabricated rather than penetrating and closely studied observations of the contemporary styles of collegiate life, the ostensible subject of his book. Such criticisms must be especially rankling for Wolfe, since he has expressly agitated for a return to the sort of realist novel that takes account of the conditions of social reality as they unfold. Nevertheless, for our purposes, the criticism of Wolfe's novel is pertinent apart from its accuracy because it shows that with respect to the practice of certain kinds of art, there is the institutional expectation that knowledge, including knowledge of mores, be something the author deliver. And where the author fails to dispatch that charge, he/she is justifiably deserving of criticism. The case of Wolfe merely

confirms that this is a *donnée* of the language game in which realist novels are created, consumed and evaluated.

17 Edith Wharton, *House of Mirth*, Harmondsworth 1995, p.122. Also cited in 'Lamarque and Olsen on Literature and Truth', by M.W. Rowe in his *Philosophy and Literature*, Aldershot 2004, p.133.

18 See Peter Kivy, *Philosophies of the Arts: An Essay in Differences*, New York 1997.

19 For an overview of recent philosophical discussions of the relation of art and ethics, see Noël Carroll, 'Art and Ethical Criticism', *Ethics* 110 (2000), pp.350–87.

20 The author would like to take this opportunity to thank Sally Banes, Diarmuid Costello, Dominic Willsdon, Nigel Warburton and Adrian Piper for their suggestions regarding this paper. However, they are not responsible for any remaining errors.

Response to Noel Carroll

pages 110–118

1 All citations are from Noël Carroll, 'Art and Alienation', and are paginated in the text.

2 Carroll thinks that the 'politicised art' of Barbara Kruger, Jenny Holzer and Mary Kelly 'has not neutralised the effect of two centuries in which the ideology of autonomy of art held sway.' (106–107) Objecting that an artist's work is ineffective in neutralising two centuries worth of bad aesthetic theory is like complaining that a fly swatter is ineffective in neutralising a mushroom cloud.

Political Art and the Paradigm of Innovation
pages 119–133

1   © Adrian Piper Research Archive 2005. Portions of this essay are excerpted from *Rationality and the Structure of the Self, Volume I: The Humean Conception* (forthcoming).

Do Artists Speak on Behalf of All of us?
pages 139–156

1   Immanuel Kant, *Critique of Judgement*, translated by Werner S. Pluhar, Indianapolis 1987, p.162. Emphasis mine.

2   Immanuel Kant, *Critique of Judgement*, translated by J.H. Bernard, New York 1951, p.77. Translation slightly modified.

3   Bernard, p.133.

4   Thierry de Duve, *Kant after Duchamp*, Cambridge, Massachusetts 1996.

5   See Hal Foster (ed.), *The Anti-Aesthetic*, Port Townsend, Washington 1983; and Hal Foster, *The Return of the Real*, Cambridge, Massachusetts 1996.

6   'Seminar II', *Art International*, vol.18, no.6, Summer 1974, p.73.

7   Clement Greenberg, 'Can Taste Be Objective?', *Artnews*, February 1973, p.92.

8   Pluhar, p.161.

9   Pluhar, p.160. Translation slightly modified.

10 Thierry de Duve, *Voici – 100 ans d'art contemporain* (2nd edn), p.251; English Translation, *Look – 100 Years of Contemporary Art*, Ghent 2001, p.251.

11 Pluhar, p.174.

The Destruction of Art
pages 162–173

1   Cited in Pierre Centlivres, 'Life, Death, and Eternity of the Buddhas in Afghanistan', in Bruno Latour and Peter Weibel, *Iconoclash: Beyond the Image Wars in Science, Religion and Art*, Cambridge 2002, p.75.

2   For a comprehensive analysis of these and other iconoclastic acts, see the work of Dario Gamboni, above all *The Destruction of Art: Iconoclasm and Vandalism since the French Revolution* and his later reflection 'Image to Destroy, Indestructible Image' in *Iconoclash*, pp.88–135.

3   Luc Boltanski offers another perspective in 'The Foetus and the Image War', *Iconoclash*, pp.78–81.

4   Anne Baldassari, *Picasso and Photography: The Dark Mirror*, exh. cat., Houston Museum of Fine Arts, Houston, 1997, p.116. Unfortunately it was not feasible to reproduce Picasso's documents of this work here; see Baldassari's catalogue for reproductions.

5   Anne Baldassari considers there to have been two negatives, one slightly displaced to the left to give a 'stereoscopic' dimension to the studio scene. However, given the extent to which Picasso manipulated the print stage of the photographic process, it is equally plausible that the prints issue from the same negative, one cropped to the left the other to the right. For Baldassari the existence of two exposures is important since it enhances the documentary status of the images – as stereoscopies they gain both a 'sculptural dimension' and document an 'installation'. If they are considered to issue from one manipulated negative, their documentary status is reduced and they become technically continuous with the technique of papier collé that Picasso had pioneered in 1912: the 'cut photos' become works rather than documents. A close inspection of an oblique detail such as the white shape towards the front of the table suggests that the 11.8 x 8.7, the 7.8 x 5.8 and the 11.4 x 8.8 prints share the same negative while that of the 11 x 9 print is from another negative.

6   'First' for the purposes of discussion – the orientation of the print to the right does not constitute a claim to chronological priority.

7   The name of the venue 'Galerie Thannhauser' is partially legible towards the top left of the poster.

8   Baldassari, op cit. p.251.

9   Ibid.

Cloning Terror: The War of Images 2001–04
pages 179–207

1   For further discussion, see Sandor Hornyk, 'On the Pictorial Turn', *Exindex*, 25 February 2005. The original essay version of 'The Pictorial Turn' appeared in Artforum, March 1992, pp.89ff. The German translation appears as the first chapter in Privileg Blick: Kritik der visuellen Kulturen, ed. Christian Kravagna, Berlin 1997, pp.15–40.

2   The raptors of Jurassic Park are, in fact, the terrorists of the park. They are 'clever girls' who hunt in packs, and are 'figuring things out', including how to open doors designed for human hands.

3   'Autoimmunity', in Giovanna Borradori, *Philosophy in a Time of Terror: Dialogues with Jurgen Habermas and Jacques Derrida*, Chicago 2003.

4   'Clones symbolize modern homosexuality', notes Martin P. Levine, in Gay Macho: *The Life and Death of the Homosexual Clone*, New York 1998; see also Roger Edmondson, *Clone: The Life and Legacy of Al Parker, Gay Superstar*, Los Angeles 2000.

5   www.weeklyworldnews.com/conspiracies/5895?page=4. 18 November 2005. *The Weekly World News* also reports that the terrorists have perfected a bomb that will turn everyone within 30 miles of its detonation point into a homosexual.

6   See Derrida, 'Autoimmunity', op. cit.

7   Baudrillard, *The Spirit of Terrorism*, trans. Chris Turner, New York 2002, pp.38, 40.

8   See David Simpson, 9-11 and the Culture of Commemoration, Chicago 2005, for a critique of the 'memory industry' around 11 September.

9   See Kevin Clarke's website for a discussion of this image: http://www.kevinclarke.com

10 Ruggiero, 'Terrorism: cloning the enemy', *International Journal of the Sociology of Law* 31 (2003), pp.23–34; 33.

11 Clarke, *Against All Enemies*, New York 2004, p.138.

12 The photo opportunity of Bush's 'Mission Accomplished' speech was, of course, quickly disavowed by the White House when it became evident that this image was becoming the subject of parody, and had even been cloned as an 'action figure'.

13 *The Vital Illusion*, New York 2000, p.4.

14 See the film *Control Room* for al Jazeera's television coverage of this event, denounced by the Pentagon for aiding the enemy. Al Jazeera's reporters noticed that the crowd assembled to celebrate the destruction of Saddam's statues was quite tiny, and contained very few Iraqis. Evidently it was mustered by the US military to produce the proper backdrop to this photo op.

15 Translated by G.E.M. Anscombe, Oxford 1953, p.178.

16 Or alternatively, 'the presence of photographers may have inflamed the crowd's passions', according to David Klatell, dean of Columbia University's Graduate School of Journalism. *Chicago Tribune*, 2 April 2004, p.11.

17 See Michael Taussig's discussion of symbolic mutilations in Columbia, 'The Language of Flowers', *Critical Inquiry* vol.30, no.1, Autumn 2003.

18 The distinction between modernist 'shock' and post-modern 'trauma' is discussed by Tanya Fernando in her PhD dissertation, University of Chicago 2005.

19 'Powerful Images Debated', Chicago *Tribune*, 2 April 2004, p.11.

20 Sheik Farzi Nameq 'condemned the mutilations of the four Americans' as 'un-Islamic desecrations'. He also warned that this would bring destruction to the city. 'Cleric in Fallujah Decries Mutilations', Chicago Tribune, 3 April 2004, p.3. It seems unlikely that this declaration was based on any notion of the human body as an imago dei. That is

a doctrine more attuned with Christian theology, and especially with the incarnation and the Catholic doctrine of the resurrection of the body. From an Islamic point of view, mutilation of the dead body is primarily a social sin, explicitly defined as such by the prophet himself, one to be avoided because of its capacity to mobilize revenge from the enemy. I am grateful to Abdolkarim Soroush for his advice on Islamic prohibitions on mutilation.

21 Patai's The Arab Mind is used in the training of US military personnel.

22 Danner, 'Abu Ghraib: The Hidden Story', NYRB, 7 October 2004, p.50.

23 On Abu Ghraib and American prisons, see Jean Snyder; on the background of American lynching photographs, see Hazel Carby.

24 See Danner, op. cit., p.45.

25 Actually, the man under the hood was suspected of nothing more than car theft, and (like most of the prisoners at Abu Ghraib) probably had nothing to do with the resistance. It now appears that he was a minor Baath Party official who managed a parking lot near Baghdad. He has since become an advocate for victims of American occupation forces, and says that he forgives the people who tortured him. See Hassan M. Fattah, 'Symbol of Abu Ghraib Seeks to Spare Others His Nightmare', *New York, Times*, 11 March 2006, pp.A1, A7.

26 Capobianco Gallery, San Francisco. The owner, Lori Haigh was forced to close her gallery after several attacks of vandalism.

27 Danner, *NYRB*, p.44.

28 Another image that resonates with Haacke's Stargazer is the cover of the leading German magazine, Der Spiegel, immediately after the Presidential election of November 2004. The cover shows the Statue of Liberty blindfolded with the American flag, accompanied by the caption, 'Augen zu und durch' ('Close your eyes and plunge forward'). A less literal, but more poetic translation, is offered by the title of Stanley Kubrick's last film, *Eyes Wide Shut*.

Dying, Seeing, Feeling: Transforming the Ethical Space of Feminist Aesthetics
pages 213–235

1 Bracha Ettinger, 'Transcryptum: Memory Tracing in/for/with the Other', in Bracha Ettinger, The Eurydice Series, Drawing Papers 24, ed. Catherine de Zegher and Brian Massumi, New York 2001, p.111.

2 Bracha Ettinger in 'Working Through: A Conversation between Craigie Horsfield and Bracha Ettinger', in The Eurydice Papers, op. cit., p.54.

3 Dominick LaCapra, History and Memory after Auschwitz, Ithaca: Cornell University Press 1998 and Writing History, Writing Trauma, Baltimore 2001.

4 Roland Barthes, 'The Photographic Message' [1961] in Image-Music-Text, translated and edited by Stephen Heath, London 1977, p.30.

5 See Barbie Zelizer, Remembering to Forget: Holocaust Memory through the Camera's Eye, Chicago 1998. Verbal reports expressed their own inadequacy before atrocities never before encountered that photographic images alone could confirm and convey.

6 Yitzah Arad, The Pictorial History of the Holocaust, New York 1990, p.200

7 Robert Neuman with Helga Koppel, The Pictorial History of the Third Reich, New York 1962, pp.178–9.

8 On lack of scholarly precision, see Sybil Milton, 'Images of the Holocaust', Part I and Part II, Holocaust and Genocide Studies, vol.1 no. 1 and no. 2, 1986. New texts include Barbie Zelizer, Remembering to Forget: Holocaust Memory through the Camera's Eye, Chicago 1998; Andrea Liss, Trespassing through Shadows: Memory, Photography & the Holocaust, Minneapolis 1998; Janina Struk, Photographing the Holocaust: Interpretations of the Evidence, London 2004; Ulrich Baer, Spectral Evidence: The Photography of Trauma, Cambridge, Massachusetts 2002; Marianne Hirsch, Family Frames: Photography, Narrative and Postmemory, Cambridge 1997.

9 Since completing the original research for this paper, I have located the original photograph and established its

apparent history. The inscription Aktion in Ivangorod, Ukraine, 1942 appears on the back of the photograph, now in a private collection in Poland. It was apparently a photograph sent by a German soldier to his family, interrupted in transmission by the Polish underground who took a copy of it. The complete image indicates two further shooters to the left of the image. In the new historical installation at Yad Vashem, a huge blow-up of the single soldier and the woman with her child is once again selected for its 'iconicity.' A copy is now held in the United States Holocaust Memorial Museum. I am grateful to Nina Springer-Aharoni for this information.

10 Elisabeth Bronfen, *Over her Dead Body: Death, Femininity and the Aesthetic*, Manchester 1992.

11 Contrast, for instance, Eugène Delacroix, *Massacre at Chios* 1824.

12 Janina Struk, 'Introduction,' op. cit. where the author also traces a recurring image, difficult to identify, of an execution of three men she calls 'The Death Pit' photograph.

13 The case for this argument is made in another place using the images of London poverty by Scottish nineteenth-century photographer John Thomson collected as *Street Life in London* in 1876. Amid the failure of this collection to find a rhetoric in which to figure the marginal and abjected figures of London street sellers, pub-drinkers and flood victims, one image has become iconic. It shows an elderly woman seated on a stone step with a baby in her arms. My question was what were the registers both social and psychic that made this equally casual and painful image work and its troping become ubiquitous in the photographic call to charitable action from Oxfam to other famines and tragedies. *The Crawlers*, I suggest, weaves together a social otherness with the deeper sense of the maternal-feminine body as lack and thus the feminisation and maternalisation of poverty and social pain becomes visually bearable.

14 The Orphic look and the idea of a non-Orphic feminist aesthetics is explored in my 'Painting as a Backward Glance That Does not Kill: Fascism and Aesthetics,' *Renaissance and Modern Studies*, no..43, special issue on Fascism and Aesthetics, pp.116–44, and 'Abandoned at the Mouth of Hell: Bracha Lichtenberg Ettinger's *Eurydice* 1992–6', in Griselda Pollock, *Looking Back to the Future*, London 2001, 113–176.

15 Susan Sontag, *On Photography*, London: Penguin Books 1977; *Regarding the Pain of Others*, New York 2003.

16 Dori Laub, 'An Event without a Witness: Truth, Testimony and Survival', in Shoshara Felman and Dori Lamb (eds.) *Testimony: Crises of Witnessing in Literature, Psychoanalysis and History*, London and New York 1992, pp.75–92.

17 Susan Sontag, *On Photography*, op. cit., pp.19–20.

18 Ibid., p.20.

19 Ibid., p.20.

20 In 'Beyond the Pleasure Principle' Freud identifies the traumatising compulsion to repeat that perplexed him in the cases of the shell-shocked soldier whose dreams and hallucinations appeared to return the subject to the scene of horror as indicating the attempt the psyche to handle the shock by generating the protective shield of anxiety that can at least prepare the subject for the blow. I am suggesting that our familiarity with the image renders the photograph not an indexical event, but an icon, a connotative rather than a denotative sign, and thus with every viewing we become better prepared to anticipate and thus tame the horror once so novel. S. Freud, 'Beyond the Pleasure Principle', *On Metapsychology: The Theory of Psychoanalysis*, vol.11, Penguin Freud Library, London 1984, pp.245–69.

21 Louise J. Kaplan, *Lost Children: Separation and Loss between Parents and Children*, London 1995, pp.224–5; Judith Kestenberg, 'Psychoanalytical Contributions to the Problem of Children of Survivors of Nazi Persecution', *Israel Annals of Psychiatry and Related Disciplines*, vol.10, 1972, pp.249–65.

22 This concept was first advanced in 1992 in 'Matrix and Metramorphosis', *Differences*, 1992, vol.4, no.3, pp.176–208. For a fuller range of the theoretical writings, see Bracha L. Ettinger, *The Matrixial Borderspace*, Minneapolis 2005.

23 Nicholas Abraham and Maria Torok, *L'écorcé et le noyau*, Paris 1987.

24 Bracha Ettinger, 'Transcryptum: Memory Tracing in/for/with the Other',' in *The Eurydice Series*, p.111.

25 Bracha Ettinger, 'Art as the Transport-Station of Trauma,' *Artworking 1985–1999*, Gent 2000, p.91.

26 For a fuller exploration of this theme, see Griselda Pollock, 'The Graces of Catastrophe' in *Encounters in the Virtual Feminist Museum: Time, Space and the Archive*, London 2007.

27 Brian Massumi, 'Painting: The Voice of the Grain', in *Artworking 1985–1999*, op.cit, pp.9–32, and Bracha Ettinger, *The Eurydice Series*, pp.7–18.

28 Bracha Ettinger, 'Art as the Transport-Station of Trauma', p.91.

29 Bracha Ettinger, 'Transcryptum', p.112.

Response to Griselda Pollock
pages 236–240

1 Hassan M. Fattah, 'Symbol of Abu Ghraib Seeks to Spare Others His Nightmare', *New York Times*, 11 March 2006, pp.1A, 7A.

List of Contributors

J M Bernstein is Chair and University Distinguished Professor of Philosophy at the New School for Social Research, NYC. His books include: *The Fate of Art: Aesthetic Alienation from Kant to Derrida and Adorno* (Penn State/Polity,1992); *Adorno: Disenchantment and Ethics* (Cambridge, 2002); (as editor), *Classic and Romantic German Aesthetics* (Cambridge, 2003); *Against Voluptuous Bodies: Late Modernism and the Meaning of Painting* (Stanford, 2006). He is currently working on a book provisionally titled *Torture and Dignity*.

Judith Butler is Maxine Elliot Professor in the Departments of Rhetoric and Comparative Literature at the University of California, Berkeley. Her books include: *Subjects of Desire: Hegelian Reflections in Twentieth-Century France* (Columbia, 1987); *Gender Trouble: Feminism and the Subversion of Identity* (Routledge, 1990); *Bodies That Matter: On the Discursive Limits of "Sex"* (Routledge, 1993); *The Psychic Life of Power: Theories of Subjection* (Stanford, 1997); *Excitable Speech* (Routledge, 1997); *Antigone's Claim: Kinship Between Life and Death* (Columbia, 2000); *Precarious Life: Powers of Violence and Mourning* (Verso, 2004); *Undoing Gender* (Routledge, 2004); and *Giving an Account of Oneself* (2005). She is currently working on essays pertaining to Jewish Philosophy, focusing on pre-Zionist criticisms of state violence.

Noël Carroll is the Andrew Mellon Professor of the Humanities at Temple University. His latest book is the *Philosophy of Motion Pictures* (Blackwell, 2008) and he has just completed *On Criticism* for Routledge's Thinking in Action series. His previous books include: *Comedy Incarnate* (Blackwell, 2007); *Engaging the Moving Image* (Yale, 2003); *Beyond Aesthetics* (Cambridge, 2001); *Philosophy of Art* (Routledge, 2000); *A Philosophy of Mass Art* (Routledge, 1999); *Interpreting the Moving Image* (Cambridge 1998); *Theorizing the Moving Image* (Cambridge, 1996); *The Philosophy of Horror or Paradoxes of the Heart* (Routledge, 1990), *Mystifying Movies* (Columbia, 1988); and *Philosophical Problems of Classical Film Theory* (Princeton, 1988).

Howard Caygill is Professor of Cultural History at Goldsmiths, University of London. He is currently completing a book the history of energy. His previous books include *Art of Judgement* (Blackwell, 1989), *A Kant Dictionary* (Blackwell, 1995), *Walter Benjamin: the Colour of Experience* (Routledge, 1998) and *Levinas and the Political* (Routledge, 2002).

Diarmuid Costello is Assistant Professor of Philosophy and Co-director of the AHRC research project 'Aesthetics after Photography' at the University of Warwick. He works on the relation between aesthetics and contemporary art theory. He has published articles on the aesthetics of Kant, Benjamin, Heidegger, Wittgenstein, Lyotard, Danto, de Duve Greenberg, Fried and Cavell. In this context he has also published on the portrait in contemporary art photography (Ruff, Dijkstra), conceptual art (LeWitt, Weiner) and the relation between painting and photography as arts (Richter, Wall, Close). He is co-editor, with Jonathan Vickery, of *Art: Key Contemporary Thinkers* (Berg, 2007) and is completing a monograph, *Aesthetics after Modernism.*

Thierry de Duve is Professor of Art History at University of Lille 3. His work revolves around Marcel Duchamp's readymade and its implications for aesthetics, and has found a new centre of interest in the work of Manet. De Duve is the author of numerous books in French and English, including: *Pictorial Nominalism: On Marcel Duchamp's Passage from Painting to the Readymade* (Minnesota, 1991); *Clement Greenberg between the Lines* (1996); and *Kant After Duchamp* (1996). He curated *Voici–100 ans d'art contemporain* at the Brussels Palais des Beaux-Arts in 2000, and the Belgian pavilion at the 2003 Venice Biennale. He is currently reworking his aesthetic theory.

W J T Mitchell is Professor of English and Art History at the University of Chicago, and the editor of *Critical Inquiry.* He has published numerous books on topics in literature, visual arts and media, ranging from landscape aesthetics to political and religious icons and theories of representation. These include: *The Language of Images* (Chicago, 1980); *The Politics of Interpretation* (Chicago, 1984); *Iconology* (Chicago, 1987); *Landscape and Power* (Chicago, 1992); *Picture Theory* (Chicago, 1994); *The Last Dinosaur Book* (Chicago, 1998); and most recently, *What Do Pictures Want?* (Chicago, 2005), winner of the James Russell Lowell Prize of the Modern Language Association in 2006. He is completing a book entitled *Cloning Terror: The War of Images, 9/11 to Abu Ghraib.*

Adrian Piper is a first-generation Conceptual artist and Professor of Philosophy whose work investigates rationality and the structure of the self in personal, social and political contexts. She has taught philosophy at Georgetown, Harvard, Michigan, Stanford and UCSD, and presently runs the Adrian Piper Research Archive in Berlin. She introduced issues of race and gender into the vocabulary of Conceptual art, and explicit political content into Minimalism. Her sixth retrospective, 'Adrian Piper since 1965,' toured Europe from 2002 to 2004. Her philosophical publications are in Kant, metaethics and the history of ethics; and her *OUT OF ORDER, OUT OF SIGHT* (MIT) has been in print since 1996.

Acknowledgements

Griselda Pollock is Professor of Social and Critical Histories of Art and Director of the Centre for Cultural Analysis Theory and History (CentreCATH) at the University of Leeds. Bringing together fine art, histories of art and cultural studies with post-colonial feminist theory and Jewish and Diaspora cultural studies, her books include: (with R. Parker) *Old Mistresses* (Routledge, 1981); *Vision and Difference* (Routledge, 1988); *Avant-Garde Gambits: Gender and the Colour of Art History* (Thames & Hudson, 1993); *Differencing the Canon* (Routledge, 1999) and *Encounters in the Virtual Feminist Museum: Time, Space and the Archive* (Routledge, 2007). Her current research focuses on trauma, cultural memory and the 'concentrationary imaginary.' Forthcoming books include a study of Charlotte Salomon's *Leben? Oder Theater?* 1941-42.

Dominic Willsdon is the Leanne and George Roberts Curator of Education and Public Programs at the San Francisco Museum of Modern Art. He also teaches at the San Francisco Art Institute. Until 2005 he was Curator of Public Events at Tate Modern, Senior Tutor in Critical Theory at the Royal College of Art, and on the core faculty of the London Consortium. He has been a researcher in philosophy at the Universities of Essex and Paris. He is the author of essays on art and philosophy, and is on the editorial board of *Journal of Visual Culture*.

It has been a pleasure working with the authors collected here; we would like to thank them for their patience, thoughtfulness and generosity in engaging with our proposals and each other's. We are also grateful for the advice and support – first for the initial talks series, and then during the production of this book – of Caroline Brimmer, Stuart Comer and Sophie Howarth in Public Programmes at Tate Modern, and James Attlee, Alice Chasey, and Roger Thorp at Tate Publishing. We are also grateful for the advice provided at various stages by Jonathan Vickery and Katerina Reed-Tsocha, and would particularly like to thank Jim Elkins for the many helpful comments and suggestions in his reader's report to the Press.

Photographic and copyright credits

ements

Photographic and copyright credits

Hans Haacke © DACS
Wassily Kandinsky © 2006 Artists Rights
Society (ARS), New York / ADAGP, Paris
Paul Klee © 2006 Artists Rights Society (ARS),
New York / VG Bild-Kunst, Bonn
Henri Matisse © Succession H. Matisse, Paris/
ARS, NY

AP Photo/Karim Kadim fig.10, p.201
AP Photo/Laurent Tebours p.191
Bayerische Staatsgemaldesammlungen, Alte
Pinakothek, Munich fig.9, p.201
© Board of Trustees, National Gallery of Art,
Washington p.65
Courtesy Margaret Bourke-White/ Time & Life
Pictures/ Getty Images p.223
Courtesy Musees Royaux des Beaux Arts,
Brussels p.226, p.228
Digital Image © The Museum of Modern
Art/Licensed by SCALA / Art Resource, NY The
Museum of Modern Art New York, NY, U.S.A.
p.48
Gilles Mermet / Art Resource, NY Pinacoteca
Gianni e Marcella Agnelli, Turin, Italy p.52
The Philadelphia Museum of Art / Art Resource,
NY Philadephia Museum of Art, Philadeplhia,
Pennsylvania, U.S.A. p.50
Photo by Janice Misurell Mitchell p.192